I0120428

Alexander Gardner

A History of the Witches of Renfrewshire

Alexander Gardner

A History of the Witches of Renfrewshire

ISBN/EAN: 9783742844859

Manufactured in Europe, USA, Canada, Australia, Japa

Cover: Foto ©Thomas Meinert / pixelio.de

Manufactured and distributed by brebook publishing software
(www.brebook.com)

Alexander Gardner

A History of the Witches of Renfrewshire

BARGARRAN HOUSE.

A HISTORY

OF THE

WITCHES OF RENFREWSHIRE.

A NEW EDITION,

WITH AN

INTRODUCTION,

*Embodying Extracts, hitherto unpublished, from the Records of the
Presbytery of Paisley.*

BARGARREN ARMS.

PAISLEY: ALEX. GARDNER.

1877.

INTRODUCTION.

WITCHCRAFT is a subject that has bulked largely in the history of mankind. A belief in it has been by no means confined to dark ages and barbarous nations. In Jewish history it held a prominent place. The first king of Israel banished wizards and witches from his borders, but could not set himself free from faith in their spells. Many of his successors had dealings with familiar spirits; and down to the days of Christianity, Gentiles as well as Jews all over the world attributed to certain men and women supernatural powers that were generally exercised for evil. Christianity, though it gave a blow to superstition, by no means eradicated it. The influence of heathen beliefs and practices did not cease to be operative when the majority of a nation formally surrendered them. The evil one has always been regarded as the great king and master of the wizard band ; and faith in Witchcraft is yet to be found among certain followers of all religions that recognise the existence of the spirit of darkness. Bishop Hutchinson's curious "Historical Essay on Witchcraft" shews how much such superstitions have served to degrade and enslave the intellect, even during periods that have been characterised by great national progress. Pope Innocent VIII., in 1484, issued a bull which indicated the beliefs that in his day were entertained regarding the baleful influences exercised by those who were credited with having made a bargain with Satan, accepting certain gifts from him in return for the surrender of their soul's salvation. "They have intercourse with the infernal fiends; they afflict both man and beast; they blight the marriage bed; destroy the births of women and the increase of cattle; they blast the corn on the ground, the grapes in the vineyard, the fruits of the trees, and the grass and herbs of the field." To punish these obnoxious men and women he issued most cruel edicts. The Alpine valleys witnessed thousands of victims slaughtered under excruciating tortures, accused of denying Christ, dishonouring his cross, and in Satan's company maintaining his devil's Sabbath. The strongest minds did not rise above the popular delusion. Luther gravely describes his interviews with the spirit of evil, and tells of many bitter nights and much restlessness which he caused him. "I no longer wonder," he says, "that the persons whom he assails are often found dead in their beds. I am of opinion that Gesner and Œcolampadius came in that manner to their deaths." Knox, too, though of stouter mental calibre than the German Reformer, was mainly instrumental in passing a statute which discharged all persons of whatsoever estate, degree, or condition to use any manner of witchcraft, sorcery, or necromancy under the pain of death, "as well to be execute against the user, abuser, as the seeker of the response or consultation." In Scotland the belief in Witchcraft was all but universal, and was sanctioned by the highest authority. It is one of the thousand marvellous proofs of Shakespere's fidelity to truth that his witches ply their vocation on Scottish soil. King James VI. was an ardent student of Witchcraft, which his " Daemonologie," in three books, gravely discusses as a science. His was not only a theoretic speculation, but a real experience as to demoniac antipathies. When he returned from Scandinavia with his bride, there was a strong muster of the Satanic army to oppose him. In his presence many poor victims confessed to being in league with Satan, and explained the schemes which had been planned by the powers of darkness to the prejudice and damage of his Scottish Majesty. When it was declared that a wretched woman named Symson had performed the feat, of sailing with two hundred companions from Leith to North Berwick in a sieve, James had her put to torture. She was subjected to the ordeal of the witch's bridle, and to other cruelties. James, by questioning with pitiless pertinacity, elicited the admission that she and her party had baptised a black cat, and raised a dreadful storm to sink the ship that held the king, for which unholy and regicidal effort she was condemned to be burned, and died protesting her innocence, and calling upon God for "the mercy that Christian men withheld." The Scottish enactments against Witchcraft he transferred to England on his accession, and under the statute many persons perished. This Act was not repealed until 1736, when it was obliterated, yet even in 1743 the Associate Presbytery enumerated amongst other national sins that had subjected the nation to Divine wrath, that "The penal statutes against Witches have been repealed by the Parliament, contrary to the express law of God; for which a holy God may be provoked in a way of righteous judgment to leave those who are already ensnared to be hardened more and more; and to permit Satan to tempt and seduce others to the same dangerous and wicked snare." The Associate Presbytery was composed of seceders from the Scottish Ecclesiastical Establishment, and was in time incorporated into the United Presbyterian Church. The testimony just quoted may be regarded as the last ecclesiastical protest in favour of witch hunting; but it must not be supposed that among clergy of the Establishment and laymen generally there were few sympathisers with the seceders. The annals of the General Assembly bring before us several proofs that belief in Witchcraft was very general at the beginning of the 18th century. In 1699 an overture against Witchcraft or charming was transmitted to Presbyteries, and in 1707 the subject was the occasion of a protracted discussion, which resulted in an instruction to the commission to advise Presbyteries in regard to cases of witchcraft, sorcery, and charming. In 1730 William Forbes, advocate, Professor of Law in Glasgow University, methodically treated of the crime and its symptoms in a professional work, "The Institutes of the Law of Scotland," in which he excuses himself for declining to follow the English commentators who touch the matter as if it were an obsolete belief. "Nothing seems plainer to me than that there may be, and have been witches, and that perhaps such are now actually existing; which I intend, God willing, to clear in a larger work concerning the criminal law." "Witchcraft is that black art whereby strange and wonderful things are wrought by a power derived from the Devil." Learning and eminence were no defence against the popular superstition. Even Hale, wise and exemplary judge as he was, avowed his belief in Witchcraft on occasion of the trial of two women whom he sentenced to death in 1664; and John Wesley, in his journal, declared that surrender of belief in Witchcraft was tantamount to infidelity. "Giving up Witchcraft," he wrote, "is in effect giving up the Bible."

The explanation of the hold which such superstition retained over strong intellects is to be found in the extreme pertinacity with which the human mind associates the accidental surroundings of religion and its essential principles. There is an extreme repugnance to admit that any doctrine once accepted as a truth of revelation has occupied its position as an incidental accessory, and not as a substantial verity. The last witch-fire kindled in Scotland was in 1722, when a poor old woman, accused of transforming her daughter into a mare to carry her to witches' gatherings, and causing her to be shod by the Devil, so that she was lamed in hands and feet, was condemned, put into a tar-barrel, and burned at Dornoch. The poor creature is represented as having sat warming herself in the cold night at the fire which was being prepared for her execution, "while the other instruments of death were getting ready." The daughter escaped and became the mother of a son who was as lame as herself, though it does not appear that the same cause was assigned for the deformity, "and this son," wrote Sir Walter Scott in 1830, "was living so lately as to receive the charity of the present Marchioness of Stafford, Countess of Sutherland in her own right." This was the last execution for Witchcraft in Scotland, and the "Acts Anentis Witchcraft" were formally repealed, the indignant protest of the Associate Presbytery notwithstanding, in June 1736. But although Witchcraft then ceased to be regarded as a specific crime, the trials for fraudulent fortune-telling, which ever and anon are reported in the newspapers, and the many other proofs of superstitious credulity that meet us, suggest the unpleasant reflection that the belief in Witches is to a very considerable extent still prevalent. Without appealing to the evidence arising from recent trials of impostors who set up as spiritualists, and in return for hard cash professed to put their dupes in communication with the invisible world, the superstition that is still displayed in other forms may well occasion surprise. We do not hear so much of it in the busy centres of population, but in country places the credulity of many is surprising, and even in the cities any one who sets up pretentions to supernatural powers will find believers. Burns tells us that faith in the world, which his Tam O'Shanter so picturesquely describes, was not altogether a pretence on his part, but so influenced him that on dark nights, and at suspicious places his heart beat more quickly than it was wont to do in other circumstances. There are still alive Scottish peasants who maintain that there is a witch world around them with which certain men and women are in communication. The evil eye is not yet an

obsolete superstition, and the horse shoe is not an extinguished
charm against its influence. Southey, in his Common-Place
Book, preserves a cutting from the *Scotsman* newspaper of
July 1836, which describes a discovery made by boys who,
while amusing themselves in searching for rabbit burrows on
Arthur's Seat,   noticed, in a very   rugged and secluded
spot, a small opening in one of the rocks, which attracted
their attention. The mouth of this little cave was closed by
three thin pieces of slate stone, rudely cut at the upper ends
into a conical form, and so placed as to protect the interior
from the effects of the weather. The boys having removed
these tiny slabs, discovered an aperture in which were lodged
seventeen Lilliputian coffins forming two tiers of eight each,
and one on a third, just begun.   Each of the coffins contained
a miniature figure of the human form cut in wood, well executed. They were dressed from head to foot in cotton
clothes, and decently laid out with a mimic representation of
all the funereal trappings, which form the usual habiliments
of the dead.   Other circumstances, described in detail in the
extract, justified the conclusion of the writer that the arrange-
ments were made in consequence of a prevalent belief that
there were still some of the weird sisters hovering about
Mushat's Cairn or the Windy Gowl, who retained their ancient
power to work the spells of death by entombing the likenesses
of those they wished to destroy.

The history of the Witches of Renfrewshire furnishes an
interesting and characteristic exposition of the beliefs and manners of the times. The extracts from the Records of the Pres-

bytery which follow are now, we believe, for the first time fully published, and throw a striking sidelight on the narrative which was drawn up with full ecclesiastical sanction. The clergymen who took so prominent a part in the investigation were, many of them, men of note in their day. Not to mention less distinguished iniquisitors, there were William Dunlop, Principal of the University of Glasgow; Patrick Simpson, minister of Renfrew, whose reputation was great, and who was so much respected by his brethren that when age and infirmity hindered him from leaving his manse, they appointed some of their number to wait on him and consult him in connection with all matters that came before them; Robert Millar, an eminent theologian and historical writer; Thomas Blackwell, a learned scholar and author, who was transferred from the Abbey of Paisley to Aberdeen, and was afterwards appointed Principal of the northern University. All these and others entered with zest on the investigation, and the record of the manner in which they conducted it, though quite in accordance with the spirit of the age, is a sad chapter of local Scottish history. The subject was first introduced to the presbytery by Mr. Andrew Turner, minister of Inchinnan, who reported that Christian Shaw, daughter of the laird of Bargarren, was suffering from Witchcraft, and indicated the authors of her trouble. The wretched girl, whose imposture is so palpable, that we wonder how it could for a moment have deceived any being possessed of common sense, seems never to have had her good faith called in question. If any witchcraft was exercised, it was by the hysterical

Christian, who appears to have cast a glamour over parents, Presbytery, Lords of Privy Council, and all who had to do judicially with the case. From the first the poor victims of her wickedness or insanity had not a chance. Their guilt was a foregone conclusion, and the chief efforts made to obtain evidence consisted in appeals made to their consciences to confess guilt. We find no reference in the proceedings to witch-bridles or other instruments, such as King James caused to be applied to the water witches in order to extort confession; but the mental suffering to which they were subjected must have been a dreadful ordeal. The life of a reputed witch was one of constant persecution. In the case of the Renfrewshire witches, the tests usually employed to bring home conviction were probably applied. Among these, inability to shed tears; not sinking in water when thrown in with hands and feet tied across,—the right hand to the left foot, and the left hand to the right foot;—failure to repeat the Lord's Prayer without mistake or omission; excrescences on the body supposed to be the Devil's marks; their being seen with a familiar in the shape of some animal, differing from a real animal in that it could not be caught or killed, were signs accepted as infallible proofs of guilt. King James ingeniously justifies the water ordeal by stating that "God hath appointed (for a supernatural sign of the monstrous impiety of Witches) that the water shall refuse to receive them in her bosom that have shaken off them the sacred water of baptism, and wilfully refuse the benefit thereof; no, not so much as their eyes are able to shed tears, threaten and torture them

as ye please, albeit" adds his sapient majesty, "the women-
kind especially be able otherways to shed tears at every light
occasion, when they will ; yea, although it were dissemblingly,
like the crocodiles." James explains philosophically the
reason why there were so many more witches than wizards,
by the assertion that the serpent's success with Eve had
"made him the homelier with that sex sensine."

Whether such tests found place in the investigations of the
Presbytery of Paisley is not recorded, but the "dealing" with
the accused parties to which reference is frequently made was
no doubt the reason why some of them became, in ecclesiastical language, "confessants." The confession was probably
brought about by the cruel treatment to which the poor creatures
were exposed. Regarded as traitors to humanity, who had
deserted to the standard of man's great enemy, reputed Witches
received no sympathy. Every misfortune that visited a neighbourhood or homestead was attributed to their agency. Children fled when they appeared, or pursued them with yells and
execrations. No one would give them shelter or sell them
food. They were kept in perpetual motion, and if they
broke down under the fatigue, their weakness was accepted as
an evidence of guilt. The existence of a reputed Witch became so miserable that death was preferable to life. Sinclair,
in his "Satan's Invisible World Discovered," tells of several
Witches who were tried at Lauder in 1649, and all but one
condemned to execution. The one who escaped sent for the
minister and others and confessed that she had formed a
league with Satan. She was not believed, and was urged to

retract her acknowledgment of guilt, but refused, and was condemned to die with the others. When she was carried to
the stake she exclaimed, " Now all you that see me this
day, know that I am now to die a Witch by my own confession, and I free all men, especially the ministers and magistrates, of the guilt of my blood. I take it wholly upon myself;
my blood be upon my own head. And as I must make
answer to the God of heaven presently, I declare I am as free
of Witchcraft as any child, but being delated by a malicious
woman, and put in prison under the name of a Witch, dis-
owned by my husband and friends, and seeing no ground
of my coming out of prison, or ever coming in credit again,
through the temptation of the devil I made up that confession
on purpose to destroy my own life, being weary of it, and
choosing rather to die than to live."

Unquestionably very many of the confessions made by reputed Witches were obtained by torture, and the forms they
took were moulded by the questions of the examiners. The
discovery of Witches became a profession. Manuals for the
guidance of inquisitors, such as the " Malleus Maleficarum "
of Sprenger, were published, containing full directions as to
the signs of guilt, and the forms of questioning the suspected
persons. The general use of these manuals explains the
family resemblance which most of the confessions assume.
Matthew Hopkins, who was honoured with the title of Witch-
finder General, is the most famous in the annals of Witch-hunt-
ing. In 1644 and the two following years his exploits gained
for him great fame and emolument. During that time many

scores of accused persons were executed through his energetic prosecutions. His fate affords an illustration of the "engineer hoist on his own petard." It is recorded by Hutchinson that "he went on searching and swimming the poor creatures till some gentlemen, out of indignation at the barbarity, took him and tied his own thumbs and toes as he used to tie others, and when he was put into the water, he himself swam as they did. This cleared the country of him." Butler, in his Hudibras, celebrates the retribution that overtook Hopkins.

> " Has not he within a year
> Hanged threescore of them in one shire ?
> Some only for not being drown'd ;
> And some for sitting above ground,
> Whole nights and days upon their breeches,
> And feeling pain were hanged for witches ;
> And some for putting knavish tricks
> Upon green geese and turkey chicks,
> Or pigs that suddenly deceased
> Of griefs unnatural, as he guessed,
> Who after proved himself a witch,
> And made a rod for his own breech."

While, however, as a general rule, the examinations gave shape to the acknowledgments, it cannot be denied that in some cases confession was made by poor creatures who believed that they were as guilty as others considered them. The mental condition in which such confession originated is by no means a rare psychological phenomenon. Belief in Witchcraft being almost universal, it is not wonderful that persons of a hysterical or morose temperament should attribute experiences and feelings that they could not understand to a direct influence exerted upon them by Satan. If, even in our own day, hallucinations are so general that experts in mental disease are found to maintain that all men are more or less subject to their influence, we need not wonder that in an age when the mysteries of nature and of human life had not been investigated as they have been in recent times, ignorant or diseased persons should have been found imagining that they had concluded a covenant with Satan, the possibility of which was universally acknowledged. It is even now-a-days no uncommon thing on occasion of some great crime for persons altogether unconnected with it to come forward and charge themselves with its commission. Under a similar delusion men and women in the days of belief in Witchcraft voluntarily confessed their imaginary crime, as in the case narrated by Dapper of the girl who accused herself of bewitching cattle by the words *Shurius, Turius, Tirius.* The ideas prevailing among the vulgar regarding cause and effect are illustrated in many parts of the Presbytery records of the period. On the 12th November, 1695, for example, John Dougall was libelled for having taught John Hunter how to make his own corn grow and his neighbours' go back,—the important secret consisting "in sowing sour milk amongst it on Beltan day"; for having prescribed as a cure for convulsion fits, the paring of the sick man's nails, the pulling of his eyebrows, and some hairs from the crown of his head, which nail-pairings and hair clippings were "to be bound up in a clout with a halfpenny, and laid down on such a place, and that whoever found this would take the disease, and the diseased be set free"; for having prescribed for curing of John Hunter's beasts of "the

sturdie," "the cutting off a stirk's head, boiling it, burning the
bones to ashes, and burying the ashes," a remedy which, as
Dougall stoutly maintained before the Presbytery, was "most
effectual." The accused had also offered "for a 14" to teach
a man how to get a part of his neighbours' fishing and his
own too. This feat was to be accomplished by taking the
sailing pin out of his neighbour's boat. Dougall was declared
by the presbytery to be a scandalous person, and sentenced
to be publicly rebuked. That he found, however, many to
accept his doctrine is proved by the care which the presbytery took to prohibit their parishioners from resorting to, and
trafficking with him.

The Commissioners, in the report presented by them to the
Privy Council on the 9th of March, 1697, stated that there
were twenty-four persons, male and female, suspected of being
concerned in the Bargarren case, and in the list a girl of fourteen and a boy under twelve find place. Twenty of the suspected persons were condemned, but only five appear to
have been executed. Death was probably produced by
burning. It has indeed been alleged that the Witches were
hanged first, and their bodies afterwards committed to the
flames; but against this the statement found in the presbytery
records seems to militate, that "one or two of the brethren"
were assigned to each of the sentenced persons "to deal with
them, and wait upon them *to the fire.*"

Christian Shaw, whose early history was so painfully associated with Paisley, acquired a reputation of a more pleasant
nature in her after life. To her the town is indebted for

originating the trade which now occupies in it so prominent a place,—the spinning and manufacture of linen thread. At the time of the investigations she was only 11 years of age, but manifested an amount of cunning and artifice extraordinary at her years. In his statistical account of Scotland, Sir John Sinclair describes the circumstances in which the thread manufacture at Bargarren originated. Christian having acquired great dexterity in the spinning of fine yarn, conceived the idea of manufacturing it into thread. With her own hands she executed almost every part of the process, manifesting great ingenuity in the bleaching and other preparation of material. Holland was at the time the seat of extensive thread manufactories, and Christian having contrived to procure information regarding the mode of conducting the processes in that country, introduced them into her own business, and established an extensive and profitable trade. Bargarren thread obtained a wide celebrity, and, guaranteed by a stamp, held the first place in the market. From this beginning, Paisley and its neighbourhood became celebrated for this branch of industry.

In the newspapers and other publications of the time, the following advertisement found place :—

"The Lady Bargarren and her daughters having attained to a great perfection in making, whitening, and twisting of SEWING THREED, which is as cheap and white, and known by experience to be much stronger than the Dutch, to prevent people's being

imposed upon by other Threed, which may be sold under
the name of 'Bargarren Threed,' the papers in which the
Lady Bargarren and her daughters at Bargarren, or Mrs.
Miller, her eldest daughter (Christian, now a widow), at
Johnstone, do put up their Threed, shall, for direction,
have thereupon their Coat of Arms, '*azure* three covered
cups *or.*' Those who want the said Threed, which is
to be sold from fivepence to six shillings per ounce, may write
to the Lady Bargarren at Bargarren, or Mrs. Miller at Johnstone, near Paisley, to the care of the Postmaster at Glasgow;
and may call for the samen in Edinburgh, at John Seton,
merchant, his shop in the Parliament Close, where they will
be served either in Wholesale or Retail; and will be served
in the same manner at Glasgow, by William Selkirk, merchant,
in Trongate."

About the year 1718 Christian Shaw became the wife of
John Miller, a licentiate of the Presbytery of Paisley, then
minister of Kilmaurs. She was soon left a widow, as her
husband died in the autumn of 1721, when Mrs. Miller removed
to Johnstone, and, in connection with her mother, the Lady
Bargarren, and other members of the family, resumed business
as a manufacturer of fine linen thread.

EXTRACTS FROM THE RECORDS OF THE PRESBYTERY.

At Pasley, December 30, 1696.

"This day Mr. Turner represented to the Presbytery a deplorable case of Christine Shaw, daughter to the laird of Bargarren, in the paroch of Erskine, who, since the beginning of September last, hath been under a very sore and unnatural-like distemper, frequently seized with strange fits, sometimes blind, sometimes deaf and dumb, the several parts of her body sometimes violently extended, and other times as violently contracted, and ordinarily much tormented in various parts of her body, which is attended with an unaccountable palpitation in those parts that are pained, and that those several weeks by past she hath degorged a considerable quantity of hair, folded up straw, unclean hay, wild-fowl-feathers, with divers kinds of bones of fowles and others, together with a number of coal cinders burning hot, candle grease, gravel-stones, etcetera, all which she puts forth during the forementioned fits, and in the intervals of them is in perfect health, wherein she gives an account of several persons, both men and women, that appeares to her in her fits, tormenting her, all which began with her upon the back of one Kathrine Campbell, her cursing of her, and though her father hath called physicians of the best note to her during her trouble, yet their application of medicine to her hath proven ineffectual, either to better or worse, and that they are ready to declare that they look upon this distemper as *toto genere* preter-natural. All which was attested by the minister who, by the Presbytery's recommendation, had visited her in her trouble, upon all which Mr. Turner desired that the Presbytery would do what they judged convenient in such a juncture. The Presbytery being deeply sensible of the sad circumstances of that Damsel and family, does appoint the exercise of fasting and prayer to be continued as it is already set up by Mr. Turner in that family every tuesday, leaving it to him to call to his assistance whom he pleased, from time to time. And further, appoints Mr. Turner and Mr. Birsbane to repaire to Bargarren, friday next, there to take up a particular narrative of her whole trouble, of its rise and progress; and also appoints Mr. John Stirling and Mr. Andrew Turner to go to Edinburgh munday next, and to lay the whole affair before the Lords of his Maj.'s Privie Counsell, in order unto their obtaining a commission for putting those who are suspected to be her tormentors to a tryall, and in their way thitherward to go to Dr. Birsbane, and to entreat him to give a declaration of his sentiments of the foresaid trouble, in order to their more easy obtaining a Commission as said is.

At Pasley, February 3, 1697.

Anent the business of Witchcraft it was reported that the appointments anent the taking up of the narrative of Christine Shaw's trouble, and the going to Edinburgh were obeyed, and accordingly the Lords of his Majestie's Privie Counsell had granted a commission to my Lord Blantyre and some other gentlemen in the bounds for taking a precognition of that affair, who are to meet at Renfrew, the 5 instant. The Presbytery appoints Mrs. Symson, Turner, and Blackwell to wait upon the commission on the foresaid day; and the Presbytery further considering that the trouble of Bargarren's daughter continueth, therefore the Presbytery appoints thursday-come-eight days for a public day of humiliation and fasting, and Mrs. Hutcheson and Symson are appointed to joyn with Mr. Turner in that work, leaving it for them to call the next Presbytery as they shall find convenient.

At Pasley, February 17, 1697.

Reported that the fast was kept at Erskine according to appointment, by Mr. Hutcheson and Mr. Sympson joyning with Mr. Turner, who finding that the Commissioners had apprehended several persons delated by James and Thomas Lindsays, and Elizabeth Anderson, now confessant, and accused by Christine Shaw as her tormentors, and that they were to sit at Renfrew to-morrow as their last meeting before their report to the Counsell. Therefore they had called the Presbytery this day that they might consider what was incumbent upon them at this juncture. The Presbytery approved of their being called, and finding that the Commission is to meet to-morrow at Renfrew, does adjourn thither to-morrow against ten of the clock.

At Renfrew, February 18, 1697.

The Presbytery considering what was incumbent upon them at this juncture did, at the desire of the Commissioners, think meet to wait upon them at their enquiries and examinations, and to deal with the consciences of the suspected, now prisoners, to see if they could be brought to a confession, which was done accordingly; and afterward meeting together, and finding Bargarren was desired by the Commissioners to go on with their report, which was to be put in the hand of Sir John Maxwell to present to the Counsell, did think fit that one of our number should go in company with Bargarren, and accordingly did appoint Mr. Thomas Blackwell, and, failing him, Mr. Robert Taylor, to go in to Edinburgh and to represent to the said Sir John Maxwell, and, with his concurrence, to His Majestie's Advocate and other Lords of His Majestie's Privie Counsell, the *lamentable condition* of this part of the country, upon the account of the great number that are delated by some that have confessed, and of the many *murders* and other *malefices* that in all probability are perpetrated by them, and to entreat their compassion in granting a Commission for putting these persons to a tryall, and for bringing the same to an effectual and speedy issue.   And that they would order some way for maintaining those of them that have nothing of their own till the tryall be complete, or so long as they shall be detained in prison.   And the three confessants, viz., Elizabeth Anderson, James and Thomas Lindsays, the Presbytery thought fit, upon the desire of the said Commissioners for enquiry, that they should be severally keeped by turns in the houses of the ministers of the Presbytery, and that they may have opportunity to instruct and deal with their consciences in the meantime, till further course be taken with them by authority.

At Pasley, March 17, 1697.

The Presbytery this day considering that upon the giving in of the Commission's report, appointed for taking a precognition of the business of witchcraft, the Lords of His Majestie's Privie Counsell had granted a Commission for putting those who are incarcerate or suspected to a tryall, and that those commissionat are to meet to-morrow at Renfrew : therefore the Presbytery appoints Mrs. Pat. Sympson, Dav. Brown, Jo. Stirling, Andrew Turner, Tho. Blackwell to wait upon their Lordships' day and place forsd.

At Pasley, March 24, 1697.

The Presbytery, considering the great rage of Satan in this corner of the land, and, particularly, the continued trouble of Bargarren's daughter, which is a great evidence of the Lord's displeasure, being provoked by the sins of the land (exprest as the cause of our former publike fasts), so to let Satan loose among us: therefore the Presbytery judged it very necessary to set apart a day of solemn humiliation and fasting, that we may humble ourselves under God's hand, and wrestle with God in prayer that He may restraine Satan's rage, and relieve that poor afflicted damsell and that family from their present distress, and that the Lord would break in upon the hearts of these poor obdured wretches that are indited, that they may freely confess, to the glory of God and the rescuing of their own souls out of the hands of Satan, and that the Lord would conduct and clear their way that are to be upon the tryall, in order to the giving of Satan's kingdom an effectuall strok : therefore the Presbytery appoints thursday-come-eight-days to be religiously and solemnly observed, upon the accounts foresaid, in all the congregations within their bounds, and the same to be intimate the Sabbath preceding. The Presbytery also appoints the wholl members to deall with those who are indited, as they shall have occasion, in order unto their being brought to a confession.

At Irvine, April 6, 1697.

The Presbytery considering that the Commissioners of Witchcraft are to meet again, April 13, at Pasley, and the Presbytery considering how requisite it would be to have a sermon before them at their down sitting upon such an occassion, and being informed also that the same is desired and expected by those concerned in the tryalls ; therefore the Presbytery appoints their clerk to write and send an express to Mr. Hutcheson, signifying that the Presbytery hath appointed and seriously recommended to him to preach before the Commissioners at Pasley, Aprile 13.

The Presbytery appoints their Moderator to apply to the Synod that they would appoint some of the grave and experienced brethren in the several Presbyteries to join with this Presbytery of Pasley during the time of the tryall for assisting and advising with them in anything incumbent upon them at this juncture.

At Pasley, Apr. 13, 1697.

Reported that application had been made to the Synod for appointing some experienced brethren to join with this Presbytery, and according to their appointment were present—Mrs. Will. Dunlop, J. Brown, Ro. Wylie, Pa. Warner, J. Wilson, Ro. Wallace, Jo. Ritchie, Tho. Linning, with several brethren of the neighbouring Presbyteries.

Mr. Hutcheson preached before the Commissioners according to appointment on Ex. xxii. 18. The meeting, at the desire of the Commissioners, appoints Mrs. Will. Dunlop, Ja. Brown, Pa. Warner, Ro. Wylie, Jo. Wilson, Tho. Linning, Ja. Hutcheson, Pa. Sympson, And. Turner, Ja. Birsbane, to wait upon their Lordships, and to know their desires to this meeting; and further recommended it to them to deal with the consciences of those on whom the insensible marks are found, in order to their being brought to confession, as they shall, with the Commissioners, concert the method of the same.

At Pasley, Apr. 14, 1697.

Reported that those appointed to wait upon the Commissioners obeyed accordingly. The meeting considering the necessity of their representing unto the Commissioners their thoughts with respect unto this present affair, and specially of the circumstances of severals delated and suspected within the bounds, does therefore appoint Mrs. Sympson, Wyllie, and Dunlop to put the same in form against the next meeting, in order to its being represented to the Commissioners, and appoints all the brethren to give information of the particular circumstances of such persons in their respective paroches unto those appointed to draw the representation.

The meeting this day considering that the revising of the narrative of Christine Shaw's trouble was recommended unto them by the Synod, therefore they appoint Mr. Turner to cause transcribe four copies, and to send one to Principall Dunlop and Mr. Ja. Brown, another to Mr. Balantyne, another to Mr. Mr. Wylie, and another to Mr. Wilson, allowing them to advise with any of the brethren of their respective presbyteries in the revising thereof, appointing them ere they leave to meet and appoint time and place of their next meeting that they may compare their animadversions, and put the wholl relation in a suteable dress.

The meeting considering that the Synod had recommended them to think upon the expediency of having a fast day, on this occasion through the Presbyteries of the Synod, as it had been in the Presbytery of Paisley, as they should find it consistent with the dyets and issue of the Commission; and the meeting finding that the Commission is to be adjourned for some time does judge it expedient and necessary, that betwixt and the next meeting of the Commission there be a fast day throwout the whole bounds of the Synod, leaving it to the particular presbytery to concert their own days to be observed, and if their ordinary meeting fall not in timeously that they call a Presbytery *pro re nata* and appoint Mr. Warner, Mr. Wilson, and Mr. Dav. Brown to draw up some causes of the same against the next meeting.

The meeting appoints all the members that are not upon the forementioned committees to meet to-morrow, at seven o'clock in the morning, for prayer at the Presbytery House, and adjourns till to-morrow after rising of the Commission.

At Pasley, Apr. 15, 1697.

Reported that the representation of the circumstances of the bounds was given in and approven, and put in the hands of the Commissioners.

Mr. Wilson produced the causes of a fast to be kept throwout the bounds of the Synod which were read and approven, and the clerk of Pasley Presbytery appointed to send copies thereof to the severall Presbyteries.

The meeting for prayer observed according to appointment.

The meeting finding that the Commissioners have adjourned till the 11th of May, and had ordered some of the pannels to the Tolbooth of Renfrew, others of them to Glasgow, and the rest to stay at Pasley, does therefore appoint Mr. Da. Brown, Mr. Ja. Stirline, Mr. Tho. Blackwell frequently to wait upon and deal with the consciences of those that are in Pasley, and Mrs. Symson and Turner with those at Renfrew, leaving it to these five minrs., when they meet to advise with the Shireff anent the disposall of the three confessants, leaving it to the minrs. of Glasgow to converse with such of the prisoners as shall be there, and adjourns this meeting till the tenth day of May.

At Pasley, May 10, 1697.

The meeting appoints Mr. Macdowell, Mr. Turner, and Mr. Blackwell to spend some time this night and to-morrow morning in conversing with the prisoners in the Tolbooth of Pasley, and Mr. Taylor and Mr. Pasley with those in Renfrew.

This day it was reported that those appointed to revise the narrative had obeyed, and their thoughts and animadversions thereupon being this day produced and compared ; the whole thereof was committed to Mr. Sympson, Mr. Turner, and Mr. Blackwell, to draw up the whole relation *in mundo.*

It having been formerly recommended to Mr. Jo. Wilson by this meeting to draw up a preface to be prefixt to the narrative which was this day produced, read, and approven, and left in Mr. Turner's hands. The meeting resolving to wait on the Commissioners and their dyets, and to converse with the

prisoners as they had access, did leave it to the Presbytery of
Paisley to meet themselves, or to call the whole meeting as
they found cause.

At Pasley, May 19, 1697.

Mrs. M'Dowell, Da. Brown, Ja. Stirline, are appointed as
frequently as they possibly can to converse with the seven persons that are condemned to die for witchcraft.   Mr. Pa. Symson and Mr. Da. Brown are appointed to have each of them a
lecture in the Tolbooth to those that are condemned, upon
June 9, the day preceding their execution.

At Pasley, June 9, 1697.

Mr. Symson preacht this day in the Tolbooth to the condemned persons, on 2 Timothy, ii. 25, 26, and also Mr.
Brown on 1 Tim. i. 16, according to appointment.

The Presbytery did appoint the whole members to spend
some time this night with the condemned persons who are to
dy to-morrow, and did allot to each one or two of the brethren one of the sentenced persons, to be dealt with by them,
and waited upon to the Fire.

J. D.

FROM AUTHENTIC DOCUMENTS.

A HISTORY

OF THE

WITCHES

OF

RENFREWSHIRE,

WHO WERE BURNED ON THE GALLOWGREEN
OF PAISLEY.

PUBLISHED BY

THE EDITOR OF THE PAISLEY REPOSITORY.

" *Magic Terrors, Spells of mighty power,*
" *Witches, who rove at midnight hour.*"

PAISLEY :

PRINTED BY J. NEILSON,
FOR JOHN MILLAR, BOOKSELLER.

1809.

CONTENTS.

The Publisher sincerely thanks his numerous subscribers for their liberal encouragement of this work, which has far exceeded his most sanguine expectations. While he has, at a considerable trouble and expense, collected old manuscripts and other materials on the subject, besides what were promised in his Prospectus, and by that means he has been enabled to make his work complete, he has the satisfaction to think that the most of his subscribers will be well pleased with the work. However, he is not of the opinion that his book will please every person, for that is what no book has ever yet done.

The Publisher cannot, with propriety, omit returning his warmest thanks to Thomas Bissland, Esq, of Ferguslie; William M'Kerrell, Esq., Maxwellton; Robert Paterson, Esq., Provost of Renfrew, and other landed gentlemen; the Faculty of Procurators, Paisley, and particularly, Messrs. William M'Walter and Henry Wilson, writers, for the pieces he received from them, and the interest they took in the work.

TREATISE ON WITCHCRAFT.

BY

SIR GEORGE MACKENZIE, OF ROSEHAUGH,

Who was King's Advocate, and one of the Lords of the Privy Council in Scotland.

From his "*Laws and Customes of Scotland in Matters Criminal.*"

Printed in 1678.

CONTENTS.

THAT there are witches, divines cannot doubt, since the Word of God hath ordained that no witch shall live ; nor lawyers in Scotland, seeing our law ordains it to be punished with death. And though many lawyers, in Holland

and elsewhere, do think that albeit there were witches under
the law, yet there are none under the Gospel,—the devil's
power having ceased as to these as well as in his giving
responses by oracles.

I.—Wierus, that great patron of witchcraft, endeavours to
maintain his opinion by these arguments :—1. That such as
are accused of witchcraft are ordinarily silly old women whose
age and sex disposeth them to melancholy, and whose melancholy disposeth them to a madness which should render their
confessions very suspected, and in this crime there are seldom
other proofs, whereas the things confessed are so horrid, that
it cannot be imagined any reasonable creature would commit
them.—2. God can only work the miracle ascribed to witches,
He who is the author of nature being only able to alter
or divert its course ; and the devil doth but delude the
fancy of poor creatures, as fevers and melancholy misrepre-
sent objects. Nor are such as are cheated in the one more
guilty than they who are sick of the other. And it is severe
to burn men and women for doing that which is concluded
impossible to be done by them.—3. It is unjust to punish
them for doing ill by charms, except it could be first proved
that these charms produced the effects that are punishable ;
and lawyers should argue thus, those who kill or hurt men or
beasts by unlawful means, are punishable by death. But so
it is, that witches and charmers kill men and beasts by unlawful means, and therefore ought to be punished by death, of
which syllogism Wierus denies the minor ; for it can never be
proved that verses, crosses, or laying flesh in the threshold,
&c., can destroy men or beasts, these being causes very dis-
proportionable to such effects, there being no contact betwixt
the agent and patient in these cases.—4. These who execute
the will of God are not punishable, for that is their duty, and
so cannot be their crime. But so it is, that whatever the

devil or witches do, is decreed by God either for trial or punishment expressly, and without his permission nothing can be done. And if the devil were not acting here by obedience, or were at liberty, he would not leave any one man undestroyed, or any of God's works undefaced.

But that there are witches, and that they are punishable capitally, not only when they poison or murder, but even for enchanting and deluding the world, is clear by an express text, Exod. xxii. verse 18.,—"Thou shalt not suffer a witch to live." And it is observable, that the same word which expresses a witch here, is that which is used in Exod. vii. to express those magicians who deluded only the people by transforming a rod into a serpent, as Moses had done, though no person was prejudged by their cheat and illusion. Likeas, Lev. xxix. and 27. It is ordained that "a man or a woman that hath a familiar spirit, or that is a wizard, shall surely be put to death; they shall stone them with stones; their blood shall be upon them." Which laws were in such observation amongst the Jews, that the witch of Endor, 1 Sam. xxviii., was afraid to use her sorcery before the king, because the king had cut off those who had familiar spirits and wizards out of the land. And so great indignation did the eternal God bear to this sin, that he did destroy the ten tribes of Israel because they were addicted to it.

Nor were the Jews only enemies to this vice, but even the Heathens, following the dictates of nature, punished witches as enemies to the author of it; for the Persians dashed their heads against stones, as Minsing observes, ad. Item lex Cornelia inst. de pub. and Tacitus, lib. ii. Annal. tells us that Publius Marcius and Pituanus were executed for this crime; for which likewise Valerius Maximus, lib. vi. cap. iii. tells us that Publicia and Lucinia were with threescore and ten other Romans hanged. But since it is expressly con-

demned in scripture, and many general councils, such as
Aurelian, Toletan, and Anaciritan, it should not be lawful
for us to debate what the law hath expressly condemned, by
the same reason, that we should deny witches, we must deny
the truth of all history, ecclesiastic and secular. It is sure
that the devil having the power and will to prejudge men,
cannot but be ready to execute all that is in witchcraft : And
it is as credible that God would suffer men to be convinced
by these means, that there are spirits, and that by these means
he would give continued proofs of his power in repressing the
devil, and of the necessity that silly men have of depending
upon his infinite power.

To the former arguments it may be answered, that as to the
first, all sins and vices are the effects of delusion ; nor are
witches more deluded by melancholy, than murderers are by
rage and revenge.   And though it hath never been seen, that
persons naturally mad, have been either guilty of, or punished
for this crime, the devil designing in this crime to gain only
such as can damn themselves by giving a free consent.   Yet
if madness could be proved, or did appear ; it would certainly
defend both against the guilt and punishment : And therefore
such a series of clear circumstances should concur before a
person be found guilty of this crime, as should secure the
panel, and satisfy the judge fully in the quærie.   But since
daily experience convinces the world that there may be such
a crime, and that the law exacts either confession, or clear
proofs, who can condemn the law as rigorous in this case,
since, without believing these, there could be no justice administered, and whilst judges shunned to punish it in some
cases, they behoved to suffer it from the same arguments to
go unpunished in all cases.

To the second, it is answered, that though neither the devil
nor witches can work miracles, yet the offering to cheat the

world by a commerce with the devil, and the very believing that the devil is able to do such things for them, should be a sufficient crime; but much more when they believe all those things to be done by themselves, they giving their own express consent to the crime, and by concurring by all that in them is to the commission of it. Likeas, it is undeniable, that the devil knowing all the secrets of nature, may, by applying actives to passives that are unknown to us, produce real effects which seem impossible.

To the third, though charms be not able to produce the effects that are punishable in witches, yet since these effects cannot be produced without the devil, and that he will not employ himself at the desire of any who have not resigned themselves wholly to him, it is very just that the users of these should be punished, being guilty at least of apostacy and heresy.

The fourth argument is but a mere and silly sophism; for though God in his providence permits at least all things that are done, to be done, yet such as contemn either the commands of him or his vicegerents, ought to be punished.

I cannot but acknowledge that there are some secrets in nature which would have been looked upon in the first authors as the effects of magic; and I believe that in the duller nations a philosopher drawing iron with a loadstone might have run a great risk of being burned; and it is hard to give a judgment of Naudeus' learned book in favour of the Persian magicians, the Assyrian chaldeans, the Indian gymnosophists, and the druids of the Gauls; for it cannot be denied but that many true mathematicians and physicians have passed for magicians in the duller ages of the world; but as to this, there is now no fear, since learning hath so sufficiently illuminated the world, so as to distinguish betwixt these two. But I am still jealous of those sages who were frequented by

familiar spirits, though they were otherwise very excellent men,
such as Porphir, Jamblicus, Plotin, and others, who pretended
by the purity of their lives to be so spiritual, as to deserve the
friendship of spirits : for besides that the primitive fathers and
doctors of the church have testified against such as mere
magicians.   It is not intelligible how those spirits that frequented them could be good, since they were tempted to fall
from the true religion to paganism, and did offer such sacrifices as the true God did never allow ; and if such impostures
were allowed, it were easy for any to defend themselves,
being truly witches.

II.—Albeit witchcraft be the greatest of crimes, since it
includes in it the grossest of heresies, and blasphemies, and
treasons against God, in preferring to the Almighty his rebel
and enemy, and in thinking the devil worthier of being served
and reverenced, and is accompanied with murder, poisoning,
bestiality, and other horrid crimes : yet I conclude only from
this, that when witches are found guilty, they should be most
severely punished, not with scourging and banishment, as the
custom of Savoy was related to be by Gothofred, hoc tit. but
by the most ignominious of deaths.   Yet from the horridness
of this crime, I do conclude, that of all crimes it requires the
clearest relevancy, and most convincing probation.   And I
condemn, next to the witches themselves, those cruel and too
forward judges, who burn persons by thousands as guilty of
this crime, to whom I shall recommend these considerations.

1. That it is not presumable that any who hear of the
kindness of God to men, and of the devil's malice against
them, of the rewards of heaven, and torments of hell, would
deliberately enter into the service of that wicked spirit, whom
they know to have no riches to bestow, nor power to help,
except it be allowed by permission that he may tempt men :
and that he being a liar from the beginning, his promises

deserve no belief, especially since in no man's experience he hath ever advantaged any person : whereas, on the contrary, his service hath brought all who entered in it to the stake.

2. Those poor persons who are ordinarily accused of this crime, are poor ignorant creatures, and oft-times women who understand not the nature of what they are accused of; and many mistake their own fears and apprehensions for witchcraft ; of which I shall give you two instances, one of a poor weaver, who after he had confessed witchcraft, being asked how he saw the devil, he answered, "like flies dancing about a candle." Another of a woman, who asked seriously, when she was accused, if a woman might be a witch and not know it? And it is dangerous that these, who are of all others the most simple, should be tried for a crime, which of all others is most mysterious.

3. These poor creatures, when they are defamed, become so confounded with fear, and the close prison in which they are kept, and so starved for want of meat and sleep, (either of which wants is enough to disorder the strongest reason) that hardly wiser and more serious people than they would escape distraction : and when men are confounded with fear and apprehension, they will imagine things very ridiculous and absurd ; and as no man would escape a profound melancholy upon such an occasion, and amidst such usages ; therefore I remit to physicians and others to consider what may be the effects of melancholy, which hath oft made men, who appeared otherwise solid enough, imagine they were horses, or had lost their noses, &c. And since it may make men err in things which are obvious to their senses, what may be expected as to things which transcend the wisest men's reason.

4. Most of these poor creatures are tortured by their keepers, who being persuaded they do God good service, think it their duty to vex and torment poor prisoners : and I know *ex cer-*

*tissima scientia,** that most of all that ever were taken, were tormented after this manner, and this usage was the ground of all their confession; and albeit the poor miscreants cannot prove this usage, the actors being the only witnesses, yet the judge should be afraid of it, as that which at first did elicit the confession, and for fear of which they dare not retract it.

5. I went when I was a justice-depute to examine some women who had confessed judicially, and one of them, who was a silly creature, told me under secrecy, that she had not confessed because she was guilty, but being a poor creature, who wrought for her meat, and being defamed for a witch, she knew she would starve, for no person thereafter would either give her meat or lodging, and that all men would beat her, and hound dogs at her, and that therefore she desired to be out of the world; whereupon she wept most bitterly and upon her knees called God to witness what she said. Another told me that she was afraid the devil would challenge a right to her, after she was said to be his servant, and would haunt her, as the minister said when he was desiring her to confess; and therefore she desired to die. And really ministers are ofttimes indiscreet in their zeal, to have poor creatures to confess in this; and I recommend to judges, that the wisest ministers should be sent to them, and those who are sent, should be cautious in this.

6. Many of them confess things which all divines conclude impossible, as transmutation of their bodies into beasts, and money into stones, and their going through close doors, and a thousand other ridiculous things, which have no truth nor existence but in their fancy.

7. The accusers here are masters, or neighbours who had their children dead, and are engaged by grief to suspect these

---

* From certain knowledge.

poor creatures. I knew one likewise burned because the lady was jealous of her with her husband : and the crime is so odious that they are never assisted or defended by their relations.

8. The witnesses and assizers are afraid that if they escape, that they will die for it, and therefore they take an unwarrantable latitude. And I have observed that scarce ever any who were accused before a country assize of neighbours did escape that trial.

9. Commissions are granted ordinarily to gentlemen, and others in the country who are suspected upon this account ; and who are not exactly enough acquainted with the nature of this crime, which is so debateable amongst the most learned ; nor have the panels any to plead for them, and to take notice who are led as witnesses ; so that many are admitted who are *testes inhabiles,** and suspected : and albeit their confessions are sent to, and advised by the counsel before such commissions be granted, yet the counsel cannot know how these confessions were emitted, nor all the circumstances which are necessary, and cannot be known at a distance. Very many of these poor silly women do re-seal at the stake from the confessions they emitted at the bar, and yet have died very penitent : and as it is very presumable that few will accuse themselves, or confess against their own life, yet very many confess this crime.

III.—The method I shall use in treating of this crime shall be—1. Upon what suspicion witches may be apprehended. 2. What judges are competent. 3. What ditties are relevant. 4. What probation is sufficient. 5. What is the ordinary punishment. As to the first, I know it is

---

* Improper witnesses.

C

ordinary in Scotland not only that Magistrates do apprehend witches almost upon any dilation; but even gentlemen and such as are masters of the ground do likewise make them prisoners, and keep them so till they transmit them at their pleasure to Justices of Peace, Magistrates, or some open prisons. But all this procedure is most unwarrantable, for gentlemen, and such as are vested with no authority, should upon no account, without a special warrant, apprehend any upon suspicion that they are witches, since to apprehend is an act of jurisdiction; and, therefore, I think no prison should receive any as suspected of witchcraft until they know that the person offered to them be apprehended by lawful authority. 2. Since imprisonment is a punishment, and constantly attended with much infamy to the name and detriment to the affairs of him who is imprisoned, especially in witchcraft, I do conclude that there must some presumption precede all inquisition,—for the meanest degrees of inquisition, though without captor, does somewhat defame,—and that the person should not be apprehended except it appear, by the event of the inquisition, that she lies under either many or pregnant suspicions, such as—That she is defamed by other witches; that she hath been herself of an evil fame; that she hath been found charming, or that the ordinary instruments of charming be found in her house; and according to Delrio's opinion,— Lib. V., Sec. II.,—"*Ad assumendas informationes, sufficiunt levia judicia, fed gravia requiruntur ad hoc ut citetur reus, & ut judex specialiter inquirat.*" *

IV.—Witchcraft was *crimen utriusque fori* † by the canon

---

* In order to take information, light trials suffice, but particular ones are required to this one, that the person accused be summoned, and that the judge may make special enquiry.

† Crime examinable by both Courts.

law, and with us the Kirk Sessions used to inquire into it, in order to the scandal, and to take the confession of the parties, to receive witnesses against them, as is clear by the process of Janet Barker and Margaret Lawder, December 9th, 1643. But since so much weight is laid upon the depositions there emitted, Kirk Sessions should be very cautious in their procedures.

By the Act of Parliament, Q. M. 9 Parl., 73. Act. All sheriffs, lords of regalities, and their deputes, and all other judges having power to execute the same, are ordained to execute that Act against witchcraft, which can import no more but that they should concur to the punishment of the crime by apprehending or imprisoning the party suspected; but it doth not follow that because they may concur, that, therefore, they are judges competent to the cognition of the crime, since the relevancy in it is oft-times so intricate, and the procedure requires necessarily so much arbitrariness, and the punishment is so severe, that these considerations jointly should appropriate the cognition thereof solely to the Justice Court. Nor find I any instances wherein these inferior courts have tried this crime. And albeit the council do oft times grant commissions to countrymen, yet that seems dangerous; nor can I see why, by express Act of Parliament, it should have been appointed that no commission should be granted for trying murder, and yet witchcraft should be so tried by commissions. The Justices, then, are the proper judges in witchcraft.

V.—As to the relevancy in this crime, the first article useth to be paction to serve the devil, which is certainly relevant *per se*, without any addition, as is to be seen in all the indictments, especially in that of Margaret Hutchison, August 10th, 1661. And by Delrio, carpz. p. 1. quest. 47. and others; but because the devil useth to appear in the similitude of a

man, when he desireth these poor creatures to serve him ;
therefore they should be interrogate, if they knew him to be
the devil when they condescended to his service.

Paction with the devil is divided by the lawyers, *in express-
um & tacitum,* an express and tacit paction. Express
paction is performed either by a formal promise given to the
devil then present, or by presenting a supplication to him, or
by giving the promise to a proxy or commissioner empowered
by the devil for that effect, which is used by some who dare
not see himself. The formula set down by Delrio, is—" I deny
God, creator of heaven and earth, and I adhere to thee, and
believe in thee." But by the journal books it appears, that the
ordinary form of express paction confessed by our witness is a
simple promise to serve him. Tacit paction is either when a
person who hath made no express paction, useth the words or
signs which sorcerers use, knowing them to be such, either by
their books, or discourse ; and this is condemned as sorcery,
Can. 26. quest. 5. and is relevant to infer the crime of witchcraft, or to use these words and signs, and though the user
know them not to be such ; it is no crime, if the ignorance be
probable, and if the user be content to abstain, Delrio, lib. ii.
quest. 4.

VI.—Renouncing of baptism is by Delrio made an effect
of paction ; yet with us it is *per se** relevant (as was found
in the former process of Margaret Hutchison), and the
solemnity confessed by our witches is by putting one hand to
the crown of the head, and another to the sole of the foot,—
renouncing their baptism in that posture. Delrio tells us
that the devil useth to baptize them of new, and to wipe off
their brow the old baptism ; and our witches confess always
the giving them new names which are very ridiculous, as
Redshanks, Sergeant, &c.

---

* By itself.

VII.—The devil's mark useth to be a great article with us ; but it is not *per se* found relevant, except it be confessed by them that they got that mark with their own consent,—*quo casu,** it is equivalent to a paction. This mark is given them, as is alledged, by a nip in any part of the body, and it is blue. Delrio calls it stigma, or character, lib. ii., quest. 4, and alledges that it is sometimes like the impression of a hare's foot, or the foot of a rat or spider,—l. v., sect. 4, num. 28. Some think that it is impossible there can be any mark which is insensible and will not bleed, for all things that live must have blood ; and so this place behoved both to be dead and alive at once, and behoved to live without aliment, for blood is the aliment of the body. But it is very easy to conceive that the devil may make a place insensible at a time, or may apply things that may squeeze out the blood.

This mark is discovered among us by a pricker, whose trade it is, and who learns it as other trades ; but this is a horrid cheat, for they alledge that if the place bleed not, or if the person be not sensible, he or she is infallibly a witch. But, as Delrio confesses, it is very hard to know any such mark *à nevo, clavo, vel impertigine naturali,*† and there are many pieces of dead flesh which are insensible even in living bodies ; and a villain who used this trade with us, being in the year 1666 apprehended for other villanies, did confess all this trade to be a mere cheat.

VIII. Threatening to do mischief, if any evil follow immediately, hath been too ordinarily found a relevant article to infer witchcraft with us. Thus Agnes Finnie was pursued in anno 1643, upon the general article of having witched several persons, and particularly for these articles, 1. That William Fairlie having nick-named and called her Annie Winnie, she

---

* In which case.   † From a mark or a natural insensibility.

sware in rage he should go halting home, and within twenty-four hours he took a palsy.   2. That Beatrix Nisbit refusing to pay the said Agnes the annual rent of two dollars owing by Hector Nisbit her father, she told her she should repent it, and within an hour thereafter she lost her tongue, and the power of her right side.   3. That Janet Greintoun having refused to carry away two herrings she had bought from the said Agnes, and to pay for them, she told her it should be the last meat she should eat, and within a little after she fell sick; against which articles, it was there alledged that this libel was not relevant, and could not go to the knowledge of an inquest :—1. Because no means were condescended upon from which the witchcraft was inferred; and if this libel were relevant, it would be relevant to libel generally that the panel were a witch.   1. Assizers are only judges to the matter of fact, and not to what consists *in jure*;* but so it is, that if this libel were to pass to the knowledge of an inquest, all the debate *in jure* behoved to be before the assize before whom the panels' procurators behoved to debate how far *minæ &* *damnum sequutum* † are relevant, and how far any person is punishable as a witch, though no charms or other means commonly used by witches be condescended upon ; and as to the threatenings, they were not relevant, seeing they had not all the requisites which are expressed by the doctors as requisite, for they were not specific, bearing the promise to do a particular ill, as that Fairlie should take a palsy or Nisbit lose her tongue.   2. There was not a preceding reason of enmity proved, nor is it probable that for so small a matter as a herring or the annual rent of two dollars she would have killed any person, and exposed herself to hazard ; nor was

---

* In law.   † Threatening and damage following thereon.

the effect immediate, nor such as could have proceeded from any other natural cause, without all which had concurred. Delrio—lib. 5, sect. 3—is very clear that *minæ etiam cum damno sequuto** are not so much as a presumption; but though all these did concur, it is very clear both from Delrio, ibid, and Farin., quest. 5, num. 37, that all these threatenings are not sufficient to infer the crime of witchcraft. Lastly, it was offered to be proved that some of these persons died of a natural disease, depending upon causes preceding that threatening; notwithstanding of all which, the libel was found relevant, and she was burned. But I think this decision very hard, and very contrary to the opinion of all received writers, who think that albeit *minæ* be *adminiculatæ*,† with all the former advantages and *probatæ de ea quæ solet minas exequi*,‡ yet the same are only sufficient to infer an arbitrary punishment, not corporal but pecuniary. And certainly such a wicked custom as threatening is in itself a crime, and thus it was only well found to be *crimen in suo genere*§ in the process led against Katherine Oswald, Nov. 11th, 1629.

IX.—Sometimes articles are libelled wherein the malefice hath no dependence at all upon the means used; and thus it was libelled against Margaret Hutchison, August 20th, 1661, that John Clark's wife being sick, she came to the bedside when all the doors and windows were fast, and combed her head, several nights; and the last of these nights, she came to the bedside, and put her hand to the woman's pap, whereupon the child died,—which article was found relevant *per se*. And it was libelled against Janet Cock, September 7th, 1661,

---

* Even threatening with following damage.   † Threats attested.

‡ And proven concerning her who was accustomed to execute these threatenings.

§ Crime in its own kind.

that a woman called Spindie being at enmity with her, she gave
her a cuff, whereupon Spindie immediately distracted ; and
being reproved therefore by the minister of Dalkeith, he immediately distracted; which article was likewise found relevant,
being joined with fame and delation : which decisions are,
in my opinion, very dangerous, for they want a sure foundation, and are precedents whereby judges may become very
arbitrary. And against these, I may oppone a third allegiance
used in the former process against Agnes Finnie, wherein it
was alledged that the conclusion of all criminal libels should
be necessarily inferred from the deed subsumed, and that
*conclusio semper sequitur debiliorem partem : nam libellus est
syllogismus apodicticus, sed non probabilis ;* ∗ and, therefore,
except the libel could condescend upon some means used by
the panel, from which the malefice were necessarily inferred,
it could not be concluded that these malifices were done by
her, or that she was guilty of the wrong done.   Thus,
Bodin, lib. 4., does conclude, that *venefica non sunt condem-
nandæ licet sint deprehensæ cum busonibus, ossibus, aliisque in-
strumentis egredientes exovili licet oves immediate moriantur.* †
And, Perkins, cap. 6, asserts that neither defamation nor
threatenings, albeit what is threatened does follow, nor *mala
fama,* ‡ nor the defuncts laying the blame of their death upon
the person accused (called *inculpatio* by the doctors) can
infer this crime, though all these be conjoined ; for, in his
opinion, nothing can be a sufficient ground to condemn a
witch, except the panel's own confession, or the depositions

∗ That a conclusion always follows the weaker party, for a libel is an
apodictic syllogism ; but is not at all probable.

† That witches are not to be condemned with toads, bones, or other
instruments, and unless the sheep die immediately when they go out of the
fold.

‡ Bad fame.

of two famous witnesses, deponing upon means used by the panel. And it is remarkable, that in the chapter immediately subsequent to that wherein witches are ordinarily to be put to death, God hath expressly ordained that "out of the mouth of two or three witnesses every word shall be established." And in the process deduced against Isobel Young for witchcraft, February 4, 1629, and against Katherine Oswald, November 11, 1629, this point is likewise debated, it being libelled against the said Katherine, that by her witchcraft she caused a cow give blood instead of milk, and caused a woman fall and break a rib in her side. Against which it was alleged, that there was no necessary connection there, *inter terminum à quo* & *ad quem inter causam* & *effectum :* * but, on the contrary, the cow's giving blood for milk might proceed from another natural cause, viz., from lying upon an ant or emmet hill; and, therefore, I think that because we know not what virtue may be in herbs, stones, or other things which may be applied, it were very hard to find cures performed by the application of these, without the using charms or spells, to be witchcraft. But when these outward applications are used to do hurt, as for instance,—If the said Margaret Wallace, being at enmity with John Clark, and after she was forbidden to frequent his house, did continue to frequent the same, and did throw in blood or any unusual thing upon his wife's pap ; if the child who sucked the same had thereafter died, I think this article, joined with preceding defamation of her by another witch, might have been found relevant, because she was there *in re illicita.* † And since the law cannot know exactly what efficacy there is in natural causes, it may very well

---

* There were no necessary connection existed betwixt the cause and the effect.

† In an unlawful way.

discharge any such superstitious forbidden acts as it pleases, under the pain of witchcraft. Nor can those who are accused complain of severity since *sibi imputent*,* that use these forbidden things against the express commandment of the law : and, therefore, since the law and practice hath forbidden all charms, it is most just that these who use the same should be severely punished, whatever the pretext be upon which they are used, or after whatever way or manner, or to whatever end, whether good or bad.

X.—Albeit per leg. 4 cod. de mal. & Math. these magic arts are only condemned which tend to the destruction of mankind, but not these whereby men are cured or the fruits of the ground preserved, yet I have oft-times imputed this constitution to Tribonian, who was a Pagan and a severe enemy to Christians, or else that it behoved to be so interpreted, or that thereby remedies assisted by godly prayers were allowed, else what mean these words—*suffragia innocenter adhibita.* † But since, I am informed from the ecclesiastic historians, as Zozim. lib. 2, that Constantine was not yet turned Christian when he passed that constitution. But, however, this constitution is omitted in the Basilicks, and the Gloss says that ουκ εδιχου ιν τη αποκαθαρ θει it was not thought fit to be mentioned in the repurgation of the law ; and that constitution was very well reprobated by Leo's 65 Novel. And by the canon law, *tit. de forti-legiis;* and the general sanction of the former Act of Parliament leaves no place for this distinction. Suitable to all which, John Brough was convicted for witchcraft in Anno 1643 for curing beasts by casting white stones in water, and sprinkling them therewith ; and for curing women by washing their feet with south-running water, and putting odd money in the water. Several

---

* They may lay the blame on themselves.   † Aids innocently used.

other instances are to be seen in the processes led in Anno 1661; and the instance of Drummond is very remarkable, who was burned for performing many miraculous cures, albeit no malefice * was ever proved.

XI.—Consulting with witches is a relevant ditty with us, as was found against Allison Jollie, per. Oct. 1596; and this is founded upon the express words of the Act. The professing, likewise, skill in necromancy, or any such craft, is by the foresaid Act of Parliament a relevant article; for the full clearing of which Act it is fit to know that divination was either *per dæmono-mantiam*,—the invocation of Pagan gods; or *nanganiam*,—which was the prophecying for invocation of some sublunary thing. *Magnania* is divided in *necromantiam*, which was a prophecying by departed spirits; *udromantiam*, which was a divination by water, &c. All which species and kinds of divinations by any thing is comprehended under the general prohibition of necromancy, and such like acts, so that predictions and responses by the seive, and the shear, and by the book, and all such cheats and species of sorcery are punishable by death in this Act. Yet these forbidden practices may sometimes be excused by ignorance, or if it can be cleared by circumstances, that the user designed nothing but an innocent jest or recreation,—Delrio lib. 4, cap. 1, quæst. 4.

XII.—The last article in criminal libels useth ordinarily to be the being delated by other witches, which the doctors call *diffamatio*,† and we, common bruit, and open fame, which are never sustained as relevant *per se*, but only joined with other relevant articles; as is to be seen in the foresaid process of

---

* Malefice, in the Scots law, signifies an act or effect of witchcraft.
† Defamation.

Margaret Hutchison, though I think that *interloquutor* very
severe, since if any of the former articles be *per se* relevant,
they need not the assistance of fame and delation. Sometimes
likewise, but with much more reason, articles that are of themselves irrelevant, are sustained relevant, being joined with
fame and delation ; an example whereof is to be seen in the
9th article of the indictment against Janet Cock, Sep. 7, 1661,
in which article, she was accused for having recovered a
child by charms, with the help of another witch, which other
witch had confessed the same when she was confronted with
the said Janet; likeas, both of them were found lying above
the child, whispering one to another, and the blood of a dog
was found standing in a plate beside them; which article
was not sustained relevant *per se*, but was found relevant,
being joined with fame and delation.

XIII.—The relevancy of this crime being thus discussed,
the ordinary probation of it is by confession or witnesses ; but
the probation here should be very clear, and it should be
certain that the person who emitted it is not weary of life
or oppressed with melancholy. 2. Albeit, *non requiritur hic
ut constet de corpore delicti,**—this being a crime which consists
oft-times *in animo,*†—yet it ought to be such as contains
nothing in it that is impossible or improbable. And thus,
albeit Isobel Ramsay did upon the 20th of Aug., 1661, confess that the Devil gave her sixpence, and said that God
desired him to give it her, and at another time a dollar, which
turned thereafter into a slate-stone,—the justices did not find
this confession, though judicial, relevant. And to know what
things are of themselves impossible for the Devil to do, or
at least what is believed to be impossible, may be seen very

---

* Not required this as it may constitute the substance of the crime.
† In the mind.

fully treated of in **Delrio's** second book, where it is condescended that *succubi* & *incubi sunt possibiles,—id est,* that
the Devil may lie in the shape of a man with a woman, or in
the shape of a woman with a man, having first formed to
himself a body of condensed air; and upon such a confession
as this, Margaret Lawder and others were convicted. It is
likewise possible for the Devil to transport witches to their
public conventions from one place to another, which he may
really do by carrying them; and sundry witches were in
Anno 1665 burned in Culross upon such a confession as this.

XIV.—It may be, I confess, argued that spirits and im-
material substances cannot touch things material, and con-
sequently can neither raise nor transport them; but if we
consider how the adamant raises and transports the iron,—and
how the soul of man, which is a spirit, can raise or transport
the body,—and that a man's voice, or a musical sound, is
able to occasion great and extraordinary motions in other
men,—we may easily conclude that devils who are spirits of
far more energy may produce effects surpassing very far our
understanding. And yet I do not deny but that the Devil
does sometimes persuade the witches that they are carried to
places where they never were, making those impressions upon
their spirits, and acquainting them what was done there,
which is done by impressing images upon their brain, and
which images are carried to the exterior senses by the animal
spirits, even as we see the air carries the species of colours
upon it, though in a very insensible way; and thus we see,
likewise, that the fumes of wine or melancholy will represent
strange apparitions, and make us think them real. Nor
ought it to be concluded that, because those witches are only
transported in spirit or in dreams, that therefore they ought
not to be punished, since none can be punished for dreaming;
and that, because those witches desire to have these dreams

and glory in them when they are awake; nor have any these dreams but such as have entered into a preceding paction. I know that the Canon Episcopi in the Council of Anacir (or the Aquilean Council, as others call it) does condemn these transportations as false, and mere delusions, which are impressed upon the fancy of poor creatures by the Devil, & *cum solus spiritus hæc patitur, nec non in animo sed in corpore inveniri opinantur;* * but that Act of that Council does not assert all transportations to be imaginary and dreams, but only declares those who thought they followed Diana and Herodias to these public meetings to be altogether seduced, for these indeed were seduced, for Herodias being dead long since could not be at their meetings. But, from that, it is unjustly concluded that there are no real transportations,— there being so many instances of these transportations given, both in sacred and profane story, and persons having been found wounded, and having really committed murders and other insolencies during these transportations.

XV.—Whether it be possible for a witch to cause any person be possessed by putting devils into their body, may be debated; and that it is possible appears from the history of Simon Magus and many others, and is testified to be true by St. Jerome in the life of St. Hilarion. And since witches have confessed that there are devils who obey one another, and that there are different degrees amongst them, why may not those of an inferior degree be forced, by virtue of a paction with those of a superior order, to possess men and women at the desire of witches? Witches themselves have confessed that this hath been done; and I find by a decision of the Parliament of Tholodus that devils have been heard to

---

* And when the spirit of itself suffers such things, they are supposed to afflict the body as well as the mind.

complain in those that were possessed that they were put there by the enchantment of such and such women. But, upon the other hand, it is not to be imagined that devils would obey mortal creatures, or that God would leave so great a power to any of them to torment poor mortals. And the Devil, who is a liar from the beginning, is not to be believed in saying that he is put there by enchantments; and though he makes such promises to witches, yet he does in these but cheat them: and if the Devil could possess at pleasure, we would see many more possessed than truly there are.

XVI.—The Devil cannot make one solid body to penetrate another, quest. 17; and therefore I think that article libelled against Margaret Hutchison of coming to John Clark's house when doors and windows were shut, should not have been admitted to probation, since it is very probable they would have searched the house after the second or third night's fear, and she could not penetrate doors nor walls.

XVII. — The Devil cannot transform one species into another, as a woman into a cat, for else he behoved to annihilate some of the substance of the woman, or create some more substance to the cat,—the one being much more than the other; and the Devil can neither annihilate or create, nor could he make the shapes return, *nam non datur regressus à privatione ad habitum.** But if we consider the strange tricks of jugglers, and the strange apparitions that Kercher and others relate from natural causes, we may believe that the Devil can make a woman appear to be a beast, & *è contra*, † by either abusing the sense of the beholders, or altering the medium, by inclosing them in the skin of the beast represented, or by inclosing them in a body of air shaped like that

---

* When the shape is destroyed, it is impossible to restore it.

† On the other hand.

which he would have them represent, and the ordinary relation
of the witnesses being wounded when the beast was wounded
in which they were changed may be likewise true, either by
their being really wounded within the body of air in which
they were inclosed, or by the Devil's inflicting that wound
really himself, which is Delrio's opinion. But it would seem
hard to condemn any person upon the confession of what
seems almost impossible in itself; and I cannot allow instances
in the journal books where poor creatures have been burned
upon such confessions, without other strong adminicles.

XVIII.—The Devil may make brutes to speak, or, at least,
speak out of them, quest. 18.

He can also raise storms in the air, and calm these that are
raised, quest. 11. And yet it being libelled against Janet
Cock that she said to those who were carrying a witch to be
executed—"Were it not a good sport if the Devil should take
her from you?" likeas, a great storm did overtake them when
they were carrying her to the place,—it having been a great
calm both before and after; yet this article was not sustained
relevant, since it might have proceeded from folly, or jest, or
vana jactantia.*

XIX.—The Devil may inflict diseases, which is an effect
he may occasion applicando activa passivis,† and by the same
means he may likewise cure : a clear instance whereof appears
in the marriage-knot. And not only may he cure diseases
laid on by himself, as Wierus observes, but even natural
diseases, since he knows the natural causes and the origin of
even those natural diseases, better than physicians can, who
are not present when diseases are contracted, and who, being
younger than he, must have less experience. And it is as un-
true that Divus Thomas observes, who asserts that cures per-

---

* Vain boasting.   † By applying actives to passives.

formed by the Devil cannot continue, since his cures are not natural.

And since he both may make sick and make whole, it follows that he may transfer a disease from one person to another. And I find that it being libelled against Margaret Hutchison, that she took a disease off a woman to put it on a cat: it was alleged that this article was not relevant; because, 1. *Una saga non potest esse ligans & solvens in eodem morbo;* * 2. That in such transactions as these the Devil never used to interpose his skill, except where he was a gainer; and, therefore, though he would transfer a disease from a brute beast to a rational creature, yet he would never transfer a disease from a rational creature to a brute beast: both these defences were repelled. Many witches likewise confess that they cannot cure diseases, because they are laid on by witches of a superior order, who depend upon spirits of a higher degree.

Some think that they may innocently employ a witch to take off the disease imposed by another, and lay it upon the witch who imposed it, even as men may innocently borrow money from a user to be employed for pious uses, or may cause an infidel swear by his false gods for eliciting truth : and that in this manner devils are rather punished than served. But since all commerce with devils is unlawful, this practice is justly reprobated by D. Autun, p. 2, discourse 48. But yet it is thought lawful to all who are bewitched to desire the bewitchers to take off the disease, if it can be removed without a new application to the Devil, but only by taking away the old charm; or it is lawful to any to remove the charm or sign of it, if it be in their power, D. Autun, pag. 825.

---

* The same witch cannot both cause and cure a disease.

E.

XX. —Witches may kill by their looks, which looks being full of venomous spirits, may infect the person upon whom they look, and this is called *fascinatio physica, sed fascinatio vulgaris, quæ dicitur fieri per oculos tenerorum puerorum vel parvorum porcorum vana est & ridicula,** Del. lib. 3. q. 4. sect. 1.

I know there are who think all kinds of fascination by the eyes, either an effect of fancy in the person affected, or else think it a mere illusion of the Devil, who persuades witches that he can bestow upon them the power of killing by looks, or else the Devil really kills, and ascribes it falsely to their looks : whereas, others contend, that by the received opinion of all historians, men have been found to be injured by the looks of witches : and why may not witches poison this way, as well as the Basilisk doth : or why may not the spirits in the eye affect as well as the breath ? or why may not looks kill as well as raise passions in the person looked upon? nor can it be denied but that blearedness is begot by blearedness ; and that menstruous women will spoil a mirror by looking upon it.   Likeas, there seems even some ground for it in scripture ; for, Deut. xxviii. 54., " It is said that a man's eyes shall be evil towards his brother." And some likewise endeavour by consequence from Matth. xx. 15, " Is thine eye evil : " the word βασκαινω signifiying in Scripture both to bewitch and to envy. Some likewise think that St. Paul, Gal. iii. 1., alludes to this received opinion, but conjecture doth so much over-rule all this affair, that it were hard to fix crimes upon so slender grounds ; and, therefore, though where witches confess that they did kill by their looks, their confession and belief may, if they be otherwise of a sound judgment, make a very

---

* Natural witchcraft is the effects of natural causes, but that which is produced by the eyes of certain persons or animals, is vain and ridiculous.

considerable part of a crime, where it is joined with other probabilities, yet *per se* it is hardly relevant.

XXI.—It may be also doubted whether witches can, by amorous potions, inchant men or women to love; and though it may seem that these being acts of the soul, cannot be raised by any corporeal means, yet l. 4. c. de. Malef. & Mathemat. makes this possible, and punishable, *corum scientia punienda, & severissimis merito legibus vindicanda, qui magicis accincti artibus pudicos ad libidinem de fixisse animos deteguntur :* * but this law speaks only of lust, and not of love, as I conceive. Nor can it be denied, but that not only witches, but even naturalists may give potions that may incline men or women to lust. And, therefore, the question still remains, whether witches may incline men or women by potions to a fancy and kindness for any particular person ; and though potions may incline men to madness, yet it doth not follow that, therefore, they may incline them to love. And though D. Autun doth bring many arguments from history, and pretends that the Devil may raise and excite the old species of love which lies hidden in the body, and may thereby form a passion, yet these are too conjectural grounds to be the foundation of a criminal sentence. The Basilicks make the punishment of this to be deportation, and so supplies the former law.

XXII. Witches do likewise torment mankind, by making images of clay or wax, and when the witches prick or punce these images, the persons whom these images represent, do find extreme torment, which doth not proceed from any influence these images have upon the body tormented, but the devil doth by natural means raise these torments in the person tormented, at the same very time that the witches do prick or

---

* The several punishments ought to be inflicted on those who, by magic arts, force chaste persons to the commission of acts of impurity.

punce, or hold to the fire these images of clay or wax; which manner of torment was lately confessed by some witches in Inverness, who likewise produced the images, and it was well known they hated the person who was tormented, and upon a confession so adminiculate, witches may very judiciously be found guilty, since *constat de corpore delicti de modo de linquendi & inimicitiis præviis.* *

XXIII.— It is ordinarily doubted whether confessions emitted before the Kirk Sessions, in this case, be sufficient; but this I have treated more fully in the title of probation by confession. Only here I shall observe that Christian Stewart was found art and part of the bewitching Patrick Ruthven, by laying on him a heavy sickness with a black clout, which she herself had confessed before several ministers, notaries, and others, at diverse times,—all which confessions were proved; and upon these repeated confessions, she was burned Nov., 1596. Margaret Lawder was convicted upon confession emitted before the magistrates and ministers of Edinburgh, albeit past from in judgment Dec. 9, 1643,—see that book of adjournal, p. 349. And if the confession be not fully adminiculate, lawyers advise that confessors should be subjected to the torture, which is not usual in Scotland. And it is very observable that the justices would not put James Welsh to the knowledge of an inquest, though he had confessed himself a witch before the Presbytery of Kirkcudbright, because he was a minor when he confessed the crime, and the confession was only extra-judicial, and that he now retracted the same. But because he had so grossly prevaricated, and had delated so many honest persons, they ordained him to be scourged and put in the correction-house April 17th,

---

* It is evident from the nature of the crime mentioned just now, of their hatred and previous malice.

1662. It was proved against Margaret Wallace, March 20, 1622, that she said that if it could be proved that she was in Greg's house, she should be guilty of all the ditty; and, therefore, it being proved that she was in Greg's house, that probation was alleged by the advocate to be equivalent to a confession, as was found against Patrick Cheyn, to which it was replied that this could amount to no more than a lie : and in my opinion it could not have even the strength of an extra-judicial confession, but rather imported a denial of the crime.

XXIV.—The probation by witness in this crime is very difficult, and therefore *socii criminis* * or other confessing witches are adduced; but though many of them concur, their depositions solely are not esteemed as sufficient, *ne vel ad pænam extraordinariam imponendam,*† though some think the same sufficient to that end because of that general brocard, — *ex multiplicatis indiciis debilibus resultare indicia indubitata.* But Delrio asserts that the conjection of such testimonies is not sufficient; "*nunquam enim,*" saith he, "*quæ sua natura dubia sunt possunt facere rem indubitatem ut nec multa agraunum sanum nec multa non alba unus album nec multa tepida unum callidum.*"‡ And that the testimony of one confessing witch was not found sufficient to file the panel is clear by the process of Allison Jollie, who was assoilzied pen. Oct., 1596; albeit Janet Hepburn, another witch, confest that the said Allison had caused her bewitch Isobel Hepburn, whereof she died. But though witchcraft cannot be proved

---

* Accomplices in the crime.   † Not to impose extraordinary punishments.

‡ A multitude of weak evidences can never establish one undoubted fact, as many sick cannot make one in health, nor many black figures a white one, nor many cold substances a warm one.

per socios criminis,* though dying and penitent witches, yet it may be doubted if the consulting witches may not be proved by two witches who were consulted, for, if this be not a sufficient probation, it would be impossible to prove consulting any other manner of way.

The persons to whom the injuries are done by the witches are admitted to be witnesses ; thus, Katherine Wardlaw was admitted against Margaret Hutchison. But sometimes they are only admitted *cum nota*, if the probation be not otherwise weak; and thus William Young and Agnes Hutchison were only admitted *cum nota*, against Beatrix Leslie, August, 1661. And in that process, likewise, they received only Agnes Ross *cum nota*, because she was the mistress of the two women who were *maleficiat*. Neilson was admitted to be an assizer against Margaret Wallace, though he was brother-in-law to John Nicol who had given information for raising the ditty, because the ditty was not at Nicol's instance ; and yet Starling was set from being an assizer because Moore, who was alleged to be one of the persons *maleficiat*, was his brother-in-law. March 2. 1622. Dickson was there likewise admitted to be an assizer, though he assisted the bailie in taking her, which was found the office of a good citizen, and though he had deadly feud against her husband, since it was not proved he had any against herself.

Women are received witnesses in this crime, as is clear by the process against Margaret Wallace, and all the processes in August, 1661. The not shedding of tears hath been used as a mark and presumption of witchcraft, Sprenger, *mal. malef.* p. 3. q. 15., because it is a mark of impenitence ; and because several witches have confessed they could not weep : but the

---

* By accomplices in the crime.

being accused of so horrid a crime may occasion a deep melancholy; and melancholy being cold and dry, hinders the shedding of tears; and great griefs do rather astonish than make one weep.

XXV.—The punishment of this crime is with us death by the foresaid Act of Parliament, to be execute as well against the user as the seeker of any response or consultation, & de practica. The doom bears, to be worried at the stake, and burned.

By the civil law, consulters were punished by death l. 5. c. de mafef. & mathem. nemo aruspicem consulat, aut mathematicum nemo ariolum, angurum et vatum prava confessio nonticescat sileat omnibus rer petuo divinandi curiositas.* In which law, fortune-tellers are also punishable; though, with us, dumb persons who pretend to foretell future events are never punished capitally. But yet I have seen them tortured, by order from the Council, upon a representation that they were not truly dumb, but (feigning themselves to be so) abused and cheated the people. The foresaid law is renewed in the Basilicks l. 31 h. t. μηδεις ερωτατα τινα μαντικην εη αγηλλο μενον οι δε χαλδαιοι και οι μαγοι μηδε εν αυταις ταις μα.τειαις εαυτων παρεχετοσαη, αλλα δε κεφαλικη τη δ.α σι δηρον τιμωρια υποκεισθοσαν. † But Farin and others think that where no person is injured, death should not be inflicted; and that imprisonment and banishment is now practised by all nations in that case, lib. 1, tom. 3, quest. 20, num. 89, & Clarus. sect. heresis num ult. But Perezeus thinks this too favourable a punishment, except the

---

* It shall not be lawful for any one to consult a fortune-teller, or one pretending to foretell events by any mathematical rules, for all their declarations are criminal, and curiosity for divination ought to be effectually restrained.

. † Let none seek advice by the art of divination, for the Chaldeans, and magicians, by no means discover the truth, wherefore they ought to be subjected to capital punishment, or public scourging.

users of these curious arts were induced thereto out of mere simplicity, & *sine dolo malo.** But, with us, no such distinction can be allowed by the Justices, who must find all libels relevant which bear consulting with witches, and, that ditty being proved, they must condemn the panel to die,—albeit I think the Council may alter the punishment, if it be clear that the user of these acts had no wicked design nor intercourse with the devil therein.

XXVI.—By the law of England, witchcraft was of old punished sometimes by death, and sometimes by exile; but 1. Jac. this following statute was made, which I here set down, because it is very special :—

" If any person or persons shall use, practise, or exercise in-
" vocation or conjuration of any evil and wicked spirit; or shall
" consult, covenant with, entertain, employ, feed, or reward
" any evil or wicked spirit to or for any intent or purpose ; or
" take up any dead man, woman, or child, out of his, her, or
" their grave, or any other place where the dead body resteth,
" or the skin, bone, or any part of a dead person, to be
" imployed or used in any manner of witch-craft, sorcery,
" charme, or inchantment ; or shall use, practise, or exercise
" any witch-craft, inchantment, charm, or sorcery, whereby
" any person shall be killed, destroyed, wasted, consumed,
" pined, or lamed, in his or her body, or any part thereof :
" that, then, every such offender or offenders, their aiders,
" abbetters, and counsellors, being of any the said offence
" duely and lawfully convicted and attainted, shall suffer pains
" of death as a fellon or fellons, and shall lose the priviledge
" and benefit of Clergie and Sanctuary. If any person or
" persons take upon him or them by witch-craft, inchantment,
" charm, or sorcery, to tell or declare in what place any

---

* And without any evil design.

" treasure of Gold or Silver should or might be found or had
" in the earth or other secret places : Or where goods or other
" things lost or stoln, are become : Or whereby any cattell or
" goods of any person shall be destroyed, or to hurt or destroy
" any person in his or her body, albeit the same be not
" effected or done : being, therefore, lawfully convicted, shall,
" for the said offence, suffer Imprisonment by the space of a
" whole year without baile or mainprise. Once every quarter
" of the year these Mountebanks are to mount the pillory, and
" to stand thereupon in some Mercat Toun six hours, and
" there to confesse his or her errour and offence."

THE BEWITCHING

SIR GEORGE MAXWELL OF POLLOK.

Account of SIR GEORGE MAXWELL, *and his son John.*
Taken from "Crawford's History of the Shire of Renfrew."

"Mr. GEORGE MAXWELL of Pollok, obtained the honour of knighthood from King Charles II. He was a gentleman of singular accomplishments, and justly esteemed a person eminent for piety, learning, and other good qualifications. Sir George deceased anno. 1677. To whom succeeded John, his son and heir; which John was raised to the dignity of baronet by King Charles IId's letters patent, bearing date, at Whitehall, the 12th of April, 1682. He was, by King William, nominated one of his Privy Council for Scotland, upon the first constitution thereof; and afterwards, in the year 1696, was appointed one of the Lords Commissioners of the Treasury of the Exchequer; and, in 1699, constituted one of the Senators of the College of Justice, and Lord Justice Clerk.

Letter which Sir John Maxwell of Pollok sent to George Sinclair, Professor of Philosophy in the College of Glasgow, along with the account of the bewitching of his father.

Pollok, 24th June, 1684.

SIR,

I send you herewith the true account my father caused me write from his own mouth, which is the surest relations I can give, either of his own trouble or what concerns Janet Douglas, first discoverer of these pictures. There

fell out some less material circumstances in the family during her abode there,
whereby it fully appeared that she knew what was done in distant places,
and understood languages.   For instance, when a chapter in the Greek New
Testament was read, she made us understand by signs what the purposes
were, (for at that time she was dumb, whether really or counterfeitly, it is hard
to determine) and did exactly give an account to myself what we did at two
miles distant from the place where she was, without any information given
to her which I knew of.   I rest your affectionate friend,

JOHN MAXWELL.

[Taken from Sir George Maxwell's account of his being bewitched.]

Upon the 14th of October, 1676, my father was surprised
at Glasgow, in the night-time, with a hot and fiery distemper;
and, coming home the next day, he was fixed to his bed.
The physician, fearing a pleuresy and a fever, opened a vein,
and, the application of medicaments being made, the fiery
heat was abated,—he remaining for seven weeks together
under a great pain, chiefly in his right side, though not fixed
to his bed.   There had come to Pollok-town a young dumb
girl, but from whence was not known, who had remained
there for four weeks before, but seldom frequenting Sir George
Maxwell's house, till at length she came to some more
familiarity and converse with his two daughters.   And, having
observed Sir George sick and weak in his body, she signified
unto them—That there was a woman, whose son had broke
his fruit-yard, that did prick him in the sides.

And seeing this woman one day in the hall of Pollok amongst
a great many other company, she assured his daughter that
this was the woman; and the day following, she told the gentleman—That this woman (whose name was Janet Mathie, relict
of John Stewart, under-miller in Shaw-mill) had formed a wax
picture with pins in the side, which was to be found in her
house, in a hole behind the fire, offering to bring it unto them
providing she were accompanied with men to protect her from
violence.   At first they hardly understood her, till she went to

one of the gentlewoman's closets, and bringing thence a little bees-wax, she plyed it before the fire, shewing the dimensions and quantity of the picture. The gentlewomen regarded not the information, because they thought it fabulous ; yet his two servants, Laurence Pollok and Andrew Martin, knowing how much the girl loved their master, and knowing that his life was in hazard if this picture were not found, resolved at all adventures to try whether the information were true or false ; and therefore going along with her to the said Janet Mathie's house, one of them planted himself on one side of the fire, and the other on the other side, while, in the meantime, the little girl coming quickly by Laurence Pollok, putting her hand in the hole behind the fire, and then slips into Andrew Martin beneath his cloak, the waxen effigy, which had two pins in it, one in each side, but that in the right side so long as to pierce through to the other ; that in the left was not so long, nor so deeply thrust in. This picture being brought to Pollok, Sir George's son, without acquainting his father, apprehended Janet Mathie, procuring the next day the Lord Ross's order for conveying her to prison. She being interrogated touching the picture, after several subterfuges, alleged "it was the deed of the dumb girl."

It was also enquired whether Sir George or his Lady had given her at any time provocation to this malice. But it was well known they had been courteous to her ; and, upon her complaints, had rebuked some for spreading bad reports upon her name, as not appearing sufficiently well founded to a conviction. Only upon the 14th of October, above specified, before Sir George went to Glasgow, he had called before him a servant in Pollok-town that had broken his orchard in harvest last, who confessed the fact, and that Hugh Stewart, a son of Janet Mathie's, was his complice. But a bye-stander declared that he was not now in Pollok land, but in the Darnly. To whom Sir George replied,—" I hope my fingers may reach him in Darnly." This was all which could be thought a provocation to Mathie,—no harm being done in the meantime to her son, whom Sir George to this hour doth not so much as know by the face, but hath suffered him all the time of his sickness to live in his mother's house, even since her imprisonment. In the meantime Mathie, remaining obstinate, was searched for insensible marks before the Sheriff-Depute of Renfrew, and many famous witnesses, at Paisley, and there were very many found upon her.

After the finding of the picture of wax foresaid, there was some abatement of Sir George's sickness, but not to any observable degree, so low was he brought. But upon the 4th of January following, his sickness recurred with that violence that for four or five days his friends and relations had no great confidence of his life. But they were more amazed on the 7th of January, being the Sabbath Day, when they had an express from the dumb girl, who was at Pollok-town, but could not get over the water to the house, the river being so swelled at that time, signifying that John Stewart, Mathie's eldest son, had four days since formed an effigy of clay, for taking away Sir George's life. And when she was called for, she declared it was in his house, beneath the bolster, among the bed-straw.

The next day following, James Dunlop, of Househill, and Ludowick Stewart, of Achinhood, with some of Sir George's servants, went to Stewart's house, taking the little girl with them, resolving to make a very exact trial, that it might not be said that the dumb girl had brought anything hither. Wherefore they caused John Stewart himself to light a candle and hold it, while Ludowick Stewart and another, did, in his sight, lift the clay effigy from among the bed-straw, beneath the bolster (the little girl all the while standing at a distance

from the place), but the picture having been made only three
or four days before, and not sufficiently hard, did break into
two pieces. In it were three pins, one in each side, and one
in the breast. Stewart had nothing to say for himself, but that
he knew not who had put that thing there. He was instantly
apprehended, and so was a little sister of his, lately entered
into the fourteenth year of her age, named Annabil Stewart,
who was said to have whispered before somewhat of the
waxen effigy. This poor creature proved thereafter, through
God's favour, a key to the detection of making both the
pictures.

At first she was very obstinate, but the next day she confessed, " That being present in her brother's house the 4th
of January, while the clay picture was formed, the black
gentleman being present, (which was the name she gave the
devil) together with Bessie Weir, Margerey Craig, Margaret
Jackson, and her brother John." But when confronted with
her brother, she did not with confidence adhere to her confession. Upon the finding of this picture, Sir George did
very observably recover in his health, and all the pain which
was in his side, did, by degrees, wear away.

John Stewart remained, notwithstanding his sister's confession, above measure obstinate, until he was searched the
next day for insensible marks, whereof he had great plenty ;
at the finding whereof, he was so confounded, that
immediately he confessed his paction with the devil, and
almost all the other heads expressed in his judicial confession
after written ; and declared, " That his accomplices who
formed the effigy with him were the same his sister had
named." She also came to a free and full confession of her
paction with the devil, and her accession to her forming both
of the waxen pictures in her mother's house, and of the clay
one in her brother's house.

Upon information of the premises, the Earl of Dundonald
and the Lord Ross, granted a warrant for apprehending
Bessie Weir, Margaret Jackson, and Margery Craig, who had
been fellow-sisters in the aforesaid sorcery.
Margaret Jackson, a woman aged about fourscore of years,
after a day or two, confessed paction with the devil, and her
accession to the making of both the pictures, and condescended upon the accomplices above-named. Many
insensible marks were found on her body.
Upon the 17th of January last, a third portrait of clay was
found under Janet Mathie's bolster, in the prison house of
Paisley, which the dumb girl had given information of. But
it seemed to be the picture of some woman, and probably of
some of the family of Pollok. For Annabil Stewart did
freely declare, "That their malice was against the whole
family of Pollok." For turning to young Pollok and his
Lady, she said, "And against you also." This portrait was
found before four famous witnesses.
The lords of his Majesty's privy council, being informed
of these pictures and effigies, the depositions of three confessing witches being sent, did grant a commission for their
trial, and also for the trial of the other three that were
obstinate. And in regard of the singularity of the case, they
ordered the process to be very solemn, commissioning for the
trial some judicious gentlemen in the country, viz. Sir Patrick
Gauston of Gauston, James Brisbane of Bishopton, Sir John
Shaw younger of Greenock, and John Anderson younger of
Dovehill. To whom they added Mr. John Preston, advocate,
(a gentleman well seen in criminals, and who exercised the
office of justice-depute for several years), a *sine qua non* in the
commission. And that the whole process might be the
more exact, they appointed George Lord Ross assessor, with
power to vote and decide. And, further, ordered Mr. Robert

Martin, Clerk of the Justice Court, to be clerk to the process, which was to be recorded in the public books of adjournal.

What follows of SIR GEORGE MAXWELL'S *affair is mostly taken out of an Authentic Copy of the Trial of the Witches, held at Paisley, Feb. 15, 1677, touching the Bewitching of* SIR GEORGE MAXWELL, *and part is taken out of* SIR GEORGE'S *Account.*

The Commissioners of Justiciary held their first Court at Paisley, the 27th of January, 1677; before whom Annabil Stewart, of the age of fourteen years or thereby, when brought in the presence of the Justices for the crime of witchcraft, declared that in harvest last the Devil, in the shape of a black man, came to her mother's house, and required the declarant to give herself up to him; and that the Devil promised her she should not want any thing that was good. Declares that she, being enticed by her mother, Janet Mathie, and Bessie Weir, who was officer to their several meetings, she put her hand to the crown of her head and the other to the sole of her foot, and did give herself up to the Devil. Declares that her mother promised her a new coat for doing it. Declares that her spirit's name was *Enippa;* * and that the Devil took her by the hand, and nipped her arm, which continued to be sore for half-an-hour. Declares that the Devil, in the shape of a black man, lay with her in the bed under the clothes, and that she found him cold. Declares, thereafter, he placed her nearest himself. And declares that she was present in her mother's house when the effigy of wax was made, and that it was made to represent Sir George Maxwell. Declares that the black man, Janet Mathie, the

---

* Sir George Maxwell's Account says—"That the new name the Devil gave her was *Anippy.*"

declarant's mother (whose spirit's name was *Landlady*), Bessie Weir (whose spirit's name is *Sopha*), Margery Craige (whose spirit's name is *Rigerum*), and Margaret Jackson (whose spirit's name * is *Locas*), were all present at the making of the said effigy; and that they bound it on a spit, and turned it before the fire; and that it was turned by Bessie Weir, saying, as they turned it,—Sir George Maxwell! Sir George Maxwell! and that this was expressed by all of them, and by the declarant. Declares that the picture was made in October last. And further declares that, upon the third day of January instant, Bessie Weir came to her mother's house, and advised her to come to her brother, John Stuart's, upon the night following; and that, accordingly, she came to the place, where she found Bessie Weir, Margery Craige, Margaret Jackson, and her brother, John Stuart, and a man with black clothes, a blue band, and white handcuffs, with *hoggers*, and that his feet were cloven. And the declarant sat down by the fireside with them, when they made a picture of clay, in which they placed pins in the breast and sides. And declares that they placed one in every side, and one in the breast. Declared that the black man did put the pins in the picture of wax, but is not sure who put in the pins in the picture of clay. Declares that the effigies produced are the effigies she saw made. Declares that the black man's name is Ejoal. This declaration was emitted before James Dunlop of Househill, William Gremlaye, &c., January 27, 1677. *Ita est Robertus Park, notarius publicus*, &c.†

---

* Sir George Maxwell's Account says Janet Mathie, her mother, whose name was, from the Devil, *Lands lady;* Bessie Weir, whose name was *Sopha;* Margery Craig, whose name was *Rigeru;* Margaret Jackson, whose name was *Locas.*

† Sir George Maxwell's Account says this declaration was made before famous witnesses, subscribed by the two notaries public for her,—Robert

The second confession is of John Stuart, who, being inter-rogated anent the crime of witchcraft, declared that upon Wednesday, the third day of January instant, Bessie Weir in Pollok town came to the declarant late at night, who, being without doors near to his own house, the said Bessie Weir did intimate to him that there was a meeting to be at his house the next day; and that the Devil, under the shape of a black man, Margaret Jackson, Margery Craige, and the said Bessie Weir, were to be present. And that Bessie Weir re-quired the declarant to be there, which he promised; and that the next night, after the declarant had gone to bed, the black man came in and called the declarant quietly by his name; upon which he rose from his bed, and put on his clothes, and lighted a candle. Declares, that Margaret Jack-son, Bessie Weir, and Margery Craige did enter in at a window in the gavel of the declarant's house, and that the first thing that the black man required was that the declarant should renounce his baptism, and deliver himself wholly to him; which the declarant did, by putting one hand on the crown of his head, and the other on the sole of his foot. And that he was tempted to it by the Devil's promising that he should not want any pleasure, and that he should get his heart filled on all that shall do him wrong. Declares that he gave him the name of *Jonas* for his spirit's name.* Declares, that thereafter the Devil required all their consents for the making of the effigies of clay for the taking away the life of Sir George Maxwell of Pollok, to revenge the taking the de-clarant's mother, Janet Mathie. Declares, that every one of

Park, younger, Patrick Carswell in Paisley, — and subscribed by the Commissioners.

* Sir George Maxwell's Account says, "That the new name given to him by the Devil was *Jonas*."

the persons above-named gave their consent to the making of
the said effigies, and that they wrought the clay; and that the
black man did make the figure of the head, and face, and two
arms to the said effigies. Declares, that the Devil set three
pins in the same,—one in each side and one in the breast,—
and that the declarant did hold the candle to them all the
time the picture was making ; and that he observed one of
the black man's feet to be cloven ; and that his apparel was
black; and that he had a bluish band and handcuffs: and
that he had *hoggers* on his legs without shoes : and that the
black man's voice was *hough* and *goustie.* And farther declares,
that after they had begun the forming of the effigies, his
sister Annabil Stuart, a child of thirteen or fourteen years of
age, came knocking at the door, and being let in by the declarant, she stayed with them a considerable time ; but that
she went away before the rest, he having opened the door to
her. That the rest went out at the window at which they
entered. Declares, that the effigies were placed by Bessie
Weir in his bed-straw. He further declares, he himself had
envy against Sir George Maxwell for apprehending Janet
Mathie, his mother ; and that Bessie Weir had great malice
against this Sir George Maxwell ; and that her quarrel was,
as the declarant conceived, because the said Sir George had
not entered her husband to his harvest service : and also
declares, that the said effigies were made upon the fourth day
of January instant ; and that the Devil's name was *Ejoal.*
Declares, that his spirit's name was *Jonas;* and Bessie
Weir's spirit's name, who was officer, was *Sopha;* and that
Margaret Jackson's spirit's name, was *Locas;* and that
Annabil Stuart, the declarant's sister's, was *Enippa;* but
does not remember what Margery Craige's spirit's name
was. Declares, that he cannot write. This confession was
emitted in the presence of the witnesses to the other con-

fession, and on the same day. *Ita est, Robertus Park, notarius publicus*, &c.*

The confession of Margaret Jackson, relict of Thomas Stuart, in Shaws, who, being examined by the Justices anent her being guilty of witchcraft, declares that she was present at the making of the first effigies and picture that were made in Janet Mathie's house, in October ; and that the Devil in the shape of a black man, Janet Mathie, Bessie Weir, Margery Craige, and Annabil Stewart, were present at the making of the said effigies, and that they were made to represent Sir George Maxwell of Pollok, for taking away his life. Declares, that forty years ago, or thereabout, she was at Pollokshaw-croft, with some few sticks on her back, and that the black man came to her, and that she did give up herself unto the black man, from the top of her head to the sole of her foot ; and that this was after the declarant's renouncing of her baptism ; and that the spirit's name which he designed her, was *Locas.* And that about the third or fourth of January instant, or thereby, in the night time, when she awaked, she found a man to be in the bed with her, whom she supposed to be her husband, though her husband had been dead twenty years, or thereby, and that the man immediately disappeared ; and declares, that this man who disappeared was the Devil. Declares, that upon Thursday, the fourth of January instant, she was present in the house of John Stuart at night, when the effigy of clay was made, and that she saw the black man there, sometimes sitting, sometimes standing with John Stuart ; and that the black man's clothes were black, and that he had white hand-cuffs ; and that Bessie Weir, in Polloktoun, and Annabil Stuart, in

---

* Sir George Maxwell's Account says—"This confession had the same solemnities which the former had."

Shaws, and Margery Craige, were at the aforesaid time and
place of making the said effigy of clay; and declares, that
she gave her consent to the making of the same; and
declares that the Devil's name, who compeared in the black
man's shape, was *Ejoal. Sic subscribitur, ita est, Robertus
Park, notarius publicus*, &c.*

One remarkable passage which is taken from Sir George
Maxwell's account, runs thus: The Justice upon the 27th of
January, commanded the jailor to fix Janet Mathie's feet in
the stocks, that she might not do violence to her own life.
The man declared, "That the next morning he had found her
bolster, which the night before was laid at least six yards
distant from the stocks, now placed beneath her: the stocks
being so heavy, that two of the strongest men in the country
could hardly have carried them six yards: he wondering, did
ask her how she had win to the bolster; she answered, "That
she had crept alongst the floor of the room, drawing the stocks
to the same place."   And before the court, she said, "She had
gotten one foot free out of the hole, and with the other had
drawn the stocks," a thing altogether impossible—the stocks
being so weighty; nor was she able to take her foot out of
the hole.

Upon the 15th of February, 1677, the Justices being con-
vened again in court at Paisley, John Stewart, and Annabil
Stewart, with Margaret Jackson, did adhere to their former
judicial confession; but Janet Mathie, Bessie Weir, and
Margery Craige, did obstinately deny.

---

* Sir George Maxwell's Account says,—"This confession had the same
solemnities which the two former had."

Now follow the depositions of certain persons, agreeing with the confessions of the above-said witches.

Andrew Martin, servitor to the lord of Pollok, of the age of thirty years, or thereby, depones that he was present in the house of Janet Mathie, panel, when the picture of wax produced was found in a little hole in the wall, at the back of the fire. Depones, that Sir George's sickness did fall upon him about the 18th of October, or thereby. Depones, that the picture of wax was found on the —— of December, and that Sir George's sickness did abate and relent about the time the picture of wax was found and discovered in Janet Mathie's house. Depones, that the pins were placed in the right and left sides; and that Sir George Maxwell of Pollok's pains, as he understood by Sir George's complaining of these pains, lay most in his right and left sides. And depones, that Sir George's pains did abate and relent after the finding of the said picture of wax, and taking out of the pins, as is said. And depones, that the panel, Janet Mathie, has been by fame and bruit reputed a witch these several years by-past. And this is the truth, as he shall answer to God. *Sic subscrib., Andr. Martin.*

Laurence Pollock, secretary to the lord of Pollok, sworn and purged of partial counsel, depones, that on the —— day of December, he was in the panel, Janet Mathie's house, when the picture was found; and that he did not see it before it was brought to the panel's door. Depones, that Sir George Maxwell of Pollok's sickness did seize upon him about the fourteenth of October, or thereby, and he did continue in his sickness or distemper for six weeks or thereby. Depones, that Sir George's sickness did abate and relent after the finding of the said picture of wax, and taking out of the pins that were in the effigies. Depones, that by open bruit and common fame,

Janet Mathie, and Bessie Weir, and Margery Craige, are branded to be witches. Depones, that the truth is this, as he shall answer to God. *Sic subscrib., Laurence Pollock.*

Ludowick Stuart of Auchinhood, being sworn and purged of partial counsel, depones, that Sir George's sickness fell upon him the fourteenth or fifteenth of October, or thereby. Depones that he was not present at the finding of the picture of wax; but that he had seen Sir George Maxwell of Pollok after it was found, and, having seen him in his sickness often-times before, he did perceive that Sir George had sensibly recovered after the time that the said picture was said to be found, which was upon the 11th or 12th of December. Depones, that Janet Mathie and Margery Craige, two of the panels, are, by report of the country, said to be witches. Depones, that he, having come to Pollok, he did see Sir George Maxwell whose pains did recur, and that his pains and torments were greatly increased in respect of what they were before the finding of the picture of wax. Depones, that upon the 8th of January, when they left the said Sir George Maxwell, of Pollok, the deponent, James Dunlop, of House-hill, Allan Douglace, and several others, did go to the house of John Stuart, warlock, in Pollok-shaw, and there he found a picture of clay in the said John Stuart's bed-straw. Depones, that there were three pins in the said picture of clay, and that there was one in each side, and one in the breast. And depones, that being returned to Sir George's house, Sir George told the deponent that he found great ease of his pains, and that it was before the deponent, Househill, and the rest did reveal to him that they had found the said picture of clay; and further depones, that this is truth, as he shall answer to God. *Sic subscrib., Ludowick Stuart.*

What follows, is taken from SIR GEORGE'S *account.*

The justices having examined all witnesses in matters of fact, touching the effigies, Sir George's sickness, and the recovery of his health, upon the finding of the same, considering also the bad fame of those who were obstinate, and having confronted them with the confessing witches, who in their faces avowed their accession, in manner expressed in the confessions above written. Considering, lastly, all other circumstances of their case, committed them to the trial of a judicious inquest, who, being found guilty, were condemned to the fire to be burned, and their effigies with them. Only Annabil, in regard of her nonage, and the evidences she seemed to give of her penitency, was reprieved by order of the council, but to remain in prison. In the meantime, both she and her brother John did seriously exhort their mother to confession; and with tears, did Annabil put her in mind of the many meetings she had with the devil in her own house; and that a summer's day would not be sufficient to relate what she had seen pass between the devil and her; but nothing could prevail with her obdured and hardened heart.

Some account of Janet Douglas, *the girl referred to in the account of the bewitching of* SIR GEORGE MAXWELL, *of Pollok.*

Sir John Maxwell, at the end of the account which he sent to Mr. George Sinclair, Professor of Philosophy, in the College of Glasgow, says,—It is to be noted, the dumb girl, whose name was Janet Douglas, doth now speak, not very distinctly, yet so as she may be understood; and is a person that most wonderfully discovers things past, and doth also understand the Latin tongue, which she never learned.

H

The following is the extract of a letter which was sent to MR. GEORGE SINCLAIR, *Professor of Philosophy in the* College of Glasgow.

"When I was at Glasgow, in summer 1677, I was desirous to see the dumb girl, (Janet Douglas.) At my first incoming she declined to entertain discourse, but my friendly expressions, and giving her some money, I gained her. I first enquired anent her parentage. ' I do not remember,' says she, ' of my parents, but only that I was called by the name of Janet Douglas by all people who knew me. I was kept when I was very young, by a poor woman who proved cruel to me, by beating and abusing me : whereupon I deserted the woman's house, and went a-begging.' I enquired next how she became dumb. She told me by reason of a sore swelling she took in her throat and tongue ; but afterwards by the application of *Album Græcum*, ' which I thought,' said she, ' was revealed to me, I recovered my speech.' I asked her, how she came to the knowledge of witches and their practices. She answered, that she had it only by a vision, and knew all things as well as if she had been personally present with them ; but had no revelation or information from the voice of any spirit ; nor had she any communication with the devil, or any spirit of that kind ; ' only,' says she, ' the devil was represented to me, when he was in company with any of the witches, in that same shape and habit he was seen by them.'—She told me, she was altogether ignorant of the principles of religion, but had some smattering knowledge of the Lord's prayer, when she had heard the witches repeat, it seems, by her vision, in presence of the Devil ; and at his desire, which she observed, they added to the word art, the letter w, which made it run, ' Our Father which wart in heaven ; ' and made the third petition thus,—' As on earth so it may in heaven ; ' by which means the Devil made the application of the prayer to himself.——I remember, that there was a woman in the town, who had the curiosity to give her a visit, who asked her, How she came to the knowledge of so many things ? But the young wench shifted her, by asking the woman's name ; says the other, 'Are there any other in Glasgow of that name ?' ' No.' says the woman. ' Then,' said the girl, ' You are a witch.' Says the other, ' Then you are a Devil.' The girl answers, ' The devil doth not reveal witches ; but I know you to be one, and I know your practices too.' Hereupon the woman ran away in great confusion, being indeed a person suspected of witchcraft, and had been sometimes imprisoned on that account. ——— Another woman, whose name was Campbel, had the curiosity likewise to come and see her, and began to ask some questions at her. The wench, shifting to give her an answer, says, ' I pray you tell me where you were yesternight, and what you were doing? And withal,' says she, ' let me see your arm ; ' she refusing, the landlord laid hold upon the woman, with some others in the house, and forced her to make bare her arm, where

Janet Douglas shewed them an invisible mark, which she had gotten from the devil. The poor woman much ashamed, ran home. A little time after, she came out and told her neighbours that what Janet Douglas said of her was true ; and earnestly intreated them that they would shew so much to the magistrates, that she might be apprehended, ''otherwise the devil,'' says she, 'will make me kill myself.' But the neighbours judging her to be under a fit of distraction, carried her home to her house; but early next morning the woman was found drowned in the Clyde. ———— The girl likewise told me at Glasgow, being then under no restraint, that it was revealed to her she would be carried before the great council at Edinburgh, imprisoned there, and scourged through the town. All which came to pass, for about a year after, she was apprehended and imprisoned in the tolbooth of the Canongate, and was brought before the council, but nothing being found against her, she was dismissed ; but thereafter, for several crimes committed within the town of Edinburgh, she was taken again, and imprisoned, scourged, and sent away to some foreign plantation ; since which time I have not heard of her. There are several other remarkable passages concerning her, which I cannot inform you of, which others perhaps may do ; therefore I shall abruptly break off, and say no more, but that I am your affectionate friend." Mr. Sinclair says, " This information I have from a discreet understanding gentleman, who was one of my scholars at Glasgow several years ago."

OF

THE BEWITCHING

OF

CHRISTIAN SHAW.

THE PREFACE TO THE NARRATIVE OF CHRISTIAN SHAW.

WISE men do justly suspect, and are hardly brought to credit the accounts of extraordinary stories; especially anent witchcraft; because the frequent impostures which the Romanists have obtruded on the world in their miracles and legends; the many relations of odd things as done by dæmons or wizards, which yet, were either false or the ground of simple natural causes; the ignorance of several Judges and Juries, who have condemned silly creatures merely upon their ridiculous confessions, or other slender proof; and the difficulty of conceiving the manner or philosophy of some operations and appearances, though undoubtedly true in fact; are good prejudices against a sudden belief, and precautions for an exact inquiry. But they are men of weak souls, destitute of distinct thoughts; who deny all, because they have discovered error in some, or condemn as false all sects which they are ignorant how they came to exist: by the same rule of reasoning that there are no enthusiasts, because the best men have been sometimes mistaken for these; nor are there any criminals, in respect severals have suffered who were not truly such, considering that many histories are fabulous, therefore none is to be trusted: and all the phænomenas in nature, whose invisible causes they cannot comprehend, are mere delusions.

The following narrative, as to the truth of fact, is the best attested piece of history of this kind that has occurred in many ages : the most of the matters therein represented having gained the assent of private sceptics : and being proven before public judges, so that it is more surprising than the strange things of witchcraft, that any should seriously deny the being thereof, and from thence discredit such useful providences at a distance, when notoriety has dispelled all objections in the places where they did exist.

Many authors have proven at large, that there are witches and witchcraft, from reason, scripture, antiquity, and experience of all nations and ages in the world, and they have solved the difficulties which might obstruct the belief of this positive proof, by possible hypothesis of philosophy : where it is to be observed, that though any such explications of the natural manner of phænomena are subject to cavil, yet the existence of a thing which hath so certain positive evidence cannot be denied in sound reasoning ; because angels and men not being made for civil converse together in this world, and all communion with devils being interdicted us, the Scripture needed to unfold little of their way of acting ; and still the next age may discover what this could not reach, as this has already unveiled what was thought inextricable in the last, unless impossibility were presently demonstrated. Therefore such a short hint, as may somewhat illustrate the events in the subsequent discourse, may suffice in the present case ; especially since providence does, by eminent occurrences, rather design our practical instruction, than a subject of national speculation.

The devil can assume a corporeal shape and bespeak man out of it : as he did to Eve, our Saviour, and in some heathen

oracles: so that there is capacity for the entering into contract.   Satan is willing thus to insure mortals of being enemies
to heaven, earth, and their own salvation, by his indefatigable
malice against all the three: as curiosity in wits, revenge, and
disclosure of secrets in the great, covetousness in the worldling,
or power and pleasure in all whom he thinks needful, (they
being impregnable other ways), and is permitted by God, to
attack in this manner, does sufficiently blind them, to be
susceptible of his proposals thereanent.   We see daily how
criminal lusts inflamed by Satan, divert their horror, not only
of eternal, but also of temporal eminent torments: perverting
these instincts of nature which might fright them from surrender.   But further, he does commonly facilitate his
conquest on witches, by decoying them piecemeal to his lure,
through the mediation of others from among mankind that
are already embarked, till they be prepared, and he get an
opportunity of making with them an explicit transaction.

That accordingly Satan has *de facto* prevailed in making
sorcerers and witches, appears from the testimony of the wisest
and best in all states and times.

The heathens, by nature and practice, discovering this truth,
made laws against *maleficos and mathematicos,** (these last,
though they assumed the name of an art much encouraged
by the legislators, yet were known, under the cloak thereof,
to consult the Devil anent the fates of men and states) which
the Roman senate and people did execute; and even the
Persians, in some good reigns did the same.   Under the Old
Testament dispensation the magicians of Egypt and Babylon
were baffled by Moses and Daniel; Balaam and the witch of
Endor were baffled, just judgments were inflicted on Jezebel,

---

* Witches and Mathematicians.

Manasseh, and the ten tribes for their sorceries, and witchcrafts amongst other crimes ; and the laws made against such,
as distinct from other guilt under the New Testament. Simon
Magus, who bewitched the people of Samaria ; Elymas the
sorcerer, who was struck blind at Paul's rebuke : the
Pythonisse girl who seems to have been possest of consent,
because she was not tormented, but got profit thereby ; and
such as confessed shewed their deeds and burned their books
in Ephesus ; are undeniable instances of witchcraft. Finally,
there are prophecies of false Christs with signs and wonders,
able to deceive, if possible, the very elect : general councils
have made canons against these wretches; and the experi-
mental knowledge of injured mortals, with the public
sentences which did vindicate the same, in subsequent ages,
are delivered down to us by the writers thereof. Hence
Guilielmus Linensis, a popish doctor, was justly put to death,
even though he died penitent, he having confessed witchcraft,
(whereof the written covenant was found in his pocket,) and
that his share of the Devil's service was to persuade and
preach that witches were only silly deluded melancholians,
whereby their confessions were no proof. His success was
such in this work of darkness, that the people and judge's
did slack, and witches were vastly multiplied in few years,
vid. Pet. Mamorius de Lamiis, who gives an account of the
process from authentic records. Through these periods, it is
observed, that Satan has oft shifted the scene, and turned
himself to many shapes, as he found it most accommodating to
his purposes : whereby the manner of apparition of devils has
been different, according to the state of the times. So of old
Satan appeared, and was worshipped as such, for deprecating
his mischief, which is said to be retained in some of the most
barbarous places of the Indies to this day.

In the darkness of Popery the Devil was transformed into

a more innocent spirit,* in the brounies and fairies. These were then very frequent, he having impudence thus to appear openly, proportional to the knowledge of men, over whom his reign was so universal, as it is related to continue in the more northern regions at this day. But since light has broke out in our horizon, he oftener works externally by magicians and witches, and internally on the lusts of men, being now mostly restrained to his own sphere or subjects. Yet still he ensnares severals, partly by aping the ordinances of God; especially as they are corrupted in the Romish Church, whence so many monks and nuns as already prepared, have been found overcome. So he keeps with them public assemblies in the night of extraordinary merit. They formally worship him by many nimical gestures; he imprints on them a kind of sacrament; he inflicts dreadful penances on such as have not executed the commanded mischiefs; he teaches them odd words and signs, upon repeating of which exorcisms, he (it being his interest) effectuates the forepactioned operations, &c.

But though what he does of himself, or on the watch word or ensign of sorcerers or witches, may, by collection, and artful disposal of matter and form, appear surprising; yet he cannot work against nature, or so apply actives to passives, as to overturn the course thereof; since that is only competent to its author, who alone can do true miracles, or know immediately the thoughts of man. Yea, after the fall it is like, that even Satan's natural powers are come down below those of good angels; and it is certain, that he is often befooled in his designs by providence: notwithstanding whereof he retains

---

* That pretended to foretell deaths, reveal the defunct's will, discover occult murder, do other friendly offices, &c., which were subtle means of inducing to him and relying on him.

so much as (being permitted) is sufficient to bring about, by unseen natural means, most of the extraordinary appearances, that the generality of the learned have attributed to him ; and particularly those in the subsequent narrative : many of which, though they are beyond the efficiency of disease, deceit, or any visible cause ; yet may be the effects of some such unperceived means as follow.

There is no difficulty in Satan's transmitting in a short time an account of things which are past ; since it is known he goes to and fro in the earth : yea, he may have certainly foretold some future events, as Alexander's success against Persia, &c., seeing he understands and may steal the great revolutions of the world, out of the prophets, wherein they are so graphically circumscribed ; or he may discover his own resolutions whenever he is commissioned or permitted to execute a judgment ; which is the case of those, whom for seeking their horoscopes, God gives over to him to whom they do apply ; and of Saul, who got so exact an account of his own end by the Philistines. But without some such aid, Satan can only guess, like the physician by the urine, or politician by the crises of states, which is the cause that most of his oracles are ambiguous.

His transporting of witches is elsewhere explained. He can raise hurricanes, as appears in Job, which are known to carry over tracts of sea and land, very ponderous bodies ; as it is easy for him to condense a part of the vehicle, which may protect the breathing and yet cut the air, like the fence of dyvers, and beak of a sloop ; in which also he affects the magnifying of his natural powers to be no less than of good angels, who transported Ezekiel and Elijah. His covering of the witches from sight, at some times, is also cleared from the difficulties which seem to attend it, in another place, where it appears very possible that his skill in optics, reflection and

I

refraction of light, &c., to which his power and agility as a spirit subministrates materials, may effectuate all that can be proven to be true fact in the case.

But Glanvil, More, and others, lay another hypothesis in both, viz., That the soul is separable from the body in some cases without death : when by God's permission, Satan, of the parties' consent, gets power over soul and body ; whereby he may carry away the one from the helm of the other, and set it back again in its seat ; providing the vital spirits which make the body a fit receptacle, be well preserved by ointments, that constrict the pores till the return of its guest ; but death ensues from a separation, when the organs of the body are rendered altogether unapt to obey the soul's commands in its functions. If such an opinion could be true, Satan might place this captivated spirit to actuate any shape he thinks fit. But there needs not so much metaphysics to unriddle the appearances of witches as beasts and the like, since their real persons may be covered with a vehicle, which by disposal of the rays coming therefrom, may fascinate the eyes by the same impressions that come from the true sight of such. His power of representing another thing in lieu of that which is truly present, is so certain that it is found he may make up the image of persons who are not present at all. For it is undoubted that spiritual devils may sometimes be permitted to represent by phantoms the most innocent and praise-worthy men, as devils incarnate do traduce them. He that accuseth the brethern and imitates an angel of light, may likewise personate the children of light by his delusions : yet the antecedents, concomitants, and consequents of such providences, do readily propale the falsehood, so as the just man, for the most part, shall not perish in his righteousness, and God, in his ordinary providence, will not laugh at the trial of the innocent, though sometimes it fall out that the sons of Belial may swear away the life of an innocent Naboth.

There are several other things of less difficult explication. Particularly, the devil or witches might have been heard in converse by the maid, and not by others, the same way as a sound directed through a speaking-trumpet does reach the ears to which it is aimed, without dispersing towards the intermediate that are not in a straight line betwixt. The confederated devil, may, upon the witches' desire, infuse poisonous humours, extracted from herbs of the same invisible operation with the steam of mad dogs, or the pestilence, which being joined to the rapidous course of the patient's own spirits, humours, and blood, that Satan, by ingyring himself thereunto, may, through the natural means of pulsion, set in career, can very well produce these extraordinary motions which are mentioned in the following account. They delight much in the torture or destruction of young children, in envy of Christ, who is tender of such little ones; and because the crime is the greater the less the patient has offended, or can resist. They use, or make others to repeat scripture words for gaining credit, or alleviating the terror, or to disgrace the Word, by such a mock use, as they did in the time of our Saviour, and therefore their testimony was rebuted. It is observable from many passages, that he hastens sometimes, and effects their discovery, by his malice against their present temporal enjoyments, uncertainty of their continuance, and insatiable desire for their full wreck. Yet some of them, who are most maliciously bent, he thinks fit to keep here, as useful instruments; and providence permits others to live, that they, wilfully filling up their measure, under means, may be finally inexcusable.

As to those whom, in secret judgment, the devil is permitted to torment, but, in mercy, not to overcome, he may be carried thereunto from his design of perverting them by terror, whereof he is at last disappointed. And however the defacing of God's image, and especially in despight of Jesus Christ, who honoured that nature by assuming it, is his chief delight; or he is constrained to make such stupendous appearances against his will (because he is most successful when he is least known) for a visible testimony superadded to the greater gospel proofs, in gross times, that there are spirits and a devil to torment them, as it is observable that this was denied by Mr. Aikenhead (though he died in full conviction thereof) at the time when these things fell out in the country. Or providence may tolerate such sufferings, that they, though intended by the devil for an instance of malice, may, by their notoriety, be a means of moving the discovery, and bringing to justice these miscreants, whom he made use of as his instruments in them, and who may have lived long in rebellion against heaven, and destruction of mankind, by malefices of the same sort which fell out in this case. Finally, the abundant and efficacious grace of God is conspicuous in enabling a young girl to resist to the utmost the best laid assaults of the evil one, as it is certain that he shews the greatest malice in countries where he is hated and hateth most, and the nearer his reign be to an end.

There are many other profitable instructions which arise from this wonderful providence, for such dispensations have their own language, and the man of wisdom shall see God's name.

The usages of charms for men or beasts, certain characters, words, verses, and spells; the observation of times and seasons as lucky or unlucky; the belief of having success by carrying about some herbs, plants, or branches of trees, and many the like superstitions, which can have no natural casualty on the effects desired, are the very rudiments of witchcraft, and an implicit application to the devil for virtues which God has denied to things; whence they are to be abhorred as sinful in themselves and introductory to explicit engagement. So gross ignorance, profane looseness, stupid forgetfulness of God, and neglect of his worship in closets and families; malice, envy, revenge, discontent, oppressive fear of want, and distrustful anxiety of spirit; finally, a libidinous temper, curses, imprecations, and sinful curiosity, are to be evited as paving the way to the same mischief.

Let none inveigh against a profession of religion, because some under that specious covert have been found in league with the devil. It is because of the glorious lustre and excellency of our holy faith, that these miscreants paint themselves with it, whereby likewise they may be less suspected, and more able subtily to gain on others, and do their master's work. So it was no stain on the apostles that one of their number had a devil, was a traitor and cheat; nor that Satan transforms himself into an angel of light, of design that the good ways of the Lord may be evil spoken of. Neither let us be under a slavish fear and terror of that hellish tribe, in truckling to their humour, least they should do harm, which savours of worshipping and paying homage to the devil; whereas we ought only to make the Lord of hosts our fear and our dread.

There is no just ground to reflect on particular persons or families, upon account of such troubles. For no man knoweth either love or hatred by all that's before them. All things come alike to all. And suppose ye that these were sinners above all the Galileans, or above all that dwelt in Jerusalem? The infinite wise God may thus try faith, patience, and Christian fortitude. Job and our Saviour were assaulted; and seven devils cast out of Mary Magdalene, a chosen vessel unto the Lord. A daughter of Abraham's was bound by Satan eighteen years; and his messenger was sent to buffet the great apostle of the Gentiles. The woman of Canaan, Matth.

xv. 22. and the godly man, Mark ix. 24. had their nearest relations vexed in this manner; and blessed be the Lord that has left such instances on record for prevention of stumbling. Though it must be confessed that the same charity which judges well of all things cannot but alter its remark, when its proof is sufficiently clear from the way in which the person affected did formerly walk, since presumptions do always cede to truth, and lawyers have a maxim, that *in re clara non est locus conjecturis.**

These things may meet with a very different reception, especially in this unhappy age and place of the world, where Britain may be termed the unfortunate island,—Afric never having been more fertile in the production of monsters,—since 'tis observed that through all the successions of men, there was never before any society or collective body of atheists till these dregs of time, though there might have been here and there some misshapen births. But wisdom is justified of her children, and 'tis the season of Samson to awake when Delilah gives the alarm that the Philistines are upon him. What, peace! so long as the whoredoms of Jezebel and her witchcrafts are so many? But good things are hoped of our magistrates, who have already so happily begun.

The apostle said of Job's trials, ye have heard of the patience of Job, and have seen the end of the Lord. So in this narrative you have a deplorable scheme of this maid's formidable fits, and of the powers of darkness that combined, not only for ruining her body, but also for murdering her soul. In the meantime, the hearts of many were bleeding for her, and much application was made to God in her behalf. Divers solemn fasts were observed, both in her father's family, in the parish, and throughout the bounds of the presbytery and elsewhere;

---

* In this case it is evident the thing is not a conjecture.

her case was expressly minded in public addresses to the throne of grace ; till at length there was a general fast religiously kept in most parts of the synod, that God might give an effectual check to Satan's rage and dominion in the country. Boasting of prayers is to be abhorred, yet it is our duty with all gratitude, to acknowledge God the hearer, and to proclaim to the world the excellency of them upon this very occasion : For he hath not turned away his ear from us, it being the comfortable result of this history, that the girl hath been perfectly well for many months : and is not this a brand plucked out of the fire ; and have not the splinters wherewith the witches thought to have destroyed her, recoiled back upon some of themselves, and we wait execution of justice on the rest.

The devil could not enter the herd of swine, nor touch one hair of Job's head, without permission from Him whose kingdom ruleth over all : whence though our enemies be very indefatigable and invisible, yet we are under the conduct of the watchman who neither slumbers nor sleeps ; to whom darkness and light are both alike ; and greater is he that is in us, than he that is in the world. So that unless we wilfully forfeit our privileges, there is no fear of counterpoising the wicked ones, throwing down the gauntlet to all their projects or machinations, since neither angels, principalities, nor powers, shall be able to separate us from the love which is in Christ Jesus our Lord ; and though no argument can be drawn from any merit in us, yet we'll carry the day against all the militia of hell under the captain of our salvation, since he will rest in his own love. Is this the manner of man, O Lord God ? yet a little while the devil and his accomplices will be cast into the bottomless pit, and we transported into Immanuel's land.

It will not be a natural sturdiness of temper, nor a lifeless mentioning of the name of God or Christ, that can shelter us

from those devourers, as appears in the seven sons of Sceva,
Acts xix., but if the Lord be God, then follow Him ; for who
is he that will harm you if ye be followers of that which is
good ; He will give His angels charge of thee to keep thee in
all thy ways. Great peace have they that love Thy law, and
nothing shall offend them. And they wrestle most successfully
against principalities and powers who fight upon their knees,
as resisting of the devil is the way to make him flee from us.

Yet whom Satan cannot obtain to be tortured hereafter he
will (when permitted) torment in this side of time : hence, if
possessions of bodies be so great a plague, how much worse is
it to have him reign master of our souls ? Wherefore let us
watch and pray against every sin, the least of which is more
pleasing to him and worse to us than the being so corporally
tormented.

If Satan, as a spirit, may insinuate himself into our humours,
no wonder that by having such advantage in the temper, he
can influence the phlegmatic to sloth, the choleric to anger,
the sanguine to lust and sinful pleasure, the melancholic to
despair, &c. So they who think that they stand have need to
take heed lest they fall, and to pray that the Watchman of
Israel may make an hedge about them and their house, and
about all that they have on every side.

Let this not only rouse our diligence and stir up our gratitude for not being affected alike ; but let it recall our admiration and love of Jesus Christ, who hath freed our souls and
bodies from the power and slavery of Satan ; and finding ourselves too weak for him, in awarding these deluding pleasures
which procure our being deserted by God, and are Satan's
baits to this fearful thraldom ; let us run to the Rock of Ages
for protection and support, our sufficiency being only of God.

Seeing there are witches and devils, there are also immortal
souls of the first, since the last do contract for them, and take

such pains to retain them; so that the Sadducees, though they have a judicial blindness in their reason, are hereby rendered inexcusable by very sense. Evil books which stir up and ensnare curious fancies that are seldom accompanied with accurate judgments, (the soul's looking outward diverting it from diving into the depths of truth) are to be restrained; and also such ridiculous pamphlets, as no doubt, by the instigation of Satan, have lately been sent abroad, of design to frustrate any good use which might be made of such rare providences, as are contained in the ensuing narrative, by forging others, or disguising this.

This has been delayed so long to be published, partly that there might be the more narrow scrutiny made into the matters of fact; and partly, by some accidents which did retard it In it the reader is not to expect any accuracy of style, because the designed shortness did occasion the wrapping up of much matter in small bounds, and the punctual exactness of truth in every circumstance was the chief aim, so that other defects ought to be the less quarrelled.

The first edition of this Preface, Narrative, &c., was printed at Edinburgh, by James Watson in 1698, and entitled, "True Narrative of the sufferings and relief of a Young Girl, who was strangely molested by evil spirits and their instruments in the west. Collected from authentic testimonies, with a preface and postscript.

Containing reflections on what is most material or curious, either in the history or trial of the Seven Witches who were condemned and burnt in the Gallowgreen of Paisley.

K

JOB ii. 6.   *And the Lord said unto* Satan, behold, he is in thine *hand ; but save his life.*

MATTH. XV. 22.   *Have mercy* upon me, *O Lord, thou son of David; my daughter is grievously vexed with a* devil.

ROM. XV. 20.   *And the God of peace shall* bruise Satan under your *feet shortly.*"

TRUE NARRATIVE

OF THE

Sufferings and Relief of a Young Girl.

———

IT was about the end of August, 1696, when the first rise and occasion was given, (so far as can be known) to these strange things that befel the child, who is the subject of this narrative, and the manner was thus :—

Christian Shaw, daughter to a gentleman of good account, called John Shaw, laird of Bargarran,* in the parish of Erskine, within the shire of Renfrew, a smart lively girl, and of good inclinations, about eleven years of age, perceiving one of the maids of the house, named Katherine Campbell, to steal and drink some milk, she told her mother of it; whereupon the maid Campbell (being a young woman of a proud and revengeful temper, and much addicted to cursing and swearing upon any like occasion, and otherwise given to purloining) did, in a most hideous rage, thrice imprecate the curse of God upon the child; and at the same time did thrice utter these horrid

———

* "A little towards the south from the castle of Erskine, stands the house of Bargarran, the seat of John Shaw of Bargarran, whose ancestors, for nigh three hundred years, have possessed these lands, and derive their descent from a younger brother of the family of Sauchie, now represented by Sir John Shaw of Greenock (anno 1697) The intermarriages of this house have been with some of the most considerable gentry of this country ; as the families of Kelsoeland, Mains, Raiss, Woodhead, Glorat, Livingstone of Haining, Craigends, and Northbar."—*Crawfurd's History of the Shire of Renfrew.*

words, "The devil harle (that is, drag) your soul through hell."
This passed upon Monday, August 17th, in presence of several
witnesses, who afterwards made evidence of it.

Upon the Friday following, being August 21st, about sun-
rising, one Agnes Naesmith, an old widow woman, ignorant,
and of a malicious disposition, addicted to threatnings, (which
sometimes were observed to be followed with fatal events),
who lived in the neighbourhood, came to Bargarran's house;
where, finding the child Christian in the court with her
younger sister, she asked how the lady and young child did,
and how old the young sucking child was; to which Christian
replied, what do I know? Then Agnes asked, how herself
did, and how old she was; to which she answered, that she
was well, and in the eleventh year of her age.

On the Saturday night thereafter, being Aug. 22, the child
went to bed in good health; but so soon as she fell asleep,
began to struggle and cry Help, help! and then suddenly got
up, and did fly over the top of a resting bed, where she was
lying (her father, mother, and others being in the room, and
to their great astonishment and admiration) with such violence,
that probably her brains had been dashed out, if a woman,
providentially standing by, and supported by a door at her
back, had not broke the force of the child's motion; who,
being laid in another bed, remained stiff and insensible as if
she had been dead for the space of half an hour; but for
forty-eight hours thereafter could not sleep, crying out of
violent pains through her whole body, and no sooner began to
sleep or turn drowsy but seemed greatly affrighted, crying still,
Help, help.

After this the pain fixed in her left side, and her body was
often so bent and rigid, as she stood like a bow on her feet
and neck at once, and continued without power of speech,
except in some short intervals, for eight days; during which

time she had scarce half an hour's intermission together, the fits taking her suddenly, and both coming on and going off by a swerff or short deliquium, but appeared perfectly well and sensible in the intervals.

But about the middle of September, her fits returned in a manner differing from the former, wherein she seemed to fight and struggle with something that was invisible to spectators, and her action appeared as if she had been defending herself from some who were assaulting or attempting to hurt her, and this with such force that four strong men were scarcely able to hold her; and when any of the people touched any part of her body she did cry and screech with such vehemence, as if they had been killing her, but could not speak.

Before this time, as she was seized with the trouble, her parents had called for physicians from Paisley, viz.: John White, apothecary, a near relation, and afterwards Dr. Johnstone, who took blood, and applied several things, both at first, and afterwards, without any discernable effect upon the patient, either to the better or worse; and she all the while of these latter fits being afflicted with extraordinary risings and fallings of her belly, like the motion of a pair of bellows, and such strange movings of her body, as made the whole bed she lay on shake, to the great consternation of spectators.

Some days thereafter was an alteration in her fits, so far, that she got speaking during the time of them; and while she was in the fits, fell a crying that Katherine Campbell and Agnes Naesmith were cutting her side and other parts of her body; which parts were in that time violently tormented. And when the fit was over she still averred that she had seen the same persons doing the same things which she complained of while under the fit, (it being remarkable that in the intervals she was still as well and sensible as ever) and would not believe but that others present saw them as well as she! In this condition she continued with some, but not very considerable variation, either as to the fits or intervals, for the space of a month.

After which time she was conveyed to Glasgow, where Dr. Brisbane,* a physician deservedly famed for skill and experience, did by Mr. Henry Marshall, apothecary, apply medicine to her; after which, having staid in Glasgow about ten days, and being brought home to the country, she had near a fortnight's intermission. But then her fits returned, with this difference, that she knew when they were coming, by a pain in her left side, which she felt before they came; and in these fits her throat was prodigiously drawn down toward her breast, and her tongue back into her throat: her whole body becoming stiff and extended, as a dead corpse, without sense or motion; and sometimes her tongue was drawn out of her mouth over her chin to a wonderful length, her teeth setting together so fast upon it, that those present were forced to thrust something betwixt her teeth, for saving her tongue; and it was oft observed that her tongue was thus tortured when she essayed to pray. And in this condition she was for some time, with sensible intervals wherein she had perfect health, and could give a full account of what she was heard to utter while in the fit.

For several days these fits continuing with some variation, her parents resolved to return her to Glasgow, that she might there have the more conveniency of being under the doctor's oversight and care, for further discerning the nature of her trouble, and making use of the most probable natural re-

---

* The Son of the Reverend Divine, Mr. Matthew Brisbane, Parson of Erskine, who was descended from the Brisbanes of Bishopton.—*Vide Crawfurd's History of the Shire of Renfrew.*

medies. But being on her way to her grandmother's house at Northbar, she did thrust or spit out of her mouth parcels of hair, some curled, some plaited, some knotted, of different colours, and in large quantities; and thus she continued to do in several swooning fits every quarter of an hour, both in her passage to Glasgow, which was by boat on Thursday, Nov. 12th, and when she was in Glasgow ; for the space of three days ensuing she put frequently hair out of her mouth, and in as great quantities as the first day, her former swerffing or swooning fits recurring as often throughout the days as before ; and thereafter from Monday to Thursday following she put out of her mouth coal cinders about the bigness of chesnuts, some whereof were so hot that they could scarcely be handled, one of which, Dr. Brisbane being by her when she took it out of her mouth, felt to be hotter than the heat of any one's body could make it. Then for the space of two days in these swooning fits, as formerly, there was put, or taken out of her mouth, straw in great quantities, though but one straw at once folded up together, which, when put out, returned to its length, was found to be both long and broad, and it was remarkable that in one of them there was a little small pin found. Thereafter were put out of her mouth, bones of various sorts and sizes, as bones of fowls, and small bones of the heads of kine, and then some small sticks of candle fir, (a sort of fir in the country, that burns like candle), one of which was about three or four inches long ; which, when any upon sight of either bones or sticks took hold of to pull out, they found them either held by her teeth set together upon them, or forcibly drawn back into her throat; particularly Archibald Bannatyne of Kellie, younger, observing a bone in her mouth like a duck shank or leg bone, and essaying to pull it out, he declared he found something drawing it back into her throat, so that it took a deal of force to get it pulled out. It is to be noticed, that she never knew how these things were brought into her mouth, and when they were got out of it, she immediately recovered of her fit for that time.

After this, she put out of her mouth some quantity of unclean hay intermixed with dung, as if it had been taken out of a dunghill, which was so stinking that the damsel could not endure the nauseating taste and vile relish those things produced in her mouth, which did necessitate her still to rinse her mouth with water, after the putting of that sort of matter out of it. Then for more than a day's space, she put out of her mouth a number of wild fowls feathers; after that a gravel-stone, which, in the judgment of beholders, had been passed by some persons in a gravel fit, with some small white stones, and a whole nut gall, (wherewith they use to dye and to make ink), together with lumps of candle grease and egg shells; during which time she continued as formerly in her recurring swooning fits, with some intervals wherein she was in perfect health: of all which there were many famous witnesses, who, in that city, (besides those who were continually with her) came frequently to visit her.

It is to be noticed, that the damsel at the time of the putting out of her mouth the sticks above-mentioned, being in bed about eight o'clock at night, told she was to be greviously tormented with sore fits at night, which accordingly fell out. For a little thereafter, she fell into a long swoon, wherein she had no use of any sense, either of hearing, seeing, or feeling; so as though oftimes the beholders called to her with a loud voice, moving, also, and tossing her body, all was to no purpose; and when the Laird of Kellie, younger, above-named, to try the truth, gave her a very sore pinch in the arm, she had no sense of it in the time. After recovering from the swoon, but yet continuing in the fit, she fell a reasoning with Katherine Campbell after this manner: " Thou sittest there with a stick in thy hand to put in my mouth, but through God's strength thou shalt not get leave : thou art permitted to torment me, but I trust in God thou shalt never get my life, though it is my life thou designest." (And at that time calling for a Bible and candle), said, "Come near me Katie, and I'll let thee see where a godly man was given up to Satan to be tormented, but God kept his life in his own hand; and so I trust in God thou shalt never get my life, and all that thou shalt be permitted to do unto me, I hope through God's mercy shall turn to my advantage. This man was robbed of all, and tormented in body, and had nothing left him but an ill wife. Come near me, Katie, and I'll read it to thee." And reading that passage of Job, when she came to the place where his wife said to him, "Curse God and die!" the damsel considering these words a little, said,—"O ! what a wife has this been, that bids her goodman curse God and die? she who should have been a comfort to him in his trouble, turned a cross to him?" Then, after reading of the chapter to the end, she looks towards the foot of the bed and said,—" Now, Katie, what thinkest thou of that? thou seest for all the power the Devil got over Job, he gained no ground on him ; and I hope he shall gain as little on me. Thy master the Devil deceives thee ; he is a bad master whom thou servest, and thou shalt find it to thy smart, except thou repent before thou die. There is no repentance to be had after death. I'll let thee see, Katie, there is no repentance in hell." And turning over the book, citing Luke, Chap. xvi., near the latter end thereof, and reading the same over, said,—" Katie, thou seest there is no repentance in hell, for this rich man besought Abraham to testify to his five brethren, that they come not to the place of torment, where he was, but repent and turn to the Lord, for there is no winning out, if once they come there ; now, Katie, thou heard this, what thinkest thou of it ?

I'll let thee hear another place which should pierce thy very heart, and turning over the Book, said she would read about Adam and Eve. Thou knowest, Katie, the serpent the Devil, thy master, thought to have ruined mankind at the beginning, his malice was so great at that blessed state wherein they were then, seeing himself cast down from all hopes of mercy, used all means possible for him to subvert their happiness, by suggesting to them fair promises, and a prospect of advantage to them before their eyes, in causing them eat that forbidden fruit, whereby they and their posterity fell from that estate wherein they were, and were made subject to God's curse for ever. But God did not suffer them to be at this stance, but of his infinite mercy shewed them a better way, whereby they might have life eternal by revealing to them that blessed promise,—' The seed of the woman shall bruise the head of the serpent.' Now, Katie, what thinkest thou of that promise? But have mind of this, thou'lt get no advantage by it ; 'tis not made to thee, who hast renounced God's service, and taken on with the Devil,—thou art his slave; thou deniedst this, but I know thou art a hypocrite ; for I remember, when thou wast in my mother's house, thou bought a Catechism upon a pretence to learn to read, to cloak thy sin. Wilt thou hear me, knowest thou the reward of the hypocrite ? I'll let thee hear it ; remember Mr. William Gillies was lecturing the other day upon the xxiii. of Matthew, where many a woe is pronounced against the hypocrite, eight dreadful woes here, Katie, and some of them belong to thee ; but I'll tell thee more. Knowest thou the reward of the hypocrite ? they shall be cast into the lake that burns for ever, that's their portion. Dost thou hear this now ? thou turnest thy back to me, when I am telling the truth ; if I were reading a story-book, or telling a tale to thee, thou wouldst hear that. Remember it will be thy portion, too, if thou do not repent, and confess, and seek mercy." Again, turning over the book, she read about Pilate, saying,—" Pilate he made a shew of cleansing himself of Christ's blood,—he washed his hands and declared himself innocent; but for all his washing, he had a foul heart,—he would not lose his office for the saving of Christ's life. He knew well enough that Christ was an innocent person ; but he preferred his honour before Christ : therefore to please the Jews, and to quench the struggling in his conscience, he washed his hands, and then delivered Christ to be crucified by them." Thus she continued for more than two hours' space, reasoning at this rate, and exhorting her to repent, quoting many places of Scripture through the Revelation and Evangelists. And when any offered to pull her Bible from her, she uttered horrid screeches and outcries, saying,—"She would never part with her Bible as long as she lived,—she would keep it in spite of all the devils."

Before we pass from this, it will be needful to give the reader advertisement of some things. 1. That while she called for her Bible and a candle, she neither heard nor saw any of those persons who were then actually and discernably present in the room with her, and that Katherine Campbell, to whom she directed her speech, was not discernably present to any other body but herself. And the pinch she got in her insensible fit, she found and complained of the pain of it in that part afterward, but knew not how she came by it, nor blamed any of her tormentors for it. 2. That these words set down as spoken by her were the very same both for words and order as nearly as they could be gathered and remembered by the hearers without any addition of their own. 3. That although she was a girl of a pregnant spirit above her age, and had much of the Scriptures, and withal had a pretty good understanding, above what might be expected of one of her years, of the fundamental principles of religion taught in the Catechisms; yet we doubt not in so strong a combat, the Lord did, by His good spirit, graciously afford her a more than ordinary measure of assistance, both now and at other times in the like debates.

Sometime after the putting out of her mouth the trash above-mentioned, she fell into extremely violent fits, with lamentable crying,—four persons being hardly able to withhold her from climbing up the walls of the chamber, or from otherways doing herself hurt, meantime having no power of speech while in the fit, but her back and the rest of her body grievously pained, in which condition she continued four or five days, with the usual sensible intervals, in which she declared that four men, Alexander and James Andersons, and other two, of whom she gave particular and exact marks, but knew not their names, were tormenting her. It was observed that many of these she named were known to be persons of ill fame, as these two persons last named were. It is also remarkable that for some time she knew not the name of the said Alexander Henderson, till one day he came a-begging to the door of the house, where the damsel was, whom she seeing, immediately cried out, "that was he whom she had seen among the crew."

After this she fell into other fits, wherein she saw the forenamed persons with some others, and heard and saw several things that passed among them. Particularly, she sometimes told when she was to take the fits, how often she would take them, (which fell out accordingly), with some discourse that were among them relating to herself and others.

About the eighth of December, being brought home again from Glasgow, and having had six or seven days respite from her fits, she afterwards fell into frightful and terrifying fits; the occasion whereof she declared to be, her seeing the devil in prodigious and horrid shapes, threatening to devour her, and then she would fall dead and stiff with all the parts of her body distended and stretched out as a corpse, without sense or motion, which fits as they came suddenly on without her knowledge, so she did as suddenly recover and grew perfectly well; and they usually came on when she essayed to pray. In which time also other fits took her more sensibly, she knowing when they were a-coming, how long they would continue, and when they would return; in which fits her eyes strangely altered, and turned in her head to the admiration of spectators, with a continual painful working about her heart; sometimes her joints were complicate and drawn together, and her forehead drawn forcibly about toward her shoulders; which fits she took by first falling into a swoon, and after her violent fits, instantly recovered after the same manner. During this time, the fits altered again as to their times of coming and continuance; in which she sometimes endeavoured to bite her own fingers, or anything else that came in her way; also when she saw the persons before-mentioned, one or two of them about her, pointing them out to the persons present with her, though by them unseen, and sometimes declaring that she had hold of them by their clothes, particularly, December 17. She being in a sore fit, she cried out of several persons that were tormenting her; and being in the bed, grasped with her hands towards the foot of it, and cried out that she had got a grip of the sleeves of one J. P's. jerkin (or jacket) which was, as she said, duddie (that is ragged or tattered) at the elbows; and at that very instant, the damsel's mother and aunt heard the sound of the rending or tearing of a cloth, but saw or felt nothing, only found in each of the damsel's hands—which were fast closed—when they got them opened, a bit of red cloth, looking as torn off a garment; of which kind of cloth there had been none in the room at that time, nor in the whole house, nor near it that any knew of. Another particular she

told was, that there was such an one among the crew going
to prick her tongue, which thereupon was instantly pulled back
into her throat, she lying dumb for a considerable space.
Sometimes upon her recovery from her fits, she told that she
heard several things spoken and communed among her afflic-
tors, but durst not make them known; because they threatened
to torment her after this, or the other manner, if she should
make them known; and accordingly, when, by her mother or
others, she was prevailed with to begin to tell them, instantly
the torment fell out as was threatened. She told further, that
her tormentors appeared to her usually with lights and strange
sorts of candles, which were frightful for her to look to them.

Thus she continued till the first of January, 1697, not only in
the fits fore-mentioned with some alterations, but fell likewise
by swooning, into light fits, wherein she continued about two
or three hours together, sometimes more, sometimes less, with
very short intervals, in which fits she did not much complain
of pain; but had a great palpitation in her breast, and sometimes in other parts of her body, strange and unaccountable
motions, which continued in a greater or lesser degree during
the whole time of the fit, wherein she was somewhat light, and
not so solid in her mind as at other times, though in the intervals of these, as of all other fits, she was sufficiently composed; which fits as all the rest, came suddenly on, and went
as suddenly off by a swoon or swerf.

Before we proceed further in the relation, let it be noticed,
first, that the foresaid Agnes Naesmith, being brought by the
parents a second time to see the damsel, did (though not
desired) pray for her, viz., "That the Lord of heaven and
earth might send the damsel her health, and try out the
verity:" After which the damsel declared that though the
said Agnes had formerly been very troublesome to her, yet,
from that time forth, she did no more appear to her as her

tormentor, but, on the contrary, as she apprehended, defending her from the fury of the rest. Second, it is further here to be noticed, that the forenamed Katherine Campbell could by no means be prevailed with to pray for the damsel, but upon the contrary, when desired by some, cursed them, and all the family of Bargarran, and in particular the damsel and all that belonged to her, withal adding this grievious imprecation, "The devil let her never grow better, nor any concerned in her, be in a better condition than she was in, for what they had done to her." Which words she spoke before several famous witnesses. 3. That Bargarran having prevailed with the sheriff depute of the shire, to imprison the said Katherine Campbell, she from the time of her imprisonment, never appeared to the damsel; (though formerly she had ordinarily appeared as one of her most violent tormentors) except once or twice, at which times, it was found upon after enquiry, that she was not in the Tolbooth, but either in the jailor's house, or had liberty granted her to go out to church. 4. That at the time when the damsel did put out of her mouth the hair and other trash, as above related, Katherine Campbell being taken into custody, there was found in her pocket a ball of hair of several colours, which was afterwards thrown into the fire, after which time the damsel put no more hair out of her mouth. And it is to be further noticed, that she said she heard among the crew, when tormenting her, that Katherine Campbell made that ball of hair found in her pocket, of the hair of the damsel's head which had been cut when her trouble began, and which did agree in colour, &c., when compared.

Upon the first day of January, about ten o'clock at night, she fell by swoonings into fits differing from the former, in that, after the swooning fit was over, she lay quiet, as if she had been dead, making no motion at all with her body in

the bed; yet, at the same time, those present heard her
mournful talking, but with a low and hardly audible voice,
and repeating several stories in metre, which they thought to
be expressions of the rise and progress of her own trouble;
and thus, she continued, (still, withal, naming some of the
forementioned persons) till her parents and others offered to
rouse her, by touching and moving her body: whereupon,
instantly, she uttered horrid screeches, and cried as if she had
been pierced through with swords, and assaulted for her life;
after which she fell a singing, leaping, and dancing for a long
time, laughing with a loud voice, in an unusual manner, tearing down the hangings of the bed, and pulling off her head-
clothes and neck-clothes; in which extravagancies she was
acted with such a force and strength, that her father and
minister, though joining their whole strength together, could
not get her dancing and leaping hindered. But after prayer,
the minister finding her composed, inquired if she remembered what she had done in time of the fit; to which she replied, "That she distinctly remembered her miscarriages, and,
in special, her singing and dancing, saying, withal, that the
witches inclosing her in a ring (or circle), and dancing and
singing about her, was the occasion of her dancing, which she
then gladly performed with the rest. For some days after
she had fits after this manner, with some variation; in one of
which fits, as she was tearing off her head-dress clothes, her
parents resolving to see what would be the event, did make no
hinderance to her; whereupon she striped herself of all her
clothes that were upon her, not leaving so much as her
smock upon her body, if that had been permitted.
     After this, toward or about the 11th Jan., she fell into fits
different from the former, in which she was suddenly carried
away from her parents and others that were about her, with a
sudden flight, and in the first of these (to their great amaze-

ment) through the chamber and hall, down a long winding stair toward the tower-gate, with such a swift and unaccountable motion, that it was not in the power of any to prevent her,—her feet not touching the ground, so far as any of the beholders could discern, being heard in her motion to laugh in an unusual manner; but, by divine providence, the gate being shut, her motion was stopped till such time as some of the family could overtake her, who, endeavouring to carry her back, found her instantly fall as one dead, and become stiff; in which posture, being brought back to the chamber, she lay for a considerable space. And being recovered, she did declare that there were about the number of nine or ten persons who had carried her away in a shue (as she termed it, that is, as one swinging upon a rope) wherein she then took pleasure, her feet not at all touching the ground, to her apprehension.

The night following, she was suddenly carried away, as before, from her parents and others who were about her, through the chamber and hall, and sixteen large steps of a winding stair, up toward the top of the house! where she met with apparitions of strange and unaccountable things; but was carried down again, as she thought, in a shue or swing, asserting, after her recovery, that she met upon the stair the number of six women and four men, and by them was carried toward the gate again, where accordingly she was found, and was carried up as formerly, all the parts of her body distended and stiff as one dead; in which posture she lay for some time, and when recovering, declared, that both now and formerly, she had endeavoured to open the gate, and that those she saw about her were helping her, with a design to get her to the court, to drown her in the well, which she said she heard them saying among themselves they intended to do, and that then the world would believe she had destroyed

M

herself. It is observable that (these kind of fits continuing with her for some few days) in one of them she was stopped at the gate, and found in the fore-mentioned posture, which was neither locked nor barred ; yet could they not get it opened, though both she and her tormentors endeavoured it.

Before we proceed in the relation, it is not to be omitted that as soon as the damsel's affliction was observed to be extraordinary and preternatural, there were (besides times formerly set apart in a more private way) at the desire of the parents and minister, and by the presbytery's special order, a minister or two appointed to meet every week, at the house of Bargarran, to join with the family, the minister of the parish, and other good christians of the neighbourhood, in fasting and praying, which usually fell to be on the Tuesday. And upon Jan. 12th, it being the turn of Mr. Patrick Simpson, a neighbour minister, to be there, when he came to the house he found both the minister of the parish, and the brother who was to join with him had been necessarily withdrawn ; yet resolved to carry on the work with assistance of three elders, some other good people being present. When he first saw the damsel after he came to the house, he found her under some lesser fits which came and went off quickly, and when prayer began she was quiet and sober during the same, but in time of singing the xciii. Psalm, she fell into a sore fit, of greater continuance, first laughing, then making some sound like singing, after that pulling her head clothes down over her face, and lastly, turning so outrageous in her motions that her father could scarce get her holden with his whole strength, but behoved to lie over upon the bed with her in his arms until the fit abated. After her recovery from which, she was quiet and composed all the time of prayer ; and while the minister lectured on Mark ix., from 14 to 30 v., was very attentive, carefully looking in her Bible the

Scriptures quoted, so all along both in time of prayer and singing, until the whole religious exercise was ended, and some refreshment after the same taken, at the end of which she told the company, she had something to tell, which she had heard some among her tormentors saying, which she durst not reveal; but the minister and her mother urging her to be free and not to obey the Devil, she said she would tell it her mother in her ear. Then coming from the other side of the table, and placing herself betwixt her mother and aunt, she began to whisper in her mother's ear; but before she got a sentence fully pronounced, she fell into a violent fit, so as her mother and those next her could scarcely hold her till the violence thereof began to abate, and then her mother told that she was speaking of a meeting and a feast they had spoke of in the orchard of Bargarran, but was able to say no more, and after recovery, her mother desiring her to tell the rest of it, and she beginning to whisper in her ear, as before, could not get one word uttered till she was seized again of a fit as violent as the former. Whereupon the minister perceiving her torment, desired them to forbear any further troubling of her. Notice, that accordingly there was a feast and meeting in that orchard about that time of the crew, acknowledged and declared afterwards by three of them, that confessed themselves to have been there, viz.:—Elizabeth Anderson, James and Thomas Lindsays, they not knowing what either the damsel had spoken, or one of them what another had confessed relating thereunto. *See No. A. of the Appendix.*

About or within a little after this time, she was again suddenly carried from them in the former manner down a stair, which goes off from a corner of the chamber to a cellar just below it, where her brother and sister were providentially gone down a little before, to bring some drink from the cellar, and already near the stair foot, with a lighted candle, which she soon put out; but they crying and holding her by the head-clothes, quickly discovered to the rest where she was. Upon which Mr. Alexander King, minister at Bonhill, (being then in the chamber) made haste down stairs where he found her, but her brother and sister had lost hold of her, she having loosed her head-clothes and let them go; yet Mr. King having caught hold of her, kept her in his arms till a lighted candle was brought; and endeavouring to bring her up stairs, did declare that he found something forcibly drawing her downwards, but he still keeping his hold, she fell stiff, as one dead upon the stair, and was in this posture carried up and laid in bed, where she lay a considerable space. And when recovered of the fit, she declared that the occasion of her going down stairs with such force, was, that the crew had suggested to her while she was in the light fits, that the devil was in the meal chest in the cellar, and that if she would go down and put out the candle, she might force him out of it. Notice here, first, that when some fits of this kind were ready to seize her, she sometimes gave advertisement thereof to those present with her, giving signs of her earnest desire of their help to prevent her motion, which usually proved to be of good effect, wherein the divine mercy toward her is much to be observed. 2. It is also to be noticed, that about the time when she was in these flying fits, she used to utter horrid shrieks and outcries, not like those of rational creatures; in which time there were heard for three nights together when the damsel was asleep in bed, shrieks and outcries of the same kind in the court, when none of the family was without doors, to the great affrightment of those who heard them, being that they exactly resembled the cries of, and shrieks the damsel used to utter in the fits; who afterwards in one of her intervals hearing some of the family talking of these cries and shrieks, and alledging they had been utttered by some wild beast or other, said to them they were mistaken, for it was Margaret. And two others of the name of Margaret, called by the crew their Maggies, had uttered these shrieks, the devil having promised to them at that time to carry her out of the house to them, that they might drown her in the well, where there were eighteen more waiting for her.

After this she fell into fretting and angry fits (as she termed them) in which her humour was cross to all that those about her could say or do, nothing proving to her satisfaction, but everything displeasing, (her former fits withal now and then seizing her,) but when restored to a right composure of mind, she declared that her tormentors about her, did still suggest to her and advise her, to go to such and such remote places of the house alone, and bring with her a snood (which is a head-lace, such as women tie up their hair with) or a cravat or some such thing, promising her rough almonds or some kinds of sweetmeats which they named to her, and for that end, to bring her apron with her to hold them in, and accordingly when seized again with fits of this nature, did resolutely endeavour to repair to these places, having a snood or cravat and her apron with her, and would suffer none to be in her company, which put her parents and others to a necessity of detaining her by force, and she being thus prevented uttered hideous screeches and outcries, of which in this sort of fits she was seldom free.

Thursday, January 14th, at night, a young lass or girl appeared to her with a scabbed face amongst the rest of her tormentors, telling her she was to come to the house to-morrow about ten o'clock, and forbidding her to reveal it.

The next day being January 15th, in the afternoon, the damsel earnestly enquired at her mother and the rest of the family what beggars had come to the gate that day, and of what countenance and visage they were? but the family not knowing her design in such a question, gave no heed unto it; yet, she still insisting, and being in company with her mother and another gentlewoman, about four o'clock at night, said to them, she thought she might tell them somewhat (the time being now past) she was forbidden to reveal it; but beginning to tell, she presently fell a crying, that she was tormented and pricked through her whole body, yet recovering from the fit, went on and told it. The thing she had to reveal was, that a scabbed faced lass appeared to her yesternight, and was to be at the gate this day at ten o'clock. Whereupon the servants being enquired at, what sort of beggars had been there that day, did declare among others, there had been a beggar wife at the door, and a young woman or lass with her who had scabs on her face, and received their alms.

Jan. 16th and 17th, when recovered of her swooning fits, she put out of her mouth a great number of pins, which she declared J—— P—— had forced into her mouth, and a gentlewoman who had been one of her most violent tormentors.

Jan. 21. Her fits altered again, after this manner: she would fall in them with heavy sighs and groans, and hideous outcries, telling those about her that cats, ravens, owls, and horses were destroying and pressing her down in the bed; and, at the same time, her mother and another gentlewoman being in the room with her, did declare that immediately after they had taken the girl out of her bed in this condition, they did see something moving under the bed-clothes as big as a cat.

The same morning, in the interval of her fits, she said she heard her tormentors whispering among themselves, and suggest to one another, (naming J—— P—— the Andersons and other) that the Devil had promised and engaged to them to carry her over the hall window to the end they might drown her in the well which was in the court, and then they said the world would believe she had destroyed herself; and the same day, and several days thereafter, when seized with her grievous fits, did attempt with such force to get herself over that window, that spectators could scarce, with their whole strength, prevent her.

About this time, nothing in the world would so discompose her as religious exercises. If there were any discourses of God or Christ, or any of the things which are not seen and are eternal, she would be cast into grievous agonies; and when she essayed in her light fits, to read any portion of the scriptures, repeat any of the Psalms, or answer any questions of our catechisms (which she could do exactly at other times) she was suddenly struck dumb, and lay as one stiff dead, her mouth opened to such a wideness that her jaw appeared to be out of joint, and anon would clap together again with incredible force. The same happened to her shoulder blade, her elbow, and hand wrists. She would at other times lie in a benumbed condition, and be drawn together as if she had been tied neck and heels with ropes; yet on a sudden would with such force and violence be pulled up and tear all about her, that it was as much as one or two could do, to hold her fast in their arms; but when ministers and other good christians (seeing her in such intolerable anguishes) made serious application by prayer to God, on her behalf, she got respite from her grievous fits of this kind, and was ordinarily free of them during the time of prayer, though seized of them before; and albeit, usually, when ministers began to pray, she made great disturbance by idle loud talking, whistling, singing and roaring, to drown the voice of the person praying.

Particularly, Jan. 22., she was more turbulent than at other times she used to be, and continued some space after the minister began to pray, singing and making hideous noise, fetching furious blows with her fist, and kicks with her feet at the minister, uttering reproachful talk of him, and calling him dog, &c. Yet, she being composed, and her fits being over before prayer was ended, and the minister, when he had done, finding her sober and in a right composure of mind, enquired why she made such disturbance? To which she replied, she was forced to do it by the hellish crew about her; and that she thought they were none of her own words that she uttered.

Jan. 24th. She said some things relating both to herself and others had been suggested to her by her troublers; but that they had threatened to torment her, if she should offer to make them known. And accordingly in essaying to express her mind, she was cast into two grievous fits, in which she cried out of violent pains; all the parts of her body becoming rigid and extended like a corpse, her head was twisted round, and, if any offered by force to obstruct such dangerous motion she seemed to be upon, she would roar exceedingly. Sometimes her neck bone seemed to be dissolved, and yet on a sudden became so stiff that there was no moving of it; and when these grievous agonies were over, she again assayed to express her mind by write, but to no purpose, for instantly she was cast into other two very grievous fits, wherein she was struck dumb, deaf, and blind, and her tongue drawn a prodigious length over her chin. And when the fits were over, declared, the Andersons, J—— P—— the gentlewoman, and I—— D—— with the rest of the hellish crew, some of whom she could not name, had been tormenting her in the fits, and that there had been fifteen of them about the house all the last night, but were now all gone save one, who was to stay about the house till her fits were over. And, accordingly, her brother and sister did declare they saw that morning a woman in the garden, with a red coat about her head, sitting at the root of an apple tree ; but Bargarran, with most of the servants, being abroad, the matter was not further searched.

The same day, about six at night, she was seized with variety of grievous fits again, in which sometimes she lay wholly senseless and breathless with her belly swelled like a drum, as like a woman with child,—her eyes were pulled into her head so far that spectators thought she should never have used them more. Sometimes, when she was tying her own neck-clothes, her enchanted hand would tie them so strait about her neck that she had strangled herself if spectators had not given some relief unto her. Sometimes she was in hazard of burning herself in the fire, offering, with violence, to throw herself into the same. Divers times she did strike furious blows at her near relations in her fits. She would maintain discourse with her tormentors, and, asking questions concerning herself and others, received answer from them, which, indeed, none but herself perceived, reasoning with one of them after this manner :—

"O, what ailed thee to be a witch ? Thou sayest it is but three nights since thou wast a witch. O, if thou wouldest repent, it may be God might give thee repentance. If thou wouldest seek it and confess. If thou would desire me I would do what I could, for the Devil is an ill master to serve. He is a liar from the beginning. He promises what he cannot perform." Then, calling for her Bible, she said—"I will let thee see where he promised to our first parents that they should not die ;" and reading the passage, said—"Now, thou seest he is a liar, for, by breaking the commandment, they were made liable to death here and death everlasting. O, that is an uncouth word. Long eternity never to have an end,—never, never to have an end ; had not God, of his infinite mercy, ordained some to eternal life through Jesus Christ. The Devil makes thee believe thou wilt get great riches by serving him; but come near." And having uttered this word, she lost power of her speech, her tongue being drawn back into her throat; yet, beckoning with her hand to the spectre to come near her, and turning over the book, kept her eye upon that passage of Holy Scripture,—Job xxvii. 18,—and pointing with her finger at the place, and shaking her head, turned over the book again, and, recovering her speech, said—"I'll let thee see where God bids us seek, and we shall find." And reading over the place, said—"It is God that gives us every good gift. We have nothing of our own. I submit to His will, though I never be better, for God can make all my trouble turn to my advantage, according to His Word, Romans viii. 28,"—which place she then read, and thus continued reasoning for the space of an hour.

Sometimes she cried out of violent pain, by reason of furious blows and strokes she had received from the hands of her tormentors,—the noise of which strokes bystanders distinctly heard, though they perceived not the hands that gave them.

One night, the girl, sitting with her parents and others, cried out something was wounding her thigh, upon which, instantly, her mother, putting her hand in the damsel's pocket, found her folding knife opened, which had been folded when put in her pocket; but her uncle, not trusting the thing, did again put up the knife, and leaving it folded in her pocket, on a sudden she cried out, as before, the knife was cutting her thigh, being unfolded by means of J. P. and others, as she said; upon which, her uncle, searching her pocket again, found the knife opened as formerly. This happened twice or thrice, to the admiration of the beholders, though they took special notice that she nor any other visible hand opened it.

Jan. 25th. She was again seized with her swooning stiff fits, with this remarkable variation—her throat was sometimes most prodigiously extended, and sometimes as strangely contracted, so that she appeared in palpable danger of being choked, and through the violence of pain in her throat, and difficulty of breathing, struggled with feet and hands, as if some had been actually strangling her, and could speak or cry none, with which kind of fits she was frequently seized for several days, and in the intervals did declare that the fore-mentioned persons and others (whom she could not get then named) were strangling her; and that the occasion of her not having power to speak or cry in the fit was a ball in her throat, which also was visible to spectators, for they did clearly discern a bunch in her throat while in the fit as big as a pullet's egg, which had almost choked her.

Sometimes she was kept from eating her meat, having her teeth set when she carried any food to her mouth. Divers times, also, she was kept from drinking when at meat; for no sooner could she taste the drink but she was in hazard of being choked thereby, and herself sometimes would have held the cup so hard betwixt her teeth that it was not in the power of those with her to unloose it. And when any thing had fallen out amiss in the place where she was,—as the falling and breaking of a cup, anybody's receiving harm, and such like,—she would fall a-laughing and rejoice extremely, which kind of jollity was far from the girl's temper when at herself.

Feb. 1st. She essaying to tell some things she had been forbidden by her tormentors to make known, was handled with intolerable torments. At the beginning of her fits, usually she would be kept oddly looking, sometimes towards the chimney, sometimes towards other particular places in the room, but could not always tell what she saw; yet, for ordinary, she would name such and such persons, who, she said, were then come to cast her into fits. And when any desired her to cry to the **Lord Jesus** for help, her teeth were instantly set close, her eyes twisted almost round in her head, and she was thrown upon the floor with the stiffness and posture of one that had been some days laid for dead; and on a sudden recovered again, and would weep bitterly to remember what had befallen her. The same day, when her fits were over, she said she now perceived it was by the means of a charm that such restraints were laid upon her; that she could not tell what the witches had forbidden her to make known; but the charm might be found out (as she said) by searching for it beneath the bed where she lay; and she having quickly done this herself, found (to the apprehension of spectators) beneath the foresaid bed, an entire egg-shell open in the end, which being instantly thrown into the fire, did melt away after the manner of wax, without any noise as egg-shells use to make when burning in the fire. After this, the girl said she would not now be handled so severely, upon essaying to make known what the witches had forbidden her to tell, only her tongue would be drawn back into her throat, which accordingly happened. She did likewise inform her friends of many things she had not liberty to do, before the charm was found out particularly, that her tormentors had frequently solicited her to become a witch herself, and promised her great riches and perfect health also, to induce her thereunto. Which temptation, she, through the mercy of God, still resisted, reasoning with them after this manner :—"The Devil promises what he cannot perform; and granting he could fulfil his promises, yet I am sure from the Scriptures, hell and the wrath of God will be the final reward of all such as yield to this wickedness." To which she received this reply, (which, indeed, none but herself perceived) that hell and the wrath of God so much talked of, was not so formidable as was represented. She also said, the witches had importunately urged her to give them her consent, to take away the life of her young sister, who was at that time upon her mother's breast; which temptation also, she was enabled through the grace of God to resist. She told her parents likewise, there had been a charm laid upon the top of the house, where her young sister was (the child having been sent out a nursing, by reason of the continued affliction of the family) and that the charm had been placed upon the top of the house by pinched Maggy, who thereby did design the taking away of her sister's life; and that this was the cause why she had so often, for some weeks before, desired her mother to bring home her sister, constantly affirming, that the child would daily decay as long as she staid there. Whereupon her parents observing the daily decay of the infant, even to skin and bone, brought her home, where she recovered. The girl being asked how she came to the knowledge of these things? replied, something speaking distinctly as it were above her head, had suggested these, and other things of that nature to her.

Feb. 2nd. The girl being in the chamber with her mother and others, was on a sudden struck with great fear and consternation, and fell a-trembling upon the sight of John Lindsay, in Barloch, talking with her father in the hall. She said to her mother the foresaid Lindsay had been always one of her most violent tormentors, and that she had been threatened with extreme tortures, if she should offer to name him; whereupon she was desired to go towards the place where he was, and touch some part of his body in a way unknown to him, which having done with some aversion, was instantly seized with extreme tortures in all the parts of her body. After which Lindsay was put to it, and interrogated thereupon; but he giving no satisfying answer, was desired to take the damsel by the hand, which he being unwillingly induced to do, she was immediately upon the touch cast into tolerable anguishes, her eyes being almost twisted round in her head, and all the parts of her body becoming rigid and stiff, fell down in the posture of one that had been laid for some days dead, and afterwards got up in a sudden, and tearing her clothes, threw herself with violence upon him and when her fit was over, spectators did also take the damsel by the hand, yet no such effect followed.

About six at night there came an old Highland fellow to Bargarran, who, calling himself a weary traveller, said, he behoved to lodge there that night; but the servants refusing him lodging, gave him something by way of alms. At this time the damsel being in the chamber with her mother and another gentlewoman, said to the best of her apprehension ; there was one of the wicked crew in or about the house at that time : whereupon her mother made haste with her daughter down stairs towards the kitchen. And finding there unexpectedly the Highland fellow, whom the girl then accused as one of her tormentors, she desired the Highland fellow to take her daughter by the hand, which he being urged to do, the girl immediately upon his touch was grievously tormented in all the parts of her body. And this falling out in divine providence, Bargarran caused secure him.

The next morning, the minister having come to Bargarran to visit the damsel, and the matter being imparted to him, called for the Highland fellow, and having questioned him to and again about this matter, without any satisfying answer, brought the child out of the chamber, covering her face, and almost her whole body, with his cloak, and giving signs to the Highland fellow to touch her in this posture, as he had ordered him before, without the damsel's knowledge, which he having done with great aversion, the girl not knowing of his touch, was instantly cast into intolerable agonies as formerly; yet others afterwards touching her, no such event followed. And when her fits were over, she besought the Highland fellow, to allow her the liberty for to discover and tell persons that haunted and molested her, whom he had forbidden her to make known. Upon which the old fellow looking at her with an angry countenance, her mouth was instantly stopped, and her teeth set; and being desired by those present to speak her mind freely, whether he would or not, at length replied, she feared to do it. And when, through the importunity of John Maxwell of Dargavel, and Porterfield of Fulwood, and some other gentlemen there present, she essayed to declare her mind, she was seized with her fits again.

Before this time the lamentable case of the afflicted damsel and family had been represented to His Majesty's most honourable privy council, who, upon serious application made to them, worthily and piously granted a commission to a noble lord and some worthy gentlemen to make inquiry into the same. By virtue of this commission some suspected persons were seized; particularly, Feb. 4, Alexander Anderson, an ignorant, irreligious fellow, who had been always of evil fame, and accused by the afflicted damsel, by a special order from the commissioners for inquiry, was apprehended and committed to prison, as was also Elizabeth Anderson, his daughter, upon flagrant presumptions of witchcraft; for the other year, Jean Fulton, her grandmother, an old scandalous woman, being cited before the kirk-session, and accused for hideous cursing, and imprecating mischief upon several persons, which had been followed with fatal events, the forementioned Elizabeth Anderson, her grandchild, who lived in the house with her, did declare before the session she had frequently seen the devil in company with her grandmother, in

the likeness of a small black man, who usually did vanish on
a sudden within the walls of the house when anybody came
to the door. Upon this presumption was the said Elizabeth
Anderson seized with her father, and committed to custody ;
but at first most obstinately denied accession any manner of
way to the sin of witchcraft, until afterwards, when seriously
importuned and dealt with in the prison by two gentlemen,
did, before she came to Bargarran's house, confess her guilt
without Bargarran's knowledge at that time. And that she
had been at several meetings with the devil and witches, and,
amongst others, she did declare her own father, and the forementioned Highland fellow to have been active instruments of
the girl's trouble; and gave, before she was confronted with
him, exact marks of this Highland body, and though she declared she knew not his name, yet, when confronted with him,
did accuse him, and affirm he was the person she spoke of.
See No. A of the Appendix.

February 5th, a quorum of the commissioners being met at
Bargarran, and the persons then delated by Elizabeth Anderson to have been at meetings with the devil, and active
instruments of the damsel's trouble, viz., Alexander Anderson, her father, Agnes Naesmith, Margaret Fultoun,
James Lindsay *alias* Curat, John Lindsay *alias* Bishop,
Katherine Campbell were all of them (excepting John
Lindsay *alias* Bishop, who was not then apprehended),
confronted with Katherine Shaw before the Lord
Blantyre, and the rest of the commissioners at Bargarran, and
several other gentlemen of note, and ministers then present,
and accused by her as her tormentors. And they having
all severally touched her in presence of the commissioners,
she was at each of their touches seized with grievous fits,
and cast into intolerable anguishes, others then present also
touching her in the same way, but no such effect followed.

And it is remarkable, when Katherine Campbell touched the girl, she was immediately upon her touch seized with more grievous fits, and cast into more intolerable torments than what followed upon the touch of the other accused persons, whereat Campbell herself being damped and confounded, though she had formerly declined to bless her, uttered these words—"The Lord God of heaven and earth bless thee, and save thee both soul and body." After which the damsel, when the fits were over, in which she had been a most pitiful spectacle, did declare she was now loosed, and that she might freely touch any of the accused persons, or they her after this, without trouble, which accordingly upon trial fell so out; and being inquired how she came to the knowledge of that, answered as formerly in the like case,— That something speaking distinctly as it were above her head, suggested this to her; and likewise usually gave her the knowledge of the names of her tormentors, and places in which they lived.

February 6. The girl being seized with sore fits, something was seen in her mouth, to the judgment of spectators like pieces of orange pills invisibly conveyed into her mouth, which she seemed in her agonies to be chewing, and having got down her throat, as those present apprehended, she did fall down dead and stiff, as if she had been choked, struggling with her feet and hands, as if at the last gasp, her throat swelling in a prodigious manner, to the affrightment of spectators; and when recovered, but yet in the light fit, she would say,—O it was a very sweet orange pill which I got from the gentlewoman, and did constantly affirm the same, declaring also that there had been others there present with the gentlewoman, particularly Margaret L—— or pinched Maggy, whose surname she had neither power nor liberty to express, neither durst she offer to do it, lest she should be tormented as was threatened, and always fell out when she essayed to do it either by speaking or writing, which had appeared the day before in the presence of the commissioners.

About this time Thomas Lindsay, a young boy, not yet twelve years of age, was seized, upon flagrant presumptions of witchcraft. He had said before several credible persons the devil was his father, and, if he pleased, he could fly in the likeness of a crow upon the mast of a ship. He sometimes caused a plough to stand, and the horse break the yoke upon the pronouncing of some words, and turning himself about wider-shins, that is, turning himself round from the right hand to the left, contrary to the natural course of the sun. This he would do upon the desire of any body who gave him a half-penny. Upon these and the like flagrant presumptions he was apprehended, who, at first, though he continued most obstinate in denial, yet afterwards confessed to the minister in his own house, before famous witnesses, compact with the devil, and that he had received the insensible mark from the devil, which is visible upon his body ; as also that he had been at several meetings with the devil and witches, where he said were present his brother James, with others, and particularly those who had been delated by Anderson. This he confessed, with some other wickedness of this kind, before he was committed to custody in Bargarran house.

After this Bargarran made diligent search for James Lindsay, elder brother to Thomas, having been all along accused by the afflicted damsel as one of her troublers, whom she called the gley'd or squint-eyed elf (as he was indeed) for that was the name the crew about her gave him, who, when he was brought upon the place, though he did at first most obstinately deny his guilt, yet at length, through the endeavours of Mr. Patrick Simpson, a neighbour minister, ingeniously confessed the guilt he was charged with, and in his confession did agree in every material circumstance with the other two, though he knew not what they had confessed, he having not seen them before his confession, nor had he any occasion of information in conference with others thereanent, being immediately brought to the place from the tolbooth of Glasgow, where he had been some weeks before that time in prison as a vagabond beggar, upon a design to have sent him to foreign plantations.

A more particular account of what they freely confessed and acknowledged before the commissioners, for inquiry, we have for the satisfaction of the reader subjoined to the narrative, with an abstract of the report made by the commissioners to the lords of his Majesty's most honourable privy council, concerning the whole affair.

February 11. There was by the presbytery's appointment a public fast kept upon the damsel's account in the church of Erskine, in which Mr. Turner, minister of the place, began the work with prayer, expounding Rev. xii. from verse 7 to verse 13. Mr. James Hutchison, minister at Kilellan, took the next turn of prayer, and did preach upon 1 Pet. v. 8.; and Mr. Simpson concluded the work, preaching upon Matthew xvii. 20. 21, where the girl was present all day; but before she came to church that morning, she told that, while she was in one of her fits the night before, she heard the Devil speaking of that public fast, and what 'ministers were to be there, and that old man Mr. James Hutchison should stumble, and his peruke fall off as he went up to the pulpit, and all the people should laugh at him, and he should break his neck in going home. And when she came out of the church after the forenoon's work, she said the Devil was a liar; for no such thing fell out as he had threatened. She was all day very quiet in church, although, being in some of her light fits, some spectres

appeared in time of the public work, which she told of there
after.

About six at night there were present in the chamber with
the damsel Mr. Simpson with his wife, Lady Northbar, and
others, discoursing and conferring about her case ; and while
they were conferring together she told them she would gladly
make some things known if she durst for her tormentors ;
and afterwards essaying to do it, was instantly seized with a
violent fit, in which she leapt straight up, and appeared as if
she had been choked, so it was as much as one or two could
do to hold her fast in their arms ; and when the fit was over,
Mr. Simpson going about family worship, did expound Psalm
cx., and speaking of the limited power of the adversaries of
our Lord Jesus Christ, from the latter part of verse 1., she
was on a sudden seized with another grevious fit, in which
she put out of her mouth some blood, which raised grounds
of fear and jealousy in the minds of spectators, that something in her mouth hurting her had been the occasion of it ;
yet they could not get her mouth opened, though they used
means to open the same, her teeth being close set. And in
the interval of the fit, she being asked if she found anything
in her mouth that had been the occasion of her putting out of
blood ; she replied she found nothing, nor knew the cause
thereof ; but opening her mouth, those present found one of
her double teeth newly drawn out, but knew not what became
of the tooth ; for though search was made for the same, it
could not be found. After which the minister proceeded upon
the same subject, but was again interrupted by her renewed
fits, yet closed the exercise with prayer, after which, without
more trouble, she was taken to her bed.

February 12. Margaret Lang and her daughter, Martha
Semple, being delated by the three confessants, and accused
by the girl to have been active instruments in her trouble,

came of their own accord to Bargarran's house, and, before
they came up stairs, the girl said she was now bound up, and
could not accuse Margaret Lang to her face; and accordingly the girl's mother having desired some of those who
were sitting by her to feel some parts of her body, and they
having done it, found her body so stiff and inflexible, that
there was no moving of it, and immediately again, found some
parts of her body so contracted and drawn hard together, as
if by cords. After this, Margaret Lang and her daughter, having gone to the chamber to the girl, did in presence of the
ministers and others, desire the damsel to come to her, for she
would do her no harm; and laying her arms about her, spake
very fairly to her, and questioned her if ever she had seen her
or her daughter amongst her tormentors, to which the girl did
positively reply, she had frequently seen her daughter; but
declined through fear to accuse herself, saying faintly, No.
After which Margaret and her daughter returning into the hall,
and the minister enquiring at her why she said No, seeing she
had accused her before, she answered, take me contrary, upon
which she was seized with a grievous fit; yet after her recovery, being urged again by those present, to tell her mind
freely, whether or not Margaret Lang was one of her tormentors, the child thereupon essaying to say Yes, and having half
pronounced the word, was cast into inexpressible anguishes;
and again, in the interval of the fit, she essayed to express
the same thing, and saying the word, Tint (that is lost) was on
a sudden struck with another fit; and when the fit was over,
and the child returned to the chamber, Margaret Lang, who
was sitting near the hall door, spoke these words after her,
"The Lord bless thee, and ding (that is beat or drive) the
devil out of thee." A little after which words, Margaret going
down stairs, the damsel came to the hall, and said, her bonds
were now loosed, and that now she could accuse Margaret

Lang to her face, and declared the occasion of her being so restrained and bound up while Margaret was present, was her letting fall a parcel of hair at the hall door as she came in; being a charm made by her for that end, which also had been the occasion of her uttering the word tint, in the former fit; and accordingly a parcel of hair had been found at the hall door, after Margaret Lang had gone straight from the hall to the chamber, which immediately was cast into the fire and burned. And it is remarkable that it could be attested, that there was no hair, or any other thing else in that place before Margaret Lang came in; and the girl being inquired what way she knew Margaret Lang had laid the forementioned charm upon her, replied, something speaking distinctly to her as it were above her head had suggested that to her.

About eight at night she was severely handled in her fits, much after the former manner, and while she was in her swooning fits, there was seen in her mouth a pin, wherewith she seemed almost choked, but by divine providence it was with great difficulty got out. After this she was somewhat composed, and did not much complain of pain; but was distinctly heard to entertain discourse with some invisible creature about her, and the replies given by her, and heard by those who took care of her, gave them ground to conclude she was tempted to set her hand to a paper then presented to her, with promises that upon her yielding thereunto, she should never be troubled any more; as also that she should get sweetmeats, a drink of sack, a bonny handsome coat with silver lace. She was also distinctly heard say, resisting the tempter, "Thou art a filthy sow, should I obey thee; this was not the end of my creation, but to glorify God and enjoy Him for ever; and thou promiseth what thou cannot perform. Art thou angry at me for saying thou sow? what could I call thee, but thou filthy sow? Art thou not the filthy devil; for as brave as thou art

with thy silver and gold lace, wouldst thou have me renounce
my baptism? Dost thou promise to give me brave men in
marriage, and fine clothes, and perfect health, if I should consent thereunto? Dost thou say my baptism will do me no good,
because thou allegest he was not a sufficient minister that bap-
tized me? Thou art a liar; I will be content to die, before I renounce my baptism—O through the grace of God I will never do
it." And thus she continued reasoning, being both blind and
deaf, for the space of two hours; and when she came to
herself, did declare it was the Devil who first presented
himself, tempting her in the shape of a sow, to renounce her
baptism, as is hinted; and that he did chide her when she
called him thou sow, and immediately appeared to her again
in the shape of a brave gentleman, as having gold and silver
lace on his clothes, still urging her to renounce her baptism,
which temptation she, through the special assistance of the
grace of God, effectually resisted. She also said, that it had
been suggested to her by the spirit, speaking to her, as it
were above her head, after the combat with the tempter was
over, that one of her tormentors would be at the house the
morrow.

February 13. She was seized with a sore fit about twelve
o'clock of the day, in which she continued for more than two
hours space, both deaf and blind. Those in the room with
her, crying to her with a loud voice, and pinching her hands
and other parts of her body; but all to no purpose. And in
this posture was hurried to and fro with violence through the
room; and when anybody by force offered to hinder the
dangerous and violent motion she seemed to be upon, she
would roar exceedingly; sometimes she desired her father and
mother and others to come and take her home, (supposing
herself not to be in her father's house). When the girl was in
this deplorable condition Margaret Roger, who lived in the

neighbourhood, came to the house of Bargarran, enquiring for the lady; and having come up stairs, the parents of the damsel remembering what the girl had said the night before, that one of her tormentors was to come that day to the house, brought Margaret Roger to the chamber where the girl was, and so soon as she entered the door, the damsel, though she could discern none of those who were present with her, nor answer them when they cried to her; yet presently saw her, and ran towards her crying,— "Maggy, Maggy, where hast thou been? wilt thou take me with thee, for my father and mother have left me." Where-upon spectators being astonished, caused Margaret speak to the child, which she having done, the girl distinctly heard and answered her every word. After this, the three con-fessants were also brought up to the chamber where the damsel was, and so soon as they entered the door, she ran also to them laughing as if she had been overjoyed, answering them when they spoke to her; and Margaret Roger there present, being confronted with the confessants, they did declare that she had been at meetings with the Devil and witches in Bargarran orchard, consulting and contriving Christian Shaw's ruin.

The Lord's day following, being February 14, after some short intervals she was again seized with her fits, in which she said, "Margaret Lang and her daughter Martha Semple, were tormenting her and cutting her throat," which words, through violence of pain, and difficulty of breathing, she uttered with a low and hardly audible voice; and upon the naming of Margaret Lang and her daughter she was tossed and dreadfully tormented in all the parts of her body, being made sometimes to stand upon her head and feet at once, sometimes her belly swelling like a drum and falling again in a sudden, and sometimes her head and other parts of her body were like to be shaken in pieces, so that spectators feared she would never speak more. And when the fit was over she declared Margaret Lang said to her, when in the fit, "That she would give her a tosty" (which imports hot and severe handling), for naming her.

At this time she was seldom free of her light fits, which for most part were all the respite and ease she had from the unexpressible agonies she endured in her more grievous fits, unless when asleep; and while she was in these fits nobody could persuade her to pray; yet when in a right composure of mind and perfectly at herself, she would weep bitterly to remember this, expressing her fears lest that might be any evidence God would forsake her.

February 18. About two in the afternoon she being in the light fit, said, "the Devil now appeared to her in the shape of a man;" whereupon, being struck with great fear and consternation, was desired to pray with an audible voice, "The Lord rebuke thee, Satan," which she essaying to do, instantly lost power of speech, her teeth being set, and her tongue drawn back into her throat; and she essaying again, was immediately seized with another grievous fit, in which her eyes being twisted almost round in her head, she fell down as one dead, struggling with her feet and hands, and again getting up on a sudden, was hurried with violence to and fro through the room deaf and blind; yet was speaking with some invisible creatures about her, saying, "with the Lord's strength thou shalt neither put straw nor stick into my mouth." After this she cried in a pitiful manner "the bumbee has stinged me," then presently sitting down and loosing her stockings, put her hand to that part which had been nipped or pinched, whereupon spectators did visibly discern the lively marks of nails of fingers deeply imprinted on that same part of her leg. And when she came to

P

herself, she did declare "that something speaking to her, as it were above her head," told her it was M. M. in a neighbouring parish, (naming the place) "that had appeared to her, and pinched her leg in the likeness of a bumbee." She likewise did declare that the fore-mentioned M. M. "instantly after this had been suggested to her, appeared to her in her own shape, and likeness as she used to be at other times." Shortly after this, being still seized with her light fit, she whispered in her mother's ear, "the Devil was now appearing to her again in the shape of a gentleman;" and being instantly seized with her fits, in which she was both blind and deaf, was distinctly heard arguing after this manner:—"thou thinkest to tempt me to be a witch; but through God's strength thou shalt never be the better. I charge thee, in the name of God, to be gone, and thy papers too. In the Lord's strength I will not fear thee. I will stand here and see if thou can come one step nearer me; I think thou fearest me more than I fear thee." Then turning herself again, she was hurried to and fro with violence through the room, as formerly, saying,—"She was bitten or pinched very sore in the hand with teeth, and nipped with fingers about twenty-four times;" which constrained her to horrid screeches and outcries at every time she received them, shewing and pointing with her finger to these parts of her arm and leg which had been pinched and bitten, but neither saw nor heard any about her. And accordingly spectators did visibly discern the evident marks of teeth and nails of fingers upon her arms and legs. In this posture the girl continued from two till five in the afternoon, and when her misery was over, she said, "M. M. told her in the fit, that Margaret Lang, then in custody, had ordered her to handle her after that manner; and that Margaret Lang had a commanding power over her."

Friday and Saturday thereafter, being February 19th and 20th, she was frequently seized with the forementioned fits, and being violently bitten, pinched, and nipped in her hands, neck, and other parts of her body, so that the clear marks of the nails of fingers and steads of teeth, both upper and lower, with the spittle and slaver of a mouth thereupon, was evidently seen by spectators. About this time, when seized with her blind and deaf fits, a crooked fellow appeared to her, having his feet deformed, his two heels wrying inward toward one another, and the foreparts of his feet outward from one another, so that the broadside of his feet moved foremost; and upon the appearing of this fellow her feet were put in the very same posture, during the time he tormented her. It is to be noticed that there is a fellow in one of the neighbouring parishes, whose feet are exactly in that manner deformed, who has been a long time of ill fame, and given up by the confessants to have been at meetings with the Devil and the rest of the crew in Bargarran orchard.

Saturday, being Feb. 20th, the whole family being gone to bed, they had left a great quantity of peats or turf, beside the hall chimney, which the next morning they saw them burnt to ashes, though there had been no fire in the chimney nor near them, so that the plaister and stones of the wall, where the peats or turf lay, were in a great part turned to rubbish through the violence of the fire, but no other damage followed, the hall floor being laid with stones, and the peats lying within the bosom of a large chimney brace.

Feb. 27th. The chamber fire having been covered with ashes in the chimney, when the family went to bed, the next morning, though a good quantity of ashes had been left, yet they found all clean swept away, and no appearance of ashes nor fire there at all; albeit none in the family that night nor next morning had been there after the fire was gathered, before this was observed.

In fits of this kind she continued for several days there-after, naming the forementioned crooked fellow, J. R. and M. A. living in the neighbouring parishes, which two women were delated by the three confessants to be amongst her tormentors ; and particularly upon the Lord's day, being Feb. 21st, and the Monday following, the said J. R. appearing to her, grievously vexed her, withal telling her she was commissioned so to do, the gentlewoman, M. M., having a pain in her head at the time, and so not able to come forth, concerning which, it is worthy of remark, that the damsel declared M. M. to have appeared to her about two days thereafter, with her head bound up with a napkin, or handkerchief, in which like habit or posture she did not formerly appear.

Upon Thursday thereafter, being Feb. 25th, she continued in the former fits, weeping bitterly and complaining of pain in both her sides : she also told in the interval of her fits that she was that night to be in very grievous and sore fits, her tormentors being resolved to choke her by putting pins in her mouth, which (though she emptied herself of all that were in her clothes) yet accordingly came to pass ; in which she was both blind and deaf, leaping up and down in an extraordinary manner, pulling down whatever came to her hand ; and thus continued for some days, putting out of her mouth a great quantity of small broken pins, which she declared J. R. had forced in the same.

Upon the Lord's day, being the last of Feb., about five o'clock in the afternoon, she fell into grievous fits, accom-panied with hideous or loud laughing, leaping, and running with violence to and fro, and thereafter wept sore, crying out of pain, that a little Highlandman (whom she knew to be such by his habit and speech) was now breaking her leg ; which (because of pain) she scarce could get told in the fit,

and putting her hand to the part of her leg affected, spectators untying her stocking, distinctly observed a sore bruise
in her shin bone, which, when touched, did so pain her,
that she uttered horrid screeches and cries; and when
recovered, did declare that the little Highland fellow had
given her that bruise. After this, she put out of her mouth
a crooked pin, by which she told the foresaid Highland
fellow having forced it into her mouth, designed to choke
her.

The first eight days of March she continued in her former
fits with little variation, putting out of her mouth a great
number of small pins, often fainting and falling as dead upon
the ground on a sudden, again struggling with feet and hands,
by all which, her natural spirits were much weakened and ex-
hausted; sometimes also she essayed to go into the fire.
About this time, when ministers and other Christians met in
the family for prayer, she used at the beginning of the work
to make great disturbance, particularly March 2d, which day,
being set apart for fasting and prayer in the family, prayer
begun, she was for some time very composed, until of a
sudden, a strong blast of wind forced open the windows of
the room, upon which she was instantly seized with a violent
fit, the minister in the very same time supplicating God that
she might be delivered from Satan's bonds; in which fit she being both blind and deaf as to all, except her tormentors, was
hurried with violence to and fro in the room, sometimes falling down as one dead, sometimes singing and making a hideous loud noise; sometimes naming M. M. and others, who,
she said, were there present, afflicting and tormenting her
withal, naming the particular places of the room where she saw
them standing and sitting. After all which, when recovered
out of the fit, she told that a gentlewoman and a little Highland fellow came in with the blast of wind which forced open

the windows. This falling out upon the Tuesday, she continued in the light fit without any intermission till the Sabbath thereafter, not being seized with any of her sore fits; and having gone to church the Lord's day following, was perfectly well for the most part of the day; yet affirmed she saw Janet Waugh and others, in one of the windows of the church, though invisible to all others.

Tuesday, being March 9th, her mother and Margaret Campbell, her cousin, took the damsel to walk with them in the orchard; and returning back to the house, her mother entering the tower gate first, the damsel being at her back and Margaret Campbell tarrying a little while at the gate, her mother going into the kitchen supposed they had been with her, whereas the damsel was of a sudden carried away in a flight up stairs with so swift and unaccountable a motion that her absence was not in the least suspected. Her mother turning and missing her, cried, whither is Christian and Margaret Campbell? and instantly running up stairs to look for the damsel heard a noise, and, following the same, found the damsel leaping and dancing upon one of the stairs, being seized with fits, out of which, when she had recovered, she told that J. P. had carried her away from her mother's back as she entered the kitchen door (her not touching the ground to her apprehension), and that with a design to strangle her in an high wardrobe with ropes, on which the linen used to dry, but that the said J. P. could carry her no further than the place where she was found, and did therefore leave her in such a violent fit.

Upon the Lord's day thereafter, being March 14th, her fits again altered, in that her mouth and nose were prodigiously distorted and turning about while in the fit, her face being thereby strangely and horribly deformed. The same day she being in church in the forenoon, her glove falling from her, the same was again put into her hand by some invisible agent, to the amazement of beholders. To which we add here, as that which is worthy of remark, that all this while an invisible being haunted her on all occasions, suggesting many things to her both concerning herself and others, but yet never heard by any but herself.

The same day betwixt sermons, she told that she was to be violently tormented in the afternoon, which accordingly came to pass; and when in her fits she named one J. K., a woman living in the neighbouring bounds, of whom she said, that she had seen her in the church, as also that she was master of these kind of fits she was afflicted with; withal asserting that if the said J. K. were not sent for, she would grow worse and worse, which her parents finding to be true, sent in the evening for the said J. K., threatening her, if the damsel was any further troubled with her, that she should be apprehended as others had been; after which, the damsel being in the meantime in a very sore fit, the forementioned J. K. prayed (though not desired) that God might send the damsel her health, whereupon the damsel was no more troubled with these kind of fits, but did instantly recover, by falling into a swoon as she used to do before recovery out of any of her fits.

Tuesday, being March 16th, she was again seized with her other kind of fits, all the parts of her body being stiff and rigid; and sometimes in them was heard conversing with the gentlewoman (as she called her), vindicating herself of what the gentlewoman alleged against her, viz., that she had accused some innocent persons as her tormentors. To which the damsel distinctly replied that she was a liar, saying, it was you yourself and none other ever mentioned any such thing.

Thus she continued until the Friday thereafter, being never free of the light fits, now and then also falling into swoons, and appeared to be almost choked by the means of some

charms and enchantments invisibly conveyed into her mouth;
which, to the apprehension of spectators, were as if it had
been pieces of chesnuts, orange pills, whites of eggs, or such
like, all which were distinctly observed, when occasionally in
the fit she opened her mouth; and when spectators essayed
to get them out, she kept her mouth and teeth so close, that
no strength could open the same. When recovered out of the
fit, she told L. M., a woman living in the neighbouring bounds,
had put them in her mouth.

Upon Friday, being March 19th, she was violently tormented with sore fits, in which her neck was distorted and bended
back like a bow towards her heels, struggling with feet and
hands, sometimes stiff, blind, and deaf, putting out of her
mouth a great number of small pins, which she said the forementioned L. M. had put into her mouth. And about six
o'clock that same night, being violently tormented, fell a-cry-
ing, that if the gentlewoman was not apprehended that night,
it would be in vain to apprehend her to-morrow: for, said she,
I have much to suffer at her hands betwixt twelve and one
o'clock in the morning. After this the damsel lifting up her
eyelids with her hands, and looking upwards, said, what art
thou that tells me that the sheriff and my father are coming
here this night? After which the sheriff, her father, and
James Guthrie, macer to the justiciary court, instantly came
up stairs, to the amazement of those who remembered what
the damsel just now had said. The damsel continuing all
this while blind and deaf; yet was heard (the foresaid persons
being present) distinctly to discourse with some invisible being
near to her, saying, is the sheriff come,—is he near me? and
stretching out her hand to feel if any were about her, the
sheriff put his hand in hers, notwithstanding of which, she
said to the invisible being discoursing with her, "I cannot
feel the sheriff; how can he be present here? or how can I

have him by the hand as thou sayest, seeing I feel it not? Thou sayest he hath brown coloured clothes, red plush breeches with black stripes, flowered muslin cravat, and an embroidered sword-belt. Thou sayest there is an old grey haired man with him, having a ring upon his hand; but I can neither see nor feel any of them. What, are they come to apprehend the gentlewoman? is that their errand indeed?" And the girl being enquired how she came to the knowledge of these strange things, replied as formerly in the like case, something speaking distinctly as above her head suggested them to her. It is very observable here, that the foresaid persons had that same afternoon got an order from the commissioners of justiciary to apprehend the same gentlewoman, and were so far on their way to put it in execution against the next morning; but being witnesses to the damsel's trouble, and hearing what she had told, viz., that a delay in that matter would prove to her exceeding dangerous, they went straight on in their journey that same night to the gentlewoman's habitation, and put their warrant to execution.

As the damsel still continued to be violently tormented, sometimes lying with her neck and other parts of her body upon the ground, as if they had been disjointed; sometimes, also, essaying to throw herself into the fire. About ten o'clock the same night, she continuing in the fit, her father (who had not gone with the sheriff) beginning to read a part of the Word of God, she repeated the words after him, though blind and deaf in the meantime, which made spectators apprehend that the damsel had the sense of hearing in these sort of fits, at least when the Word of God was read; to find out the truth of which, her father did cease from reading, which, though he did, yet the damsel continued to repeat the following verses of the chapter, while none in the room were reading, and she herself had no book; withal being

Q

heard say to some invisible being about her,—"Wilt thou teach me a part of the Old Testament as well as the New."

The damsel still continuing in the forementioned fits, said unto the persons present, that "now it was twelve of the clock; oh! it is now past twelve," sometimes lying as one dead, through the violence of pain and decay of her natural spirits, sometimes again recovering, essayed to express somewhat, but could not; withal putting out of her mouth a great quantity of crooked pins, and the parts of her body being prodigiously distorted, she complained of great pain. Thus she continued until half-an-hour after twelve o'clock at night; when on a sudden she recovered, to the admiration of beholders, telling them she might now go to bed, being told by some invisible informer that the sheriff and the other gentleman, to wit, the macer, had now entered the gentlewoman's house, and accordingly going to bed, was no further troubled that night. It is worthy of remark here, that the sheriff and macer, at their return, did declare that it was just about that time they entered the gentlewoman's house, which the damsel condescended upon.

Saturday, being March 20th, about ten o'clock in the forenoon, she was of a sudden seized with fits, falling down as one dead, her eyes quite closed, sometimes again opening and turning in her head, she saw nor heard none about her, but was hurried with violence to and fro through the room, crying with a loud voice when any by force would hinder her motion. She being in this posture, and deprived thus of her senses, James Lindsay, one of the three confessants, was brought into the room, who no sooner had entered the door, but was perceived by her, and she, smiling, ran towards him, saying,—"Jamie, where hast thou been this long time—how is it with thee?" and answered him distinctly to every word he spake, though at the same time she neither

heard nor saw any other in the room, nor could converse
with them, albeit, tried by several experiments for that
purpose, particularly a tobacco box being held before her
eyes by a person present in the room, she did not see it; but
as soon as it was put in the hand of James Lindsay, she
inquired at him where he had got that box? She, continuing in this posture, the sheriff and her father being
present, thought it fit to confront M. M., who was now come,
thereby to try if the damsel would hear or see her, as she
had done James Lindsay, which accordingly they did. And
as soon as M. M. entered the door, the damsel (though still
in the fit) presently smiled and said,—"I see the gentlewoman now," though formerly she had never seen her
personally, but only her spectre in the fits. She likewise
heard her, when she spoke to her, answering distinctly some
questions proposed by M. M., such as, when it was she
had seen her tormenting her? to which she answered, she
had seen her the other night in her fits, and further chal-
lenged her, why she had restrained her from making known
the Highland wife's name, as also saying unto her, thou
pretends thou knowest not what I say—thou knowest well
enough. Upon all which, the gentlewoman on a sudden
(without being desired) prayed that the Lord might send
the damsel her health, saying,—"Lord help thee, poor
daft child, and rebuke the Devil." Which words were no
sooner uttered than the damsel fell down as dead, and being
in this posture carried to another room, instantly recovered
of the blind, deaf, and also of the light fit, becoming
perfectly well, and continued so for some time; and being
thus recovered, and M. M. removed into another room, the
damsel was enquired at, whom she had seen in the last fit?
to which she replied, she had seen the gentlewoman, though

in the meantime she was ignorant of the gentlewoman's ever being personally present in the room with her.

The same day the commissioners of justiciary having come to Bargarran, M. M. and the damsel were again confronted, upon which the damsel (being in the light fit), upon the first look of the forementioned M. M. was suddenly seized with sore fits, out of which, when she recovered, she accused her as being one of her most violent tormentors, particularly mentioning such and such times, in which she had in an extraordinary manner afflicted her, as also what words she spoke in her hearing while in the fit; and which is yet more remarkable, did question the gentlewoman if she did not sometime in December last, when she was tormenting her, remember how she went away from her in great haste, saying she could stay no longer, being obliged to attend a child's burial at home. In confirmation of which, we are very credibly informed, that W. R., a near neighbour of her's, had a child buried that same day, and that the gentlewoman came not in due time to attend the corpse to the burial place but the corpse being near to the churchyard ere she reached the house from whence they came, she returned again to her own lodging, and so did not accompany the burial at all.

The Lord's day following, being March 21st, she fell into swooning fits, complaining of no pain, except near to her heart, falling down as dead, not only when the fits seized her, but also when she recovered, sometimes singing after an unusual manner, withal informing spectators that J. G. constrained her to that kind of music, her own lips not at all moving in the meantime, which beholders saw to be true, only her tongue, for preventing of which she frequently put her hand into her mouth. And at this time, when either she herself, or those about her, offered to read any part of the Scripture, she was violently tormented, declaring if she did but so much as hear the word of God read that day, she would certainly be extremely tortured; in confirmation of which, when some essayed to read Heb. xi. 2, 4, 6, Isa. xl., Psal. iii. she uttered horrid screeches and outcries, complaining that she was pinched, in evidence of which, the prints or marks of the nails of fingers were distinctly seen on her arms; and being thus pinched or bitten for several times with great violence and pain, the skin itself was seen to be torn from off those parts of her arms and fingers, where the prints of the teeth and nails were observed; so that, from the deepness of the wounds, the foresaid parts affected fell a-bleeding, which blood was both seen and handled by spectators. Moreover, the damsel, while in this sad and lamentable condition, seemed to be extremely affected and oppressed with sore sickness, as one in a fever, crying sometimes to remove these dead children out of her sight; which she frequently repeated from six to nine in the morning, and she still continuing the rest of the day, it was observed that some charms and enchantments were put in her mouth as formerly, of which the damsel being very sensible, fell down on a sudden on the ground, putting her hand to some spittle which she had put out of her mouth, and lifted some trash which she again cast down to the ground, it making some noise, but yet neither seen in her spittle nor elsewhere by spectators, though while in her mouth, they observed something like orange pills, whites of eggs, and pieces of chesnuts.

Monday, being March 22d, the forementioned L. M. or J. G. came to Bargarran's house, and being confronted with the damsel, questioned her if ever she had seen her in any of her fits, withal alleging that she, viz., L. M. or J. G., could be none of her tormentors, because the damsel was not now seized with a fit, though looking upon her as she used to be, when she looked upon any of her other tormentors when confronted

with them ; upon which, the damsel being for some time si-
lent, L. M. or J. G. did again propose the same question to
her, to which the damsel distinctly replied—Yes ; upon which
L. M. replied, "perhaps you have seen the Devil in my
shape."

As to the conference, there are several things exceeding remarkable ; as first, that the damsel, upon her answering yes,
was immediately seized with a fit ; secondly, that however, after Katherine Campbell had touched the damsel in
presence of the Commissioners, upon the 5th of Feb. last,
she had ever since that time freedom to touch any of her
tormentors without being seized with her fits, as has been
hinted ; yet true it is, that in the room of that charm a
new one took place, viz., when any time she looked upon her
tormentors in the face, at the very first look she was seized
with her fits ; which charm she declared was laid by means of
the forementioned L. M. or J. G., and also taken off again by
her that very morning before she came to visit the damsel ;
and this, she said, was suggested to her by some invisible
being, speaking distinctly as it were above her head, and that
therefore the damsel now had freedom to look L. M. in the
face without being seized with fits, which for a considerable
time before she could not do when confronted with any of her
tormentors ; thirdly, it is yet more observable that in the same
morning, before ever L. M. came to visit the damsel, it was
told by the damsel to several persons in the family that L. M.
had taken off that charm of her being seized with fits when
looking any of her tormentors in the face ; but, withal, that
she had laid on another in its room, viz., that as soon as the
damsel should by words confer with any of her tormentors, so
soon should she be seized with a fit, which accordingly was
verified when she spoke to L. M. or J. G.

Tuesday, being March 23d, the damsel being asleep in the

bed with her mother, about three o'clock in the morning, was on a sudden awakened (having for some time struggled in her sleep) in great fear and consternation, and being seized with her blind and deaf fits, took fast hold of her mother, declaring to her father and her, that the Devil was standing near to the bed assaulting her, upon which she cried suddenly: "God Almighty keep me from thy meetings. I will die rather than go to them. I will never, through the grace of God, renounce my baptism; for I will certainly go to hell if I do it. Thou says I will go to hell, however, because I am a great sinner; but I believe what the word of God saith,—though I have many sins, yet the blood of Christ cleanseth from all sin; and I will not add that great wickedness to my other sins, which thou art tempting me to do. It is no wonder thou lie to me, seeing thou wast bold to lie in God's face. I know thou art a liar from the beginning; and the red coat thou promises me, I know thou canst not perform it. And although I should never recover, I am resolved never to renounce my baptism. It is God that hath kept me all this time from being a witch, and I trust he will yet by his grace keep me, not because of any thing in me, but of his own mercy; and that he who hath kept me hitherto from being devoured by thee I hope will yet keep me." This conference continued near the space of an hour, her father, mother, and others being ear witnesses to the same. And after recovery the damsel declared that it was the Devil, who (in the shape of a naked man with a shirt, having much hair upon his hands, and his face like swine's bristles), had appeared to her tempting her as aforesaid.

Until Sabbath following she continued in the light fit, but withal every morning and evening was still seized with her sore fits, continuing still to name M. M. (who was at this time set at liberty), the forementioned L. M., E. T., an Highland wife, and others as being her tormentors. It is more than remarkable here, that M. M. being set at liberty upon bail, the very day after she went home, she appeared again to the damsel tormenting her in her fits, and continued so to do several days thereafter, particularly upon the Saturday, being March 27, after she was set at liberty; the which day, the damsel was heard name her in the fits, and say to her: "Wilt thou say, God help me, poor mad or foolish child, as thou said the other day before the judges: art thou wishing the devil to take me; where is the habit thou was clothed in the other day?"

On Sabbath morning, being March 28th, the damsel through God's great mercy towards her, was perfectly recovered, both of all her sore and light fits; becoming as well, sensible, and composed as ever.

End of the Narrative of Christian Shaw.

The Editors of the first Edition of the Narrative, which was printed in 1698, have subjoined the following information, &c., to the Narrative :—

If it shall be questioned how the truth of all these strange things is attested? there is none of those particulars mentioned in the Narrative, but had, in the first draught, the witnesses inserted at the end of every particular paragraph, and attested before the commissioners for enquiry at Renfrew, by the subscriptions of the respective witnesses. But seeing the placing of them so now would have occasioned the repetition of several persons names over and over again, and would have made this Narrative swell too much in bulk, therefore we judged it fittest now to set down the names altogether at the end of the Narrative ; and the rather that, seeing these things fell not out in a private corner, but thousands in this country have been eye and ear witnesses thereof, to their admiration and raising of their sympathy, and been fully convinced beyond all debate of a diabolical influence upon the affliction of the damsel ; we shall now make mention of a few, viz., beside the father, mother, grandmother, and nearest relations of the damsel, and servants of the family, who were always present with her in her fits, such of the commissioners for enquiry and of justiciary as had occasion to be on the place of the events, particularly the Lord Blantyre, Mr. Francis Montgomery of Giffen, Sir John Maxwell of Pollok, Sir John Houstoun of that ilk, the Laird of Blackhall younger, the Laird of Glanderstone, the Laird of Craigends, Porterfield of Fulwood, John Alexander of Blackhouse, Mr. Robert Semple, sheriff-depute of Renfrew, and several other honourable persons of good sense and prying wits, such as the noble Earl of Marshall, the Laird of Orbistone, the Laird of Kilmarnock, the Laird of Meldrum, the Laird of Bishopton, elder and younger, Gavin Cochrane of Craigmure, William

Denniston of Colgrain, Dr. Matthew Brisbane, &c., and many ministers, who kept days of humiliation and prayer weekly to the family, and sometimes in the parish church with the congregation, viz., Mr. James Hutchison, minister of the gospel at Kilellan, Mr. Patrick Simpson at Renfrew, Mr. James Stirling at Kilbarchan, Mr. Thomas Blackwell * at Paisley, Mr. James Brisbane at Kilmacolm, Mr. Robert Taylor at Houston, and of neighbouring presbyteries, Mr. Neil Gillies, Mr. James Brown, Mr. John Gray, minister of the Gospel at Glasgow, while the damsel was there; Mr. John Ritchie, minister at Old Kilpatrick; Mr. Alexander King, at Bonhill; Mr. Archibald Wallace, at Cardross; Mr. John Anderson, at Drymmon; Mr. Andrew Turner, minister of the place, who was frequently there; besides Mr. Menzies of Cammo, and Mr. Grant of Cullen, advocates, who were eye and ear witnesses to several important passages of the damsel's affliction, and the convincing evidences of its flowing from the operation of the Devil and his instruments. The truth whereof is further adminiculat by the progress and issue of the trial, at which were present at several occasions not only Sir John Shaw of Greenock, Commissar Smollet, at Bonhill, Mr. John Stewart, advocate, who were concerned in the commission, with these others beforementioned; but also great confluence of several nobility and gentry out of the country, such as the Earl of Glencairn, the Lord Kilmaurs, the Lord Semple, &c.

And now we are sure that after all the pregnant evidences of the truth of this relation, as to matter of fact, they must be persons very hard of belief that can allow themselves to deny credit thereunto; and must need conclude that there is

---

* Author of the *Schema Sacrum* and *Ratio Sacra*, and afterwards Professor of Divinity in the University of Aberdeen.

nothing credible in the world that ever hath been delivered to mankind or posterity, and that they resolve to believe nothing though never so fully attested which they do not see with their own eyes, and perhaps there are some hardened in their prejudicate conceits that will not believe even these so far as they may have influence to convince them of their errors; but wisdom is, and will be justified of all her children. Among all ingenuous persons, we are hopeful this Narrative, (which plainly relates things as they fell out without any kind of disguise), will obtain such entertainment as it is truly designed for, viz. :—That we be hereby more and more confirmed in the faith of the being of God and invisible spirits, and admire and adore the wonderful works of God in the depths of His judgments, and that there is really a hellish hierarchy and combination of infernal spirits, enemies to God, and working all the mischief they can to men; whereby also, there is an evident testimony given to the truth of what is related in the Scriptures concerning the same, and withal, to lament, that through the just displeasure of our holy and righteous God, those devils get leave to break forth with so much rage and fury, and gets so many among professed christians into a hellish confederacy with themselves, to be the instruments of their malice, and the actors of so many tragedies in the christian world; to stir us up also to bless and magnify our God, that those devils and their instruments are chained and limited, that they cannot work all the evil they would, and as long as they will; and therefore to join in thanksgiving to God for His deliverance to that afflicted family and damsel. Finally, as we are to submit to such afflictions as the Lord may think fit to measure out unto us, by whatsoever instruments, as in the case of Job; so we are called to watch and pray that we enter not into temptation, while we have such adversaries going about still seeking to devour us; and to rejoice that we have a strong protector,—

the blessed Captain of our salvation, the Lord Jesus Christ,—
who hath obtained the victory over all the devils in hell, and
hath promised all His saints a share in His victory, which
they begin to have in time. 1 Epistle John, iv. 4,—" And He
hath given us hope, even through grace of a speedy and
certain accomplishment thereof." Luke xxi. 22,—" Let us
lift up our heads, because our redemption draweth nigh."

APPENDIX, No. A.

THE subscribed attestations of Dr. Matthew Brisbane, physician, and Mr. Henry Marshall, apothecary in Glasgow, did influence the belief of an extraordinary cause of these events.

The doctor, on the 31st December 1696, tells, that at first sight, when he was brought to the girl she appeared so brisk in motion, so florid in colour, so cheerful, and, in a word, every way healthful, that he could hardly be persuaded she had need of a physician; but within ten minutes he found himself obliged to alter his thoughts, for she rose from her seat, and advertised she was instantly to be seized with a fit, according whereunto he observed a considerable distention in her left hypochondre, which in a trace falling, she was forthwith taken with horrid convulsive motions and heavy groans at first; which afterwards as soon as she was able to frame words, turned into expostulatory mourning against some women, particularly Campbell and Naesmith. Yet he thought these symptoms were reducible to the freaks of hypochondriac melancholy, and therefore put her in such a course proper against that kind of malady. Upon which, being freed for some time, he was alarmed that the child was returned to town worse than ever for having his assistance. He then was frequently with her, and observed her narrowly, so that he was confident she had no visible correspondent to subminister hair, straw, coal cinders, hay, and such like trash unto her; all which upon several occasions he saw her put out of her mouth without being wet; nay, rather as they had been dried with artifice, and actually hot above the natural warmth of the body, sometimes after severe fits, and other times without trouble when discoursing with him. When she had only light convulsive motions, but to a high degree, such rigidity of the whole body, as we call τεταιο, she did not fancy, as at other times, she saw these persons already named about her; but the upcasting of the trash above-mentioned did no sooner cease, than in all her fits, when she was able to speak any, she always cried out they were pricking or pinching her. He saw her also when free of fits, suddenly seized with dumbness, &c. And this he solemnly declares himself to have seen and handled; and were it not for the hay, straw, &c., he should not despair to reduce the other symptoms to their proper classes, in the catalogue of human diseases.

Mr. Marshall, the apothecary, concurs with the doctor, and gives some particular instances of his own observation; and among the rest, that the girl having fallen headlong upon the ground, as she had been thrown down with violence, fell a reasoning very distinctly, thus:—"Katie, what ails thee at me; I am sure I never did thee wrong; come let us gree; let there be no more difference betwixt us; let us shake hands together;" (putting forth her hand said,) "well, Katie, I cannot help it, ye will not gree with me." And immediately she cried, fell into a swoon, and out of that into a rage, wherein she continued without intermission for about half an hour; and perfectly recovered. Then she told him that she saw Katie Campbell, Nancy Naesmith, &c., and many more. Campwas going to thrust a sword into her side, which made her so desirous to be agreed with her; and when the girl told him this, she instantly fell into another fit as formerly, in which she continued another half hour, &c. Dated 1st Jan., 1697.

"The lamentable case of the afflicted damsel and family, had been represented to his Majesty's most honourable Privy Council," * and on the 19th of Jan., 1697, a warrant of Privy Council was issued, † which set forth that there were

---

pregnant grounds of suspicion of Witchcraft in the Shire of Renfrew, especially from the afflicted and extraordinary condition of Christian Shaw, daughter of John Shaw, of Bargarran. It therefore granted permission to Alexander, Lord Blantyre, Sir John Maxwell of Pollok, Sir John Shaw of Greenock, William Cunnyngham of Craigens, Alexander Porterfield of Duchall, ———— Caldwall of Glanderstoun, Gavin Cochrane of Thornly-muir, Alexander Porterfield of Fulwood, and Robert Semple, sheriff-depute of Renfrew, or any five of them, to interrogate and imprison persons suspected of Witchcraft, to examine witnesses, &c., but not upon oath, and to transmit their report before the 10th of March, 1697. The Act of Privy Council is subscribed thus :—" Polwarth, *Cancellar*, Argyle, Leven, Forfar, Raith, Belhaven, Ja. Stewart, J. Hope, W. Anstruther, J. Maxwell, Ro. Sinclair."

———————

An Abbreviate of the Precognition and Report made by the Commissioners appointed by his Majesty's Privy Council for enquiry : and the confessions of Elizabeth Anderson, James and Thomas Lindsay, transmitted by these Commissioners, and presented to the Privy Council on the 9th of March, 1697.

The Commissioners for enquiry, having met at Bargarran in February, 1697, did choose the Lord Blantyre, Preses., and took the confession of Elizabeth Anderson, aged about seventeen years, as follows :—Declares " that about seven years ago she staid with Jean Fulton, her grandmother, and playing about the door she saw a black grim man go into her grandmother's house ; after which, her grandmother came to the door, called her in, and desired her to take the gentleman (as she named him) by the hand, and which she did, but finding it very cold, became afraid, and immediately he vanished.

About a month thereafter, her grandmother and she being in the house together, the said gentleman (whom she then suspected to be the Devil) appeared to them, and fell a talking with her grandmother, by rounding in one anothers ears; upon which the grandmother desired her to take him by the hand, being a friend of hers; but Elizabeth refusing, the grandmother threatened that she would get none of the clothes promised to her unless she should obey; yet Elizabeth withstood, saying, "the Lord be between me and him," whereupon he went away in a flight, but she knew not how. Elizabeth was not troubled for a long time thereafter, till her father desiring her to go with him a begging through the country, and she saying that she needed not to seek her meat, seeing she might have work; her father pressed her to go alongst, and took her to a moor in Kilmalcolm, where were gathered together, at that and other subsequent meetings, Katherine Campbell, Margaret Fulton (her grandaunt), Margaret Lang, John Reid, smith, Margaret and Janet Rodgers, the three Lindsays (besides the two confessant ones), &c., and several whom she did not know, and the foresaid gentleman with them. He came to Elizabeth, bidding her to renounce her baptism, promising that if she would consent thereunto, she should get better meat and clothes, and not need to beg. But (as she declared) she would not consent. Then he enquired what brought her hither; she answered, that she came with her father; whereupon the devil and her father went and talked together apart, but she knew not where about. Declares, that in that meeting was concerted the tormenting of Mr. William Fleming, minister at Innerkip, his child. Elizabeth confesses she was at another meeting with that crew above the town of Kilpatrick, with the foresaid gentleman, whom they called their lord; and that she went with her father to the ferry boat of Erskine, where the Devil, with the rest of the band, overturned the boat, and drowned the Laird of Brighouse, and the ferrier of Erskine, with several special circumstances thereanent; particularly that some of the crew would have saved the ferrier, but one of them, viz., his mother-in-law, gainstood it, in regard he had expelled her out of his house a little while before the meeting. Acknowledges she was present with them at the destroying of William Montgomerie's child, by strangling it with a sea napkin; where they, having entered the house, lighted a candle, which was somewhat bluish, and Agnes Naesmith saying, "what if the people awake?" Margaret Fulton replied, "ye need not fear;" as also declares, that about five weeks before the date, her father brought her on foot to Bargarran orchard, into which they entered by a slap in the dyke, and where were present the persons before-named, &c., and the Devil, who told that nobody would see them, at which they laughed. At this meeting they, with their lord, contrived the destruction of Christian Shaw; some being for stabbing her with a touck, others for hanging her with a cord, a third sort for choking her, and some intended to have her out of the house to destroy her; but fearing they might be taken before the next meeting to that effect, their lord (as they called him), gave them a piece of an unchristened child's liver to eat (but the declarant and the other two confessants slipped the eating of it), telling them that though they were apprehended they should never confess, which would prevent an effectual discovery; and further, several of them being afraid that the declarant would confess, and tell of them as she had done formerly on her grandmother, they threatened to tear her all in pieces if she did so; and particularly, Margaret Lang threatened her most. After two hours or thereby, they disappeared in a flight, except the declarant, who went home on her foot. Confesses likewise, that one night her father raised her out of her bed, and they having gone to the water side, took her on his back, and carried her over the river in a flight; from whence they went on foot to Dumbarton, and in Mr. John Hardy, minister, his yard, the crew and their lord being met, they formed the picture of Mr. Hardy, and dabbed it full of pins, and having put it amongst water and ale mixed, roasted it on a spit at a fire, &c. After which her father and herself returned in the same manner as they went. Declares the particular persons that were employed, and most industrious in the several facts before mentioned, &c."

James Lindsay, aged 14 years, declares, "That one day he met with the deceased Jean Fulton, his grandmother, at her own house, where she took from him a little round cape and a plack; but being grieved, he required them from her again, and she refusing, he called her an old witch and ran away, upon which she followed him and cried that she should meet him with an ill turn. About three days thereafter, he being a begging in the country, he met his grandmother with a black grim man, &c., whom she desired him to take by the hand, which James did, but found it exceeding cold, and was straitly griped; whereupon the said gentleman (as she termed him) asked the declarant if he would serve him, and obey him, and he should have a coat, hat, and several other things, to which James answered, "yes, I'll do it." And after this the foresaid gentleman (whom the declarant knew thereafter to be the Devil), and his grandmother went away, but knows not how. Acknowledges he was frequently thereafter at meetings with the Devil and witches, particularly these mentioned in Elizabeth Anderson's confession: that their lord came to James at the first public meeting, took him by the hand, and forbade him to tell: that they contrived beforehand at the said meeting, the drowning of Brighouse, and concurs with Elizabeth Anderson anent the design of saving the ferrier, which his mother-in-law did divert. He being interrogate, declared he did not see J. K. and J. W. at committing of the foresaid fact, (and indeed they were then in prison): that they with a cord strangled Matthew Park's child: and that the person who waited on the child, finding it stiffled cried out, 'Matthew! Matthew! the bairn is dead.' Elizabeth Anderson concurs in this particular, and tells, that when they had done, they took the cord with them. Declares, that he was present at strangling William Montgomerie's child with a sea napkin, and heard Agnes Naesmith say, 'draw the loup,' &c. That about five weeks since, he was carried to them in Bargarran's orchard, and concurs with Elizabeth Anderson in what was treated there, anent destroying Christian Shaw, and the charm against confessing. Likewise the meeting in Dumbarton, anent Mr. Hardy, is acknowledged by him; and that he has several times appeared to Christian Shaw, both in Glasgow and Bargarran, with the others that did torment her, and put in her mouth coal cinders, bones, hay, hair, sticks, &c., intending thereby to choke her: that he and they did oftentimes prick and stab her in this manner, viz., he had a needle which, if he put in his clothes, her body would be pricked and stabbed in that place where he fixed the needle, and if he put in his hair, that part of her head would be tormented: that he saw her put out the pins they had put in, at which time he cried these words, 'Help, J. D.' who was also then present: that when the ministers began to pray in Bargarran's house at several occasions, the Devil and they immediately went away," &c.

Thomas Lindsay, being below pupilarity, declares, "The same Jean Fulton, his grandmother, awaked him one night out of his bed, and caused him take a black grim gentleman (as he called him) by the hand; which he felt to be cold;

and who having enquired if Thomas would serve him and be his man, and he would give him a red coat, the declarant consented; and the gentleman (whom he knew thereafter to be the Devil) gave him a nip in the neck, which continued sore for ten days. Thereafter, one day after his grandmother's decease, coming by her house, he thought she appeared to him clapping his head, and desiring him to be a good servant to the gentleman to whom she had gifted him, and forbidding him to reveal it. Declares, that one night lying in bed in the house of one Robert Shaw, he was awakened out of his sleep and carried in a flight to Matthew Park's house, where were present the particular persons named by him, and concurs to the manner of strangling of the child with James Lindsay his brother; and that another night, being in the house of Walter Alexander, he was brought to the strangling of William Montgomerie's child, and agrees likewise in the manner of it with his brother, only, he says the sea napkin with which they committed the fact was speckled. He likewise concurs as to the meeting in Bargarran's orchard about five weeks ago, and what was acted therein : as also anent Mr. Hardy; with this addition, that himself turned the spit whereon the picture was roasted," &c.

It is to be noticed that the three confessants were separately apprehended upon several occasions, so they (after the obstinacy to discover was abated) did emit these confessions in several distinct places, without communication with, or knowledge of, another's confession in manner mentioned in the preceding narrative. The commissioners did examine them upon other trying questions that were new, thereby to make experiment of their consonancy or disagreement, but still found them strangely to accord. The facts did fall out in the manner declared by them, particularly the strangling of the children, death of the minister, drowning of those in the boat, and torture of Bargarran's daughter mentioned in the confessions before expressed. Further, the commissioners did confront them both with Christian Shaw, the afflicted girl, and the persons declared (whom they caused apprehend), and both the girl and confessants did accuse these to their faces, and bind them in circumstances with great steadiness and congruity, though separately brought in. The commissioners did also try some experiments anent the girl, her falling in fits on approach of the accused, as is expressed in the Narrative, and examined her with those who staid commonly about her upon the particulars of her sufferings. They tried to cause her write (since she could not say out), the name of a person whom she first called Margaret or pinched Maggie, and asserted to be one of her chief bourriers, yet upon writing Margaret, and the letter L of her surname, the girl was presently taken with a fearful convulsion, the pen being struck out of her hand, and herself falling as dead, with groans heavier and sorer than ordinary. After some recovery, whereof some ministers pointed to her a passage of the Bible, but upon essaying to cast her eyes on it, she fell into vehement pangs, till one of the commissioners desired the book might be closed, and that being done, she immediately came to herself, &c. Lastly, the commissioners called before them those persons who had signed the passages of the several days in the written journal of the girl's sufferings; and having examined them thereupon, transmitted the same, with the declarations of the three confessants and several of the passages that occur in the precognition, to His Majesty's Privy Council, by whom they were appointed for that effect.

The Commissioners represented that there were twenty-four persons, male and female, suspected and accused of

Witchcraft, and that further enquiry ought to be made into this crime.*

Agreeable to this report, a new warrant was issued by the Privy Council on the 5th April, 1697, † to most of the Commissioners formerly named, with the addition of Lord Hallcraig, Mr. Francis Montgomery, of Giffen ; Sir John Houston of that Ilk ; Mr. John Kincaid of Corsbasket, advocate ; and Mr. John Stewart, younger, of Blackhall, advocate, or any five of them to meet at Renfrew, Paisley, or Glasgow, to take trial of, judge, and do justice upon the foresaid persons; and to sentence the guilty to be burned, or otherwise executed to death, as the commissioners should incline. It further ordained the commissioners to transmit to the Court of Justiciary an authentic extract of their proceedings, to be entered upon its records ; and contained a recommendation to the Lords of the Treasury to defray the expenses of the trial. The Act of Privy Council is subscribed thus : " Polwarth, Cancellar, Douglas, Lauderdale, Annandale, Yester, Kintore, Carmichael, W. Anstruther, Archd. Mure."

Hugo Arnot, Esq., author of a collection of celebrated Criminal Trials in Scotland, from which I have taken the copy of the warrants, dated 19th Jan., 1697, and 5th April, 1697, says, " The commissioners, thus empowered, were not remiss in acting under the authority delegated to them. After twenty hours were spent in the examination of witnesses, who gave testimony that the malefices libelled could not have proceeded from natural causes, and that the prisoners were the authors of these malefices—after five of the unhappy prisoners confessed their own guilt, and criminated their alleged associates —after counsel had been heard on both sides, and the counsel

* Vide Records of Privy Council, 9th March, 1697.
† Vide Records of Privy Council, 5th April, 1697.

for the prosecution had declared that ' he would not press the jury with the ordinary severity of threatening an assize of error,'* but recommended to them to proceed according to the evidence; and loudly declared to them, that although they ought to beware of condemning the innocent, yet if they should acquit the prisoners, in opposition to legal evidence, 'they would be accessory to all the blasphemies, apostacies, murders, tortures, and seductions, whereof these enemies of heaven and earth should hereafter be guilty.' After the jury had spent six hours in deliberation, seven of those miserable persons were condemned to the flames."

Mr. Arnot further says, "The order of Privy Council for recording the commissioners' proceedings in the books of justiciary was not complied with. I am therefore unable to give any further particulars of the catastrophe of these miserable persons, or of the criminal absurdity of those who committed them to the flames."

Mr. Arnot further says, "These instances afford a sufficient specimen of the mode of prosecution against the multitude of miserable persons who were sacrificed at the altar of the fatal sisters,—Ignorance, Superstition, and Cruelty. But it is impossible to form an estimate of the number of the victims. For not only the Lords of Justiciary, but bailies of regalities, sheriffs of counties, and the endless tribe of commissioners appointed by the Privy Council, and sometimes by Parliament, officiated as the priests who dragged the victims to the altar."

Mr. Arnot further says, "The last person who was prosecut- before the Lords of Justiciary for Witchcraft, was Elspeth Rule, who was tried at Dumfries, in 1709. The last person who was brought to the stake in Scotland for the crime of

---

* Vide the Advocate's speech to the inquest.

Witchcraft was condemned by Captain David Ross of Little Daan, Sheriff-depute of Sutherland, A.D. 1722."

Doctor Brisbane being adduced upon oath in the trial, he adheres to his former subscribed attestation, and in respect of what is mentioned in that attestation, and some other specialities, the Doctor depones, that in his opinion the things mentioned in his attestation, did not proceed from natural causes arising from the patient's body.

The sum of the confessions of Margaret and Janet Rodger, who confessed during the trial of the rest beyond expectation.

During the dependence of the trial, Janet and Margaret Rodgers confessed in this manner: The commissioners had adjourned for two several diets, and though they were to meet on the third, yet it was not expected that they would proceed till providence might clear the prisoners' guilt by further testimonies of those who might come to confess. The very morning of the third term, the Rodgers did confess, which was a surprise to every one that came up to attend the court, since these, as they were women, and were not formerly noticed as others were: so they confessed of free motion, without any persons desiring it of them at the time; they had not such means of instruction as were administered to others: and the conjuncture of many circumstances were altogether singular. Their confessions did coincide as to the meetings and things acted therein, with the three former confessants, and the other evidences of the visible matters of fact: only they were so pointed as to condescend upon some of the panels whom they did not see at these rendezvouses; and great care was taken, to compare their testimonies which had been already discovered, and to expiscate their certain knowledge, by new interrogators, when they were separate from one another, &c. The whole crisis had such an evidence, that now the commissioners, with the general approbation of the most intelligent of the country, who came in to attend the court, allowed the going on of the process to debate of the relevancy, and putting seven of the best known criminals, for whom an advocate appeared, to the knowledge of an inquest : according whereunto there were some days allowed for the panels giving in their informations upon the relevancy ; and at the term, there was a great time spent in adducing the probation, an account whereof is referred to Appendix No. B.

APPENDIX No. B.

An account of Two Letters which were written after the persons were condemned, and before they were executed, which contain a Summary of what appeared most Material or Curious, in the Trial of the Seven Witches, who were condemned to be burned on the Gallowgreen of Paisley.

THE truth of the strange things mentioned in the preceding Narrative was at first carefully searched into only by private persons, but at last became so notour that, upon application founded on a journal of these extraordinary events, attested by many of the gentry in the country, the council gave a commission for enquiring thereanent.

The honourable persons to whom this was recommended did, with great impartiality and exactness, make a report which, in providence, proved a means of moving the Government to notice the execution of justice on some of these witches, who otherwise might have lurked without being discovered.

For, hereupon, the Council directed a second commission, for trial of those who appeared to them to be most loaded

T

by the preliminary probation adduced on the first. Several of these judges were not only persons of honour, but also of singular knowledge and experience; conform whereunto they did proceed with singular caution, and were so far from precipitancy in the affair, that, after several diets of Court, they adjourned to a longer term, that, in the meantime, the prisoners might be provided of advocates.

Accordingly an advocate compeared for them, and managed their defence with all the accuracy that could be expected. There were about twenty hours employed at one diet in examination of witnesses; and the inquest being enclosed, did consume about six hours in comparing the probation. Whereupon seven of the most notorious criminals were convicted and condemned.

The crimes libelled and found proven against them, were not mere spectral imaginations, but open and obvious facts, viz.:—The murders of some children and persons of age, and the torturing of several persons, particularly Bargarran's daughter; and both these, not at a distance, but contiguously, by natural means of cords, pins, and the like, besides the other ordinary works of Witchcraft, such as renouncing baptism, entering in contract with, and adoring the Devil under a corporeal shape, &c., which could not but be sustained relevant in Scotland, since there is an express statute, Parl. 9th, Act 73, Queen Mary, appointing the pain of death to such.

To make the probation the more convincing, it was adduced orderly in three periods. The first consisted of unsuspected witnesses, who proved facts. From whence it was necessarily inferred that there was Witchcraft in the case. The second did include also unexceptional witnesses, who deponed upon facts; which made it probable if not necessary, that the panels were the Witches. The third did comprehend six positive testimonies of these who did see and hear these Witches committing the malefices libelled.

The only valuable subject of debate, was anent the import of these last testimonies; five whereof were by confessants who had been at the meetings in which were committed the crimes libelled; and the sixth of Bargarran's daughter, who was one of the persons maleficiat. The antecedent part of the probation was by witnesses beyond exception; and the judges upon a long debate did sustain four of these six only *cum nota*, and two of them to be examined without oath, so nice were they in favour of the panels' lives, since some of these witnesses might have been admitted in such a crime without any quality by the most scrupulous judicatory in Europe. But all things were carried on in this procedure with tenderness and moderation, for even the advocates, who were sent to prosecute the indictment by his majesty's council and advocate, did not act with the bias of parties; but, on the contrary shewed an equal concern to have the panels assoilized, if it could be found compatible with justice.

This is the reason for which the publisher doubts not, but the two following Letters (the one whereof gives a compend of the advocate's speech to the jury, and the other of their answers to the objections against the confessant witnesses) will afford a satisfying view of the chiefest part of the trial, since the objections which were or might have been made, are therein stated and answered, or anticipate and prevented; and the intended brevity would not permit to print at this time the whole process, which being extant upon record, any who are curious may have easy access thereunto.

There is scarcely need to take notice of a late scurrilous pamphlet that had been printed in England, and pretends to give an account of those proceedings; for any who reads it may easily find that the author has been either fool, knave, or

both, there being neither good language, sense, nor truth, in
the most part of it.

The above Preface to the Letters was printed in 1698.

LETTER I.

SIR,—You having told me, that the odd passages which
occur in the west, have put many of your neighbours and
yourself upon reading all the books you can get treating of
Witchcraft; and therefore desired me to transmit to you my
observations at the court. I shall not pre-occupy your opinion
by giving them in my own form, but herein I send to you
the exactest duplicate of the advocate's speech to the inquest
that I could obtain; and by the next post you shall have
something more curious, viz., A collection of their answers to
the objections against the six last witnesses, that were
adduced for concluding the proof: having these, you will
want little that could be agreeable to such an accurate gust
as yours is.

The Advocate's Speech to the inquest was of this import :—

GOOD MEN OF INQUEST,—You having sitten above twenty
hours in overhearing the probation; and being inclosed,
where, it is like, you will take no small time to reconsider and
compare it, we shall not detain you with summing up the
same in particular; but shall only suggest some things,
whereof it is fit you take special notice in your perusal of it,
viz., 1st, The nature of your own power, and the management
thereof; 2dly, The object of this power which lies before you,
wherein you are to consider in the first place, whether or not
there has been Witchcraft in the malefices libelled? and in
the next place, whether or not these panels are the
Witches?

As to your power, it is certain that you are both judges and witnesses, by the opinion of our lawyers and custom; therefore you are called out of the neighbourhood, as presumed best to know the quality of the panels, and the notoriety of their guilt or innocence. Your oath is, that you shall all truth tell, and no truth conceal; which does plainly imply, that you are to condemn or assoil, conform to your proper conviction. Such is the excellent constitution of juries in England, and ought to hold more specially in this circumstantiate case, where there is such a chain of different kinds of probation concurring against the same panels, as will appear by the review thereof in its proper place.

We are not to press you with the ordinary severity of threatening an assize of error, in case you should absolve; but wholly leave you to the conduct of God and your own conscience, and desire that you proceed with all the care of the panels' lives that is possible for you; as the honourable judges have set to you a desirable pattern, in their great caution thereanent.

As to the probation itself, you see that it is divided in three parts, viz. :—The extraordinariness of the malefices; the probability of the concurring adminicles; and the clearness of the positive probation.

As to the first part, the malefices, or *corpora delicti*, are proven by unexceptionable witnesses, to have fallen out in such an odd and extraordinary a manner, that it points out some other causes than the ordinary course of nature to have produced these effects.

For clearing of this, particularly in relation to the torments of Bargarran's daughter, you may consider not only the extraordinary things that could not proceed from a natural disease, which lie proven before you; but also several other matters of fact, which is notour, have been seen by some of yourselves, and lie here in a journal of her sufferings; every article whereof is attested by the subscriptions of persons of entire credit, before the honourable commissioners appointed by his Majesty's Privy Council for making enquiry thereanent.

This girl's throwing out of hairs, pins, and coals of greater heat than that of her body or blood; as also so dry that they appeared not to have come out of her stomach; nor had she any press of vomiting at the time; that she declared the same to have been put in her mouth by her tormentors, is deponed by Dr. Brisbane, in his opinion, not to proceed from a natural cause.

She was not tormented by any of the panels after their imprisonment, except two nights by Katherine Campbell; which being a surprise, it was thereafter discovered, that these two nights the jailor's wife had got out Katherine Campbell to spin in her house.

She having been speaking to one of her tormentors as present (though invisible to the bye-standers), and asking how her tormentors had got these coloured red sleeves; she suddenly gets up, takes hold of them, the company hears a shried, and she pulls away two pieces of red cloth, which all the bye-standers beheld with amazement, in her hand; nor was there any other piece of this kind of cloth to be found in the room at that occasion.

She told that her tormentors were giving her a glass of sack, an orange pill, &c. (thereby ensnaring her to accept of a favour from them), and, accordingly, she was seen to move her lips, and to have an orange pill betwixt her teeth; though there was no visible hand that could have done it.

She advertised beforehand that one of her tormentors was to be at the door at a particular hour, and that another of them was in the kitchen before any did tell her thereof;

which accordingly fell out. And these being brought to her presence, became obnoxious to the ordinary means of discovery.

When her glove fell down from her, at a time when several persons were about her; it was lifted again by a hand invisible to them.

She was not only transported through the hall and down stairs without perceiving her feet to touch the ground; but also was hurried in a flight up stairs: and when a minister endeavoured to retain her, he found a sensible weight, besides her own strength, drawing her from him.

When she complained that her tormentors had bitten and scratched her, the steads of the nails and teeth were seen upon her skin, with blood and spittle about the wounds, which were above twenty-four; while neither her own, or any other teeth that were visible, could have done it.

She was most vehemently distorted upon attempting to tell or even write the names of her tormentors; yet that ceased as to any of them how soon the person was delated; and particularly she had liberty, after many painful attempts, to accuse Margaret Lang, how soon a charm of hair to restrain her, which Margaret had left behind the door, was found and burned; the girl having told it to have been tint, in manner mentioned in the deposition.

She did throw out no more hair after the finding the ball of hair, of the same colour and kind with that thrown out by the girl, in Katherine Campbell's pocket, with pins in it, and the burning of it.

After Agnes Naesmith had prayed for her, she did appear to her, but not torment her.

She foretold that her tormentors had concerted to throw her in a fit (whereof they did premonish, of design to fright her to renounce her baptism by the terror) at a certain hour, and had left one of their number to execute it ; according whereunto, there was a woman with a red coat seen under a tree in the orchard, and the torment was brought on at the time appointed.

When she told there was something tormenting her under the clothes, the spectators saw the bed clothes move in an extraordinary manner, after the girl had been raised out of them.

When she complained she was beaten, the bye-standers heard the noise of the strokes.

She cried out at a time, that her thigh was hurt ; and one of the company having searched her pocket, found a knife, but unfolded : however, having folded up the same, and put it in a second time, she cries of new ; and upon the second search, (it, though secured by the spring) is found open, to the great wonder of beholders; since they did watch, that no visible thing could have possibly opened it.

She told of a charm under the bed ; and accordingly it was found in the shape of an egg, which melted away being put in the fire : she told also that her sister, who was boarded abroad, had charms put above her in the house, and would not recover of the decaying sickness till she was brought out of it. According whereunto, the child being brought home, she straightway recovered.

She told of their meeting in the yard of Bargarran, for consulting anent the destroying of her; and accordingly the confessants have deponed that they did meet and consult her ruin in that place.

The story anent her telling that the commissioners, though at three miles distance, had granted a warrant to the sheriff to apprehend one of her tormentors ; her telling so perfect an account of the sheriff and of Mr. Guthrie who was with him, while her eyes were tied and fast ; her being in excessive torments, (as she foretold) till that person was apprehended, and immediately thereupon, though at many miles distance, her telling that her tormentors were now taken, betwixt twelve and one o'clock in the morning, and the sheriff, when he returned, did declare the seizure to have been about that time, is so notour, and so well attested, that we need only to put you in mind thereof.

Her falling in fits upon the sight or touch of her tormentors, was no effect of imagination; for she was fully hood-winked with a cloak, so as she saw nobody whatsoever; yet upon the approach of her tormentor, she immediately fell down as dead : whereas she remained no ways startled upon the touch of any other; which experiments were tried for ascertaining this means of discovery.

Finally, she is naturally sagacious and observant, and discovered her integrity in face of court; for when the president asked, whether or not she knew one of the panel's name that was to be pricked? she answered, that though she knew her well enough of herself, yet one had told her the name of this panel when she was sent for to be confronted with her. So far did this girl discover her aversion from any thing that might seem intended to aid unfairly the natural evidence of truth, and her firmness to the outmost against temptations of becoming a witch, particularly against the last assault of Satan, wherein he persuaded her at least to go to their meetings; and she answered, that she would not follow such a base fallen creature ; and he rejoining, that she would go to hell, however, for her other sins ; and she answering, that he was a liar from the beginning ; and the blood of Jesus would cleanse her from all iniquity : whereupon he disappeared, and she perfectly recovered upon the Sabbath thereafter; was an happy end put this fearful tragedy of Witchcraft, and confirms to conviction the reality of it.

As to the murdering of the children, and the minister

libelled; you may observe several extraordinary things appearing in them; particularly, the witnesses depone the minister to have been in excessive torments, and of an unusual colour, to have been of sound judgment; and yet he did tell of several women being about him, and that he heard the noise of the door opening, when none else did hear it. The children were well at night, and found dead in the morning, with a little blood on their noses, and blaes at the roots of their ears; which were obvious symptoms of stranglings: besides, that it is testified that the keeper of one of them cried out, "Matthew! Matthew! the child is dead." And the house of the other was whitened within, with sifting of meal the night before; both which particulars were told and discovered by the confessants, before the witnesses which now concur with them in it were examined.

The second part of the probation consists of several adminicles, proven by unsuspected witnesses, which lead us to suspect those panels to be Witches, as so many lines drawn from a circumference to a centre, and as an avenue to the positive probation thereafter adduced; and these either strike at the whole panels in general, or some of them in particular. In general, we need not enumerate all these adminicles, but remit you to the probation, which is so full thereanent; only you will be pleased to notice, that it is clearly proven that all the panels have insensible marks, and some of them in an extraordinary manner; that most of them have been long reputed witches, and some of them delated in 1687, by a confessing witch, whose subscribed confession has been produced. You see that none of them doth shed tears; nor were they ever discovered to do it since their imprisonment, notwithstanding of their frequent howlings; so that it is not a sudden grief or surprise. And finally, that the girl fell into fits of torment upon the panels approach to her, and that she did name them all frequently, either out or in her fits.

In particular, you see how Katherine Campbell was provoked by this girl's discovering her theft; whereupon she has brought in the rest of her confederates to act the following mischiefs. How, thereupon, Campbell did curse and imprecate in a terrible manner; how she staid out of her bed at night, and was frequently drousy in the morning; how she was named by the girl, particularly the two nights that she was out of prison. The ball of hair was taken out of her pocket and burned; whereupon the girl's throwing out of hair did cease; she could not express one word, even when on her knees, of prayer for the girl's recovery; and the insensible marks on her were remarkable.

Agnes Naesmith did not torment the girl after she had prayed for her. She was reputed a witch and hath the marks. She came early in the morning to Bargarran's close, when, by refusing to go in, it appeared she had no business; yea, it is plain that she had a resentment for her not getting a greater alms the last time she was there. The girl declared, *ex incontinenti*, that Naesmith asked her health and age, which, in these circumstances, was a shrewd presumption of her evil design; and she acknowledged herself to have done this when she asked the age of another child, wherein by Providence she was befooled, since that which she thought would have been an excuse, tended to discover her guilt. And lastly, after this appearance of Agnes Naesmith, the girl did take her first fit, and nominate her among her first tormentors.

Margaret Lang, that great imposter, has been a great master-piece of the Devil. She has confessed unnatural lust, which is known to some of your number; she sat near the door where the charm of hair was found, which the girl declared did keep up her tongue; and upon burning thereof, it was loosed. The girl fell in fits upon her approach ; she has notable marks, particularly one which the confessant declared she lately received; and, by inspection, it appears to be recent. When she came from her private conversation (no doubt with the Devil) she raged as if she had been possessed, and could not but declare that she expected a violent death. She looked in the face of James Millar's child and asked her age, whereupon that child sickened the same night, and named Margaret Lang on her death-bed. It appears she was ready to show to Janet Laird a sight of her mother, who had been three years dead. And finally, she has been taken in several lies and gross prevarications; particularly you may remember how six hours ago, when the witnesses were examined on the ball of hair found with Katherine Campbell, a gentleman, (Mr. Stewart of ——) heard her say to Katherine in the ear, "This is well waird on you, because you would not put it away when I desired you," &c. Which the said Mr. Stewart did openly testify in court upon oath; notwithstanding whereof, this impudent wretch had the confidence to deny it, though Katherine Campbell also confessed that she pulled at her, and had spoke somewhat to her, to which she did not advert. This was no wonder, the witnesses deponing at the same time, being close against Katherine.

Margaret Fulton was reputed a Witch, has the mark of it, and acknowledged, in presence of her husband, that she made use of a charm, which appeared full of small stones and blood ; that her husband had brought her back from the fairies ; and her repute of being a Witch is of an old date, besides her being often named by the maleficiate girl.

As to the Lindsays, they all have the mark, and were all of a long time reputed to be Witches. John Lindsay, in Barlock, was accidentally discovered by the girl's taking a fit upon his coming to the house. John and James Lindsay were delated

by a confessing Witch in anno 1687, which confession is publicly read before you, and there was money given to the Sheriff-
depute for delaying of the pursuit. James Lindsay appeared
to William Semple suddenly, and flew about like a fowl, for an
opportunity to strike him, in revenge of the quarrel mentioned
in the deposition, and at last prevailed to strike him dead
over a dyke. And finally, which is a remarkable indication
both to truth and providence, the very witnesses adduced in
the exculpation for the Lindsays, deponed so clearly against
them, even beyond the pursuer's witnesses, that their advocate
was stunned thereat, and thereupon desisted from craving any
more witnesses to be examined on the exculpation.

It is true some of these indications may be in one, and
others of them in another, either from nature or accident, and
yet that person not be a Witch; but it was never heard nor
read, that all these indications, which are so many discoveries
by providence of a crime that might otherwise remain in the
dark, did ever concur in one and the same individual
person that was innocent; yea, on the contrary, they, by the
wisdom and experience of all nations, do also convincingly
discover a Witch, as the symptoms of a leprosy concerted by
all physicians do unfold the person affected with the same to
be leperous, but *esto*, they are not sufficient of themselves; yet
their tendency and meaning, being cleared and applied to
their proper cause, by a liquid and positive probation, there
wants no more to determine you anent the panel's guilt, and
therefore,

Thirdly,—As to the third part of the probation, we remit
the positive depositions of the confessants, and against whom
they do concur, wholly to your own perusal or examination;
only you would be pleased to notice, 1st, Something which
do very much sustain the credibility of their testimonies
arising from their examination in court; 2dly, We shall ex-

plain to you the import of the word *Nota*, which is added to the interlocutor of the judges admitting these last witnesses.

First, Elizabeth Anderson is of sufficient age, being seventeen; but so young and pointed, that her deposition appears no effect of melancholy; she accused her father to his face when he was a-dying in the prison, as now there are two of her aunts in the panel, which certainly must proceed from the strength of truth, since even Dives retained a natural affection to his relations; she went on foot to the meetings with her father, except only that the Devil transported them over the water Clyde, which was easy to the prince of the air, who does far greater things by his hurricanes; she tells that Montgomerie's house was meally when his child was strangled; and declares, that she never renounced her baptism, but was carried along by the concussion of the parent, so that nothing can be objected against her testimony in any judgment, much less an excepted crime.

James Lindsay, it is true, is of less import; yet by his weeping when he came in and was admonished of the greatness of his guilt, it appears that he had a sense of it. He hath a natural precipitancy in what he speaks, yet that is commonly the concomitant of ingenuity, as importing his expressions not to be forethought. He concurs in most things with the others, and yet he has declared, that he saw not Margaret Fulton at Dumbarton, &c., which implies that he does not file the panels all at random, but tells what occurred to his senses, &c.

Janet and Margaret Rodgers are instances of a singular providence; for they did confess the same morning that the court did last sit, of their own proper motive, there being neither ministers nor judges beside them at the time. Agnes Naesmith is Janet's relation, and she tells that she never saw Katherine Campbell, as Margaret declares that she did not see John Lindsay in Barloch; which plainly demonstrates that they tell only the dictates of their natural conscience, arising from discretion and knowledge of the true matters of fact: they both professed their repentance last Sabbath in the church, and do persist with great firmness, as you see their deportment, in deponing to the congruous and exact.

Thomas Lindsay and Christian Shaw being under pupilarity, we did not press their being put to an oath; yet you saw that they did declare in court againt those panels in such an harmony with the rest of the deponents, and gave such a cause of their knowledge, that it is certain their own youngness in years adds extremely to the credit of their testimony; because thereby it is incredible that they could have contrived or executed the acting of concert.

As to the second, since these witnesses are admitted by the judges, it necessarily implies that they meant them to be probative; only they adjected the words *cum nota*, that is, you must notice, or *notandum est*, that there must something else concur to prove the guilt of the panels, by and atour the depositions of any two such witnesses; but so it is that all the adminicles on which you have seen probation led, for more than sixteen hours of your time, are strengthening evidences of those witnesses' credibility, and cannot but have been noticed by you, as illative of the same things which they depone. Whereby the *nota* is fully taken off by the concurrence of four other positive testimonies, agreeing with that of two of these witnesses; by the extraordinariness of the *corpora delicti;* by the probability of the adminicles; and, finally, by the whole chain of this affair, and the sparkles of an infernal fire which in every place hath broken out of it.

It is true, there are some few of the adminicles that are proven only by one witness, but as to this you may consider, 1st, That a witness deponing *de facto proprio*, is in law more credited than any other single witness, and this is the present case as to some of the adminicles ; 2dly, The antecedent concomitant and subsequent circumstances of fact, do sustain the testimony and make the *semi plenary* probation to become full; but 3dly, The other adminicles undoubtedly proven by concurring witnesses, are *per se*, sufficient ; and therefore you saw us, at the desire of the Judges, forbear to call the far greatest part of our witnesses, because the time had already run to so great a length, and it was thought that there was already enough proven of presumptions ; for it may also reasonably be imagined, that the most regular and curious scheme had emerged from the fortuitous concourse of atoms, roving without rule, as that so many indications should concenter against each of these panels, and yet they remain innocent of Witchcraft.

Now upon the whole, you will take notice that presumptions, being vehement, make a more certain probation than witnesses ; because presumptions are natural emanations of the thing itself, which cannot be bribed ; whereas witnesses are obnoxious ; so in our law there was one condemned for theft, another for falsehood, and a third for murdering of a child, merely upon presumptions, as is related by M'Kenzie in his Criminal Treatise, much more may presumptions abstract the faith of, and take off the *nota* from positive witnesses ; for it is a gross mistake that several proofs which have each of them some import may not be joined to make a full evidence, the same way as two small candles in a dark room will not suffice, yet several others being added to them will make a sufficient light to discover the murderer ; two boys will be able to carry a weight which one of them would not be able to sustain, as two units make a full number : one witness of whatsoever dignity proves nothing ; yet out of the mouth of two or three witnesses every truth shall be established. And finally, though one coal make not a fire that can do the work, yet several coals added to it, increase the flame, which is hoped will be sufficient for the operation.

We shall, therefore, leave you with this conclusion, that as you ought to beware of condemning the innocent, and ought to incline to the safest side; so if these panels be proven legally guilty, then *quad* bygones, your eye ought not to spare them, nor ought you to suffer a Witch to live; and as to the future, you, in doing otherwise, would be accessory to all the blasphemies, apostasies, murders, torture, and seductions, &c., whereof these enemies of heaven and earth shall thereafter be guilty when they have got out. So that the question seems simply to come to this, whether upon your oath *de fideli*, you can swear that the panels, notwithstanding of all that is proven against them, are not guilty of Witchcraft; in the determination whereof, we pray God may direct you to the right course.

The inquest being inclosed near six hours, brought in their verdict to Court that they found the libel proven.

LETTER II.

Sir,—I have collected, according to my promise, what appeared to me most specious in the reasonings, either in Court or private conversation, anent receiving of the confessants as witnesses. You are not to imagine that the panels were condemned on the faith of these; for I do believe the probation by unexceptionable witnesses, led antecedent to this last, was so pregnant that the panels might have been condemned on it, though these last had not been adduced.

I may have misled the energy of the argument sometimes, in a case which in itself is abtruse; however, you have it in such a manner as I was able to penetrate thereunto, as follows :—

In order to the more satisfactory answering of the objections made against these last witnesses, we shall first lay before you the state of the case, and then clear up the determination of it. As to the first, the question is not whether partners in the crime, or others mentioned in the objections, can be a concluding proof of themselves, though two of them would concur as to the same act of witchcraft; but whether the *corpora delicti* appearing already to imply witchcraft, and the extrinsic adminicles being so pregnant, to infer that these panels are the Witches; their concurring such characters, as by observance of all nations and ages, are the symptoms of a Witch; particularly the marks, fame, not shedding of tears, &c., which are discoveries of providence of such a crime, that like avenues lead us to the secret of it. And finally, when six persons of different ages and stations, five confessants, and the girl, do, when separately examined, agree in their answers to every material question that is put to them, even though it be new, so that it could not be concerted : we say, whether or not in such a case, may witnesses be received to put the copestone on the evidence by a positive probation, of a matter of fact, which is the object of sense, though otherwise they may be liable to exception, if such extraordinariness of the *corpora delicti*, clearness of the adminicles, and of the diagnostics of Witches, did not precede them as you have seen proven before you that they do.

The cases are not, whether these witnesses would be habile in an ordinary crime, which commonly falls to be exposed to other witnesses than those concerned in it ; but whether they can be received in this extraordinary, occult, and excepted crime of Witchcraft, wherein there are two special cases to be noticed, viz. : sometimes the acts thereof are open and admit the choice of witnesses, such as charms used in the day time, when the actor is visible. But that part of Witchcraft, whereby Witches meet in the night time, adore their lord, contrive their malefices, and accordingly thereafter execute them when other witnesses are asleep, or the Witches themselves are covered from sight, we say this can be no otherwise proven than by these that are intimate to it, joined to the positive proof and adminicles before mentioned.

We do not allege that persons altogether destitute of knowledge and natural conscience are not to be admitted in any case, such as infants, furious, fatuous, &c. Neither do we contend that Thomas Lindsay and Christian Shaw, who are under pupilarity, should be put to an oath; for they are only to be examined separately before the court, upon interrogators, by which it may appear, whether or not they coincide with the four other confessants that are to depone before them; and this is the panels' advantage in case of disagreement. But we insist, that any person above pupilarity, giving evidences of considerable knowledge and natural conscience (which is a sufficient fund for all the credit that we need in this case, that is already almost fully proven) it is to be received as a witness.

As to the second, we shall make this as clear as noon. 1st. From reason and the nature of the thing; 2dly, Our own customs and decisions; and 3dly, The singularity of the circumstantiate case.

As to the first, the going to and coming from meetings, especially on foot; the falling down and worshipping the Devil there, under a corporeal shape (which he had when he tempted our Saviour to do it). The actual murdering of children by a cord and napkin; and the tormenting of others by pins, &c., are plain objects of sense; and therefore the senses are to be believed anent

them. For as reason hath things intelligible, and faith
things supernatural; so the senses have things corporal
for their objects, whereanent they are to be trusted,
aye, and while it be proven that the appearance is impossible, or that the witness of it is an impostor. It is
a part of the Witches' purchase from the Devil, that they
cannot be seen at some occasions; so that the abominations
committed then would remain unpunished if such witnesses
were not admitted. It cannot be thought that Witches (who
of all criminals are the most obstinate to confess) would ven-
ture the loss of their own lives by deponing against others,
against whom they have no special pique; yea, for whom
they have particular affection, as several of the panels are
some of the witnesses' relations. Nor has the Devil any
peculiar interest to instigate them thereunto; for several of
the panels have confessed other execrable crimes; whereby it cannot be supposed that Satan would be divided against
himself. God, in his ordinary providence, has taken such
care of public judgments that the enemy of justice, his special
power ceases thereabout, as appears by the Witches not
being able either to do more harm, or escape after God's
ministers being to counteract Satan's instruments by imprisonment. And finally, the oddness of the malefices, the
concurrence of the adminicles, and the existence of matters
of fact wherein these confessants (though not knowing the
same otherwise) do agree with other unexceptionable witnesses, &c., do sufficiently abstract their credibility. For as
falsehood being a crime is ever presumed, so a person found
true in many things is still presumed to continue such till
the contrary be evinced.

As to the second, we have the testimony of our famous K[ing]
J[ames], 6th, Demon. lib. 2. C. ult., telling us that it is our law
that boys, girls, infamous persons, &c., are not to be rejected

any more in Witchcraft than in human lese majesty, even though they assert others to have been present at imaginary meetings; because this supposes their having entered into a precontract. He says that Satan's mark and the want of tears are pregnant aids to the discovery. He gives an instance of a girl who, having named Witches in her fits, they were all condemned upon other concurring adminicles. This not a common author, but a man who as curious, was exact; as prudent, did not publish such things without the approbation of the best divines and lawyers; as a prince, is to be credited anent the law of his own country; and as a king, has determined any dubiety that might have remained in this point as far as the law of our government will permit.

But further, our judges and lawyers have followed his Majesty; for in all the processes in the journals, fame and delation, and the mark, are still sustained as most pregnant presumptions; whereupon, and a very small probation besides, Witches have been frequently condemned. So in the processes against the bewitchers of Sir George Maxwell of Pollok, and Hamilton of Barnes, Anno 1677, *socius criminis*, though under age, is sustained to be a witness; and witnesses are adduced before the inquest for proving that the mark was found upon some of the Witches. Women and minors have been received by multitudes of decisions cited by M'Kenzie, Tit. prob. by witnesses, and Tit. Witchcraft. And he also cites decision, where in parallel cases, *socii criminis*, and others inhabile, were admitted, particularly in treason and in falsehood; and all lawyers conclude that Witchcraft is as much an excepted crime as these.

As to the third, whatever inhability these witnesses might be under, it is fully made up, and they rendered unexceptionably habile by the chain of this whole business. It is true one man, through the concurrence of corrosive humours,

may have an insensible mark ; another be enviously defamed;
a third may, through sudden grief or melancholy, not be
able to weep, &c. ; a fourth may be loaded with suspicious
circumstances, when extraordinary things fall out in the
country; a fifth may be deponed against by two false witnesses, though neither of these separately be truly Witches ;
but by the known observation and experience of mankind,
none except Witches have had the unhappy medley and concourse of all or most of these *indicia*, and ordinarily, and for
the greater part, Witches have them ; so that since the rules of
judgment are established upon that *quod plerumque sit*,
which does obtain till an exception be apparent in a special
case, the conjunction of these in one person does as plainly
give his character, as the most certain symptoms of the
plainest disease being universally concerted in all parts of the
world, points out to us that the haver of them is a person
truly affected with that disease, whereof he hath the concur-
rent diagnostics. In a word, one or other of these may concur in the innocent; but no writers do attest that all of them
have concentred in any other person in the world but a Witch ;
and on the other hand, they, taking place in Witches through
all parts in the world, must proceed from a common, and
not from a peculiar humour or cause.

   The specific aptitude of some of the nicest of the *indicia*,
which appeared from the probation already led to discover a
Witch, do serve to clear the ground of the world's observation
anent them. Particularly the devil as aping God, imprints a
sacrament of his covenant ; besides that, commonly this mark
being given at the first meeting, does, by its intolerable pain,
force the Witch to a second rendezvous for curing it, at which
the poor wretch, being under this furious necessity, fixes the
paction by renewing it with deliberation, having been diverted
in the meantime from considering the horridness of the first

engagement by the pain. The inhability to shed tears may be characteristic of hardening, though not always in the case of Christians; yet in those who have ceased to be such, least the Devil giving them such words of Scripture and prayer as many have, it should be impossible to discover their hypocrisy; and that is not Satan's own interest, since by this discovery, occasion is given to buffoon the profession of holiness. A report often arises without ground, but a constant repute that keeps footing, implies for the most part a surer cause, especially when it is of persons below envy, and by persons above calumny. The girl falling in fits at approach of the panels might proceed from antipathy, arising from the poisonous steams of the Witch accustomed to produce that effect through a virtue affixed thereto by the Devil, by conjunction of natural causes (the same way as the invisible pestilence does operate) or his promise of casting the girl in fits at the Witch's presence, might have been general; whereby the Witch was eventually befooled and discovered, as it often falls out : for Satan envies even their temporal felicity, and fears, lest by continuing here, they should be reft out of his hands by conversion, when they come to perceive the delusion of his promises to make them rich, &c.

There was one thing further which was tried before your lordships, viz. :—None of the panels that were tried (though most sagacious and knowing, and perfect in memory, so that it could not proceed from ignorance or forgetfulness) could make out the attempt of saying the Lord's prayer; which may either bê a secret judgment for renouncing their first Lord, after whom it is peculiarly denominate, or by restraint of their new lord, who may think that too special an homage to his adversary. But we have hindered you too long with that which is not necessary; for this being incontrovertible law and custom, there needs no philosophy to support it;

since legislators do reason, but subjects must obey : and both
the fool and lazy (who have neither read nor thought enough
to understand this subject) are to be left to their own chi-
meras ; yet lest they should insult, we shall answer in their
fashion such of the objections as the panels' advocate thought
anywise worthy to be repeated in this place.

Whereas it is objected that Delrio, sect. 5. § 4. says, that *socii*
are not to be admitted witnesses *ad condemnandum*, especially
considering that the probation ought to be *luce meridiana
clarior*.

It is answered, that the place itself confutes this inference
in the present case ; for it says, *ex his solis non est procedendum
ad condemnationem scio contrarium communius teneri & in praxi
obtinere, &c.*, so it is evident, 1st, The common opinion and
custom is in the contrary, even where there is no other probation, but by the partners of the crime ; yet, 2dly, We are
not so straitened, but subsume in his very words, *ex his
solu*, we do not desire the panels should be condemned ; but
your lordships see these witnesses we are to adduce are not
soli or alone ; for the probation led these last sixteen hours,
are so many concomitants and discoveries of providence,
which abstruct and make up any defect in their credit that can
be desiderate ; 3dly, Hence the meaning of that maxim
(which is metaphorical, as appears by the words *clarior luce
meridiana*, an equal clearness being sufficient) is fully answered,
and takes place in the present case ; for the extraordinariness
of the *corpora delicti*, pregnancy of the adminicles and pointed-
ness of the positive probation, being conjoined, there is not
a clearer proof upon record in any nation, than that to which
it is hoped these will amount.

Whereas this allegance is enforced, by pretending it were of
dangerous consequence to allow such witnesses to prove

meeting with the Devil, since Satan might have represented others by their false shapes.

It is answered,—1st. That we are not straitened in this, because there are many other articles proven which could not have been falsified; but if we give some scope to reasoning, even in this point, it is to be considered that the rules of judgment are established upon that which, for the most part, does still obtain,—and rules are to be followed till an exception be proven in a particular circumstantiate case. But so it is by the experience and observation of the wisest divines, lawyers, philosophers, physicians, statesmen, judges, and historians, at home and abroad (that are too wise to be imposed upon, and too ingenuous to deceive us when they all concur in the same matter of fact), besides the testimony of Witches themselves everywhere, make the apparitions of Witches to be commonly and mostly real ; and, therefore, the testimony of the senses is always to be credited anent them, aye and while it be canvelled. For single or few instances of false representations to the senses, esteeming them to be true, or a possibility of appearances being false, can nowise invalidate the rule established upon experience, which is common, and, for the most part, whereby no exception is to be presumed till it is proven in a special case ; since a wonder does not subvert the proof drawn from a common course of nature ; logic admits not to argue a *particulari*, or from possibility to existence ; law puts the burden of proving simulation on the affirmer, and that which seldom occurs is not considered by the legislators.

For illustrating of which, it is further to be considered that for the most part and ordinarily, the Witches are personally existant in the places where they appear, because it is more easy for the Prince of the Air to transport them in his hurricanes which he can raise, as is plain in the instance of Job (who was put in his power, *i. e.* his natural power without

w

delegation) forming a fence upon their face, whereby the
violence of the air may be diverted from choking them, then
to form the curious miniature of such various transactions on
their brain : the difficulty whereof is the greater, that all their
fancies are not disposed at all times the same way, and they
have not the seeds of this work, unless they had once acted it
in reality. It is both the greater crime and pleasure to act in
truth ; which therefore the Devil and Witches do rather choose
(unless the place be far distant, or the party indisposed) and
this *de facto* is attested to be so by the writers and Witches
in all nations and ages, as said is.

2dly. Notwithstanding that the rule must hold till an exception of exculpation be evinced, *quoad* a particular person,
by evidencing that the real appearance was in that special
case a true mistake ; yet this exception is sufficient for safety
of the misrepresented, since the same providence which permitted the affliction will order the outgate and exculpation,
either by the ærial bodies not biding the touch, or some other
distinction, as providence commonly allows the Devil to personate only with a cloven foot ; or that the apparition was
folly to one single witness who cannot be a proof ; or that
the innocent can prove *alibi ;* or finally, the notour character
of a Samuel will purge and dispel the aspersions of Satan,
contrived of purpose to discredit the evidence of sense, by
which alone his instruments can be discovered. Especially
this character being joined to the other circumstances of the
providence, such as, when good men are disguised, they are
mostly passive in the scene and outwith thereof: whereas
Witches are personally active in their common life by such
words and deeds as (in conjunction with these appearances)
conspire to make us know and distinguish them from the truly
good ; since these Witches' open profanity, naughtiness, or
unveiled hypocrisy, being cleared by fame, sealed by the mark,

and confirmed by the other discoveries of the adminicles that lie proven before you, do still make a land mark betwixt the children of darkness and light. So Delrio, lib. 5. sect. 16. N. 5. tells of Athanasius and St. Germanus, against whom probation was adduced for sorcery, but providence did canvel it. It is a famous instance of Susanna, represented by the elders, which, though not in the case of spectre, yet agrees in the rational. The representation of Pharoah's magicians had concomitants, by which they were discovered and confounded. But lastly, suppose that God, in the depths of his wisdom (to convince the error of nimious self-confidence) should permit all necessary probation to concur against an innocent; yet the judge, following the faith of proofs established by divine and human laws, is altogether innoxious. Since this case being very rare, the evil is less than the establishing a principle, by which most of all these monsters could not be cut off.

Upon the whole, it is certain that as though oft-times false witnesses set on by the Devil have taken away a harmless life, by accusing it of other crimes, yet the testimony of witnesses must still be credited till they be redargued; so these appearances of Witches with the other specialities before expressed, being proven, ought to be esteemed real till the fallacy be established. Especially seeing there are examples in ancient and modern history of Satan's representing the best of men, committing murder, buggery, &c., in effigy, so Delrio, lib. 5. sect. 16. N. 5. relates that St. Silvanus was represented by the Devil, as committing a common capital crime; and the like of a monk; whereof there are several modern parallel instances; yet this cannot enervate the rule and faith of public judicatures, founded on no more but upon the sight of the like appearances; and any argument against the probation in Witchcraft will equally hold against the probation of any other crime whatsomever;

wherefore the rules of them both must be common, as to believing the senses fortified *ut supra*, till their error be individually discovered.

Finally, the certainty is noways diminished by the extraordinariness of the appearance to the senses ; for in law and nature reality, and not simulation, is presumed, till the contrary be made appear that it is actually false. This is answer enough to those who place a great part of their small wit in nonsensical arguing against all divine authority ; but writers further illustrate that the extraordinariness of a matter of fact does not exclude its realities being the subject of the testimony of witnesses in our Saviour's miracles, transfiguration, walking on the waters, standing in the midst of the disciples while the doors were shut, and arguing assurance by their senses, that a spirit had not flesh and bones, though indeed the surer word of prophecy did put these beyond doubt.

Nor could it be alleged for the panels (though they had the last word, as perhaps they have not, in objections against witnesses, since therein *rei fiunt actores* by attacking the witnesses' presumed hability) that it is not conceiveable, how the girl or witnesses could see what the by-standers could not behold ; beside the impossibility of the real bodies entering at close doors and windows, or not intercepting the sight of what is at its back.

For this it would be answered,—1st, Proven facts must not be denied, though philosophers have not yet certainly reached the invisible manner of their existence ; so in nature the loadstone draws the iron, the compass turns always to the poles, &c. In Scripture the angel (and the Devil was once such, retaining as yet his natural powers) smote the Sodomites, that they could not see the door, though they saw the house. Balaam's ass perceived the angel that stood undiscovered to himself; and the rod thrown down by the magicians of Egypt, was no doubt seen by themselves, though invisible to the by-standers, which holding of their eyes, interpreters explain to have been done by natural means; and yet the manner thereof is certainly difficult.

However, it is also certain, that if a possible way can be proposed, the reality of a proved fact is not to be contra-dicted; and this can be done in the present case.

For, 2dly, Satan's natural knowledge and acquired experience, makes him perfect in the optics and limning; besides that, as a spirit, he excels in strength and agility, whereby he may easily bewitch the eyes of others, to whom he intends that his instruments should not be seen in this manner as was formerly hinted, viz., he constricts the pores of the Witches' vehicle, which intercepts a part of the rays reflecting from her body; he condenses the interjacent air with grosser meteors blown into it, or otherwise does violently agitate it, which drowns another part of the rays; and lastly, he obstructs the optic nerves with humours stirred toward them; all which joined together, may easily intercept the whole rays reflecting from these bodies, so as to make no impression upon the common sense: and yet at the same time, by the refraction of the rays gliding alongst the fitted sides of the volatile couch, wherein Satan transports them, and thereby meeting and coming to the eye, as if there were nothing interjacent, the wall or chair behind the same bodies may be seen; as a piece of money lying out of sight in a cup becomes visible, how soon the medium is altered by pouring in some water on it. Several of your number do know, that the girl declared that she saw and heard the doors and windows open at the Witches' entry, when, no doubt, the Devil had precon-densed a soft postage on the eyes and ears of others, to whom that was unperceived.

So Apolonius escaped Domitian's flight, and Giges became invisible by his magical ring. John of Sarisberrie tells us of a Witch that could make anything not to be seen; and Mejerus relates another that had the like power. Some Italian Witches of greater than ordinary wit, confessed to Grilandus the Devil opening doors and windows for them, though the more ignorant, by a fascination, think themselves actors of this ; whence it ought not to be doubted by any reasonable man, what in all times and places is so incontestible fact.

Finally, the panels could not insist that these confessants are to depone only on their imagination, which can prove no more against themselves or others than a dream.

For still it is to be minded that there are other proofs to which this is only necessary as a consonant adminicle. But further, *Arg. causa*, it is answered that the allegiance is a mistake, seeing they are plain matters of fact, obvious not only to one, but several of their senses, viz.—some of them went the greatest part of the way to these meetings on foot ; they there saw and touched their confederates ; they heard their combinations to destroy and torture the infants, girl, and ministers : they returned on foot again, and even when they were carried fore or back, they knew on the next day that it was no dream, the same way as all other mortals discover the difference. But, moreover, this is adminiculate by some real effects of a personal presence, as you have seen in the probation : and yet it is further cleared by the journal of Bargarran's daughter's sufferings, which was attested before the former commissioners, and is notour in the country, particularly the glass of sack and orange pill, the pieces of the clouted sleeves, the words expressed by the keeper on the sudden murder of the child, which are constantly told by some of the confessants ; as also the house being meally that night ; the girl, though hoodwinked at the time, her falling in fits at their approach, &c., and others which shall be pointed at to the assize, conjoined together, can be ascribed to no other cause than the real existence of the Witches' persons in the place, unless it be said that Satan might possibly have foisted and suborned all these; and thence it be concluded that the Devil did actually so, in which case the objectors are the persons that bottom their opinion on imagination, without any positive ground of the reality of what they fancy; yea, against positive grounds of belief in the contrary, which, arguing from possibility to existence, is already sufficiently exploded.

Whereas for sustaining the objection, it is likewise alleged that the confessants having been in the Devil's service, and renounced Christ, they are not capable of the religion of an oath. .

1st, In the rules of charity, &c., the confessants, though once Witches, yet now they, at least the majority of them, have ceased to be such, having had the use of means by the ministers and word, and actually declared their repentance, and the Devil ceasing to molest them; particularly Elizabeth Anderson was only carried alongst violently by her father, and stood out to the last against her renouncing of her baptism, or consenting to these crimes which were contrived in their meetings. Janet and Margaret Rodgers do testify a great remorse, and avowed the same last Sabbath, in the face of the congregation. So those three are sufficient, whatsoever it might be said against the other two, especially if we join the improbability either of hazarding their own lives, or the Devil's sending them out against the panels, of their destroying their own relations as was remarked before.

But, 2dly, Whether they remain Witches or not, it is certain, by reason and experience, that the Devil's peculiar influence ceaseth in and about judgment by the common course of providence ;· and, therefore, the authors before cited admit Witches whether penitent or not.

3dly, All the defects of their hability is supplied, and the entireness thereof completed, by their testimonies being so wonderful adminiculate; particularly the confessants are constant from the first discovery; uniform in so various circumstances, not only with themselves, but with the girl; they declare nothing but what is probable, most of the panels have been reputed Witches, all of them having the mark; and one or other of them (to whom the associates delighted in mischief, never missed to join,) having had particular irritation to take revenge by the torture and deaths libelled; besides the other adminicles of guilt already proven before you. The confessants were threatened to retract by the panels themselves and their friends; besides the bad usage from others in the country. They concur with the maleficiat's testimony, and amongst themselves, even when interrogate singly; and upon new things, as several of your number have tried the experiment; the reiteration of the acts which they declare anent some persons whom they never saw except in these congresses; yet whom they know now on the first sight, is unaccountable if they were falsaries. And that they are not such, is further abstructed by some of the panels being delated by a confessing Witch in anno 1687. And you know that others delated by these confessants were lately brought in guilty by the verdict of a former inquest, &c., which are so many joint proofs of these witnesses' integrity, and makes a chain of evidence and moral demonstration, both against error in themselves, and delusion in relation to others, &c.

There were some things objected out of the law of Scotland, of which I shall give you some touch.

Whereas it was alleged, that *irretiti criminibus capitalibus,* and so under the pursuer's power cannot be admitted to be witnesses, conform to a statute in *Regiam Majestatem*.

To this it was answered, that we need not say that these statutes have not the force of law, except in so far as they are received by custom, unless conform thereto. A laik [layman] cannot witness against a clerk, or *e contra*, &c. Nor need we make use of that which is obvious, viz., that these statutes are only common rules in the ordinary crimes, such as Withchcraft, &c. *Nam omnis regula subverti potest*, and particularly this rule, is actually so restricted in the case of Witchcraft, by the opinion of lawyers and customs before-mentioned, which are the best interpreters of laws; for if this application should hold, *socius criminus* could never be admitted; but we positively deny that those confessants are under our power or influence, seeing Elizabeth Anderson is not guilty of Witchcraft for anything that doth appear, the Lindsays were never indicted for it, and the diet was deserted against the Rodgers. As the whole commission is to expire against the first of June, betwixt and which time they are to proceed no further than this particular trial. So that this objection vanishes to smoke.

Whereas it is pretended that the Rogers cannot be received, because not given out in the list of witnesses, conform to the regulations whereby the panels might have proven their objections by their exculpation.

It was answered,—1st, This objection ought to be repelled, because, besides that the act speaks only of criminal libels, and not indictments, which with the list of witnesses, may be given in far shorter time than the additional list has been given to the panels, being prisoners; this act is interpreted by the common custom of the justice court; of giving additional lists after the first, upon shorter time than this has been given; as it is particularly attested by James Gutherie, macer, who has given them, and, who being a person in office, his testimony is to be credited in what relates to his office ; so that the old custom, confirmed by a decision, August 3d, 1661, where Alexander Forrester was cited *apud acta* against a Witch, continues *quoad* this point, as is related by M'Kenzie, page 529 ; but, 2dly, Any objection that the panels pretend against these witnesses, is *in jure*, or may instantly appear ; 3dly, the case is altogether extraordinary and circumstantiate, for the witnesses had not confessed, and so were not existent under that redublication when the principal list was given out, whereby the Act of Parliament can only be understood of witnesses that were then existent ; and finally, the panels got a general warrant of exculpation for citing of any witnesses they pleased, and they have had several days since they got this additional list, so that they might have cited witnesses to prove their objections, were it not, the truth is, they have none besides these that are common and before answered.

Thus I have given you hints that your own reasoning (which I know to be refined) may improve and apply, so as to dissolve the quibbles which the petty wits, who have not soul enough to penetrate into the true light of what is recondite, may raise against it ; it being their common talent either to skip over the surface of mines, or otherwise to tear asunder some apurtenances of a scheme, and then presently pronounce it mortally maimed.

I must confess that none could be more sceptical anent the truth of such odd things as I have heard, nor inquisitive for canvasing the reality and explications of them, than I was before my attendances on Bargarran's house, and the several diets of court, and my conversation with some of those concerned thereanent. But now, after all I have seen, reasoned, and heard, I do acknowledge myself entirely captivate by the dictates of natural understanding and common sense, into a sound mind and persuasion that, as there is such a thing as Witchcraft, so it was eminent in its forementioned effect; and the seven panels were some of the Witches.

I have troubled you little with my proper observations; yet lest you should think me either too lazy or peevish, I shall make one, and it is, that I do not think the greater part of the condemned prisoners will ever fully confess; of which conjecture I have two chief grounds, viz.,—that they are neither ignorant nor melancholic; but on the contrary, some of them would seem to have been once enlightened before they fell away; so that, if this be a sin unto death, there is no appearance that they will glorify God by acknowledgement.

Several of them are of singular knowledge and acuteness beyond the common level of their station; particularly, Margaret Lang did make harangues in her own defence, which neither divine nor lawyer could reasonably mend; yet I thought that when they spoke in a matter of any concern, their eyes stood squint and fixed, as if they had been turning their ears and attentive to a dictator. Their answers to the trying interrogatories put to them, were surprisingly subtile and cautious; though, indeed, by the industry of some of the Judges and lawyers, they were at occasions involved in lies, prevarications, and contradictions, which might have proceeded either from natural or preternatural causes. Some of them were esteemed in the country very sagacious and exact in their business,—Margaret Lang having been a midwife, and one of the Lindsays having acquired a considerable fortune by his tillage and trade; yet it was noticed, something odd either of iniquity or affectation; and Lindsay did finely get off from the sheriff when he was formerly accused in 1687.

Melancholians are lovers of solitude; Witches of society

and feasts ; those are commonly pale and heavy ; many of these corpulent and voluptuous. Witches are hard to confess as knowing their guilt ; melancholians delight to discover their horridest damps, because they think them no crime ;— the one's confessions everywhere are uniform, the others' phantasms are as various as their humours. Finally, Witches teach their trade ; whereas conceits would die with them, and could be no more conveyed than the humour which is the specific cause thereof. As these distinguishing characters do hold in general, so it is already manifest, that the real effects in several passages of Bargarran's daughter, were not possibly producible by any imagination or humour ; and it is special in this case, that neither the panels nor confessants were distempered by being kept from sleep, tortured, or the like, which were too usual in former times ; but all the measures were strictly observed that are the requisites of a truly impartial judgment.

Indeed, not to have sent unto you the doubles of the depositions themselves ; because it is not denied that the depositions are such as they are represented in the pleadings ; the chief question being anent the hability of the last de-ponents. Neither was you to expect the defenders' part of the debate, separately by itself, in respect that what was dispersed here and there for them, is faithfully repeated and implied in what you have, as to those points which I thought worthy the notice.

Upon the whole, I do believe that there is scarcely a more rare providence of this nature in any true history,—a more exact caution in any enquiry or trial of this kind,—a more clear probation without confession of the panels themselves,—or a more just sentence, putting together all circumstances upon record.

APPENDIX No. C.

An Account of the Confession and Death of JOHN REID, *Smith in Inchinnan, who made a discovery conform to the former witnesses after the trial was over.*

Upon the 21st of May, 1697, after the trial of the seven Witches, there is an attestation subscribed by Mr. Patrick Simpson, Minister at Renfrew, Walter Scott, Bailie there, &c., of this import:—John Reid, Smith in Inchinnan, prisoner, did, in the presence of the said persons and some others, declare that about a year ago the Devil (whom he knew to be such thereafter) appeared to him when he was travelling in the night-time, but spoke none to him at the first encounter. At the second appearance, he gave him a bite or a nip in his loin, which he found painful for a fortnight. That the third time he appeared to him as a black man, &c., desired him to engage in his service, upon assurance of getting gear and comfort in the world, since he should not want anything that he would ask in the Devil's name; and then he renounced his baptism, putting the one hand to the crown of his head, and the other to the sole of his foot, thereby giving himself up to Satan's service; after which the pain of the bite or nip ceased. He told that hitherto there were no others present; but thereafter he was at several meetings, particularly that in Bargarran's yard, about the time when there was a fast for Christian Shaw, where the Devil appeared in the same kind of garb as he first appeared to him, and they consulted Christian's death, either by worrying or drowning her in the well; and the Devil said he should warrant them that they should neither be heard, seen, nor confess; to which end he gave every one of them a bit of flesh, that the declarant got, but let it fall and did not eat it. Thereafter, in the presence of the Laird of Jordanhill, the Minister, Mr. Andrew Cochran, Town Clerk, and Bailie Paterson, he owned his former confessions; and being enquired of Jordanhill how they were advertised of their meetings, he said that ordinarily at their meetings the time of the next was appointed; but for particular warning there appeared a black dog with a chain about his neck, who, tinkling it, they were to follow, &c. And being enquired by the minister, if he did now wholly renounce the Devil (for he had formerly told how Satan had not performed his promise) and give himself to Jesus Christ, and desire to find mercy of God through him, he assented thereunto. It is to be observed that John Reid, after his confession, had called out of the prison window, desiring Bailie Scott to keep that old body Angus Forrester, who had been his fellow prisoner, close and secure; whereupon the company asked John when they were leaving him, on Friday's night the 21st of May, whether he desired company or would be afraid alone; he said he had no fear of any thing. So being left till Saturday's forenoon, he was found in this posture, viz. :—Sitting upon a stool, which was on the hearth of the chimney, with his feet on the floor and his body straight upward, his shoulders touching the lintel of the chimney, but his neck tied with his own neckcloth (whereof the knot was behind) to a small stick thrust into a clift above the lintel of the chimney; upon which the company, especially John Campbell, a surgeon who was called, thought at first in respect of his being in an ordinary posture of sitting, and the neckcloth not having any run loup, but an ordinary knot, which was not very straight, and the stick not having the strength to bear the weight of his body or the struggle, that he had not been quite dead; but finding it otherwise, and that he was in such a situation that he could not have been the actor thereof himself, concluded that some extraordinary cause had done it, especially considering that the door of the room was secured, and that there was a board set over the window, which was not there the night before when they left him.

APPENDIX No. D.

I am much obliged to John Stewart, near Neilston, for favouring me with the curious old manuscript volume, from which the following Sermon is extracted. I understand that this curious old manuscript volume came into Mr. Stewart's possession from his forefather's. This book was originally the property of A. Mathie, who, probably, was a Student in the University of Glasgow between the years 1707 and 1709, for these dates are written on it.

In this Sermon, besides such ancient orthography, as, *ane* for *an* and *one*, *doe* for *do*, *hes* for *has*, *hiest* for *highest*, &c., a great number of contractions also occur, as, *J*. X for *Jesus Christ*, *qch.* and *wc*, for *which*, *qm.* for *whom*, *qn.* for *when*, *qo.* for *who*, *qr.* for *where*, *wt.* for *with*, *ye.* for *the*, *ym.* for *them*, *yn.* for *then* and *than*, *yr.* for *their* and *there*, *ys.* for *this*, *yse.* for *these*, and *yt.* for *that*.

APPENDIX.

A SERMON,

Preached by Mr. David Brown, at Paisley, on Wednesday the
9th of June 1697 years, being the day before the execution
of several persons condemned for witchcraft.*

1. Timothy i. Chap. 16. v.—"Howbeit, for this cause I obtained mercy,
that in me first Jesus Christ might shew forth all long suffering, for a
pattern to them that should hereafter believe in him to life everlasting."

MAN by nature, since the fall, is a guilty creature, and being
guilty is ready to be jealous of God, as if all his designs were
designs of wrath against him; yea, oftentimes so suspicious is
man of God, that he is jealous of the hardness of his design
in that which is one of the greatest instances of his love in
the world, and that is in sending his Son Jesus Christ into
the world to save sinners. To obviate this, the Apostle tells
us, John iii. 17., *God sent not his Son to condemn the world, but
that the world might be saved through him.* Even Luther
himself, as is reported of him, was so suspicious of God this
way, mistaking that place of Scripture, Rom. iii. 25, 26.,
*Whom God hath set forth to be a propitiation, and through
faith in his blood to declare his righteousness,* he understood it
as if the words, *to declare his righteousness,* had been that God
sent forth his Son to the world, to set forth his judgments
upon the world. I say, sometimes man comes so great a
length in this, that he thinks it impossible God can find in
his heart to forgive, and therefore the Apostle shews, in

---

* It is probable that this Minister was the David Brown who was Minister
of Neilston between 1689 and 1693, and was afterwards translated to another
Parish, and who was an elder brother of Thomas Brown, Mr. Blackwell's
colleague at Paisley.

opposition to this, that Christ had put him in the ministry, in the 12th verse, and that, notwithstanding of the bad life he had lived before his conversion, in the 13th verse, *and that the grace of our Lord was exceeding abundant*, in the 14th verse, which was the matter of his joy and rejoicing, 15th verse. And here he gives account why God was pleased to call and justify him, and that is, that he might set him forth as an instance of the glory of God, and be an encouragement to others, who were great sinners, to believe in Christ to life everlasting.

In the words ye have two things considerable. (1.) The great mercy conferred upon this Apostle Paul, in this expression, *Howbeit, I obtained mercy;* and no doubt he speaks here of pardoning mercy; for mercy supposes misery on the sinner's part, and free favour on God's part, and here it supposes sense of the one and the other too in Paul's case.

(2.) Ye have the reason of this dispensation of mercy in these words, *that in me first Jesus Christ might shew forth all long-suffering, for a pattern to them that should hereafter believe on Him to life everlasting;* in which ye have three things. First, the author of this pardoning mercy, *Jesus Christ.* Second, the end for which he obtained mercy, and that is, *that in me he might shew forth all long suffering for a pattern.* Third, the end for whom, and that is, *for a pattern to them that should hereafter believe on him to life everlasting.*

I return to the first of these. The author of this pardoning mercy *Jesus Christ.* Ye know Jesus Christ is not only the meritorious cause of pardoning mercy, but the author also of eternal salvation to as many as believe on Him. John xvii 2., *that he should give everlasting life*, by his death, *to as many as thou has given him:* so that he hath promised everlasting life by his death; yet he hath also power to give everlasting life, and to forgive sin.

Y

Again, secondly, ye have the end for which he obtained
mercy ; *that in me first he might shew forth all long-suffering for
a pattern*, where ye have three things.   1. That he might
shew forth all long-suffering.   2. That he might shew it forth
for a pattern.   3. That he might shew it forth in me first. First,
That he might shew forth all long suffering, ye have three
things.   1. That he might shew forth, that is, that he might
make manifest.   There are some sovereign steps of his grace
and mercy hid, and out of the common observation of men,
and therefore he says that he might shew forth all long-suffering.   2. That he might shew forth long-suffering, that is, that
he might shew forth patience to me that had sinned so long.
3. That he might shew forth all long suffering, that is, that he
might shew forth patience to me, in a great and eminent
degree ; a patience becoming, and like unto God.

2. Ye have in this part of the verse, "That he might shew
it forth for a pattern," that is, for a copy, that others might
take me for an example of God's patience,—that they might
take me for a copy to encourage them that will believe on
Christ to life everlasting.

Again, that in me first, that is, in me the chief of sinners,
as in the 13th verse ; or me, that is among the first rank of
sinners ; or, in me first, that is, that having put me into the
ministry, he might make of me a special instance of grace,
who was a gross sinner ; therefore he pitched on such an one
as me to send among the Gentiles who were gross sinners.

Again, ye have the end for whom the Apostle was made an
instance of grace, and that is, *for them that should hereafter
believe on Christ to life everlasting;* where ye have something
implied, and something expressed.   That which is implied is
in these two things.   1. That there are some who shall believe,
that do not yet believe on Christ Jesus.   2. That everlasting
life is attainable by them that believe on him.   That which is

expressed is, that the reason of making him an instance of grace, was to be a pattern for the encouragement of great sinners to believe on Christ Jesus to life everlasting.

The observation I make on the verse, That God is pleased to give some rare instances of his mercy, for the encouragement of the worst of sinners to believe on Christ Jesus to obtain life everlasting. This ye see exhausts the substance of this verse, that the Lord is pleased to give some rare instances of his grace and superabundant mercy for the encouragement of the worst of sinners to believe in Christ Jesus to obtain life everlasting. In clearing of this doctrine, I would, 1. Give you some instances of the great riches of his grace. 2. What way these instances of grace may have influence upon the greatest of sinners to believe on Jesus Christ to life everlasting. 3. I would shew you why God is pleased to give such instances of grace for the encouragement of the greatest of sinners to believe on Jesus Christ to life everlasting. 4. I would shew you what it is to believe on Christ Jesus, which these instances of grace calls sinners to do in order to obtain life everlasting. 5. What everlasting life is, which is the consequent of believing on Jesus Christ.

Now for the first of these. To shew you some instances of the great riches of his grace, I shall begin with the same Apostle, and lead you to one place where he gives a full accompt of himself, Acts xxvi. 10, 11, in which ye have seven or eight sad aggravations of his own case. There he tells you, that he gave his voice against them that were put to death; that he compelled the saints to blaspheme; that he persecuted them to strange cities; and that he had authority from the high priest against them; and that he persecuted them in a constant track, and yet he obtained mercy, because he did it ignorantly; but all that this will say is, that therefore his sin was pardonable, because he had not sinned wilfully against the knowledge of the truth ; but certainly this made him a great instance of the grace of God, that yet he obtained mercy.

2. Another instance you have in Acts xix. 18, 19. Ye see there, that many of them that believed came and confessed their deeds, and many of these were such as used curious arts,— devilish magical arts,—and yet the grace of God brake in upon them. There is a great instance of the grace of God.

3. Another instance you have in Luke vii. 37, where you see a woman who was a sinner comes to Christ. Now a sinner in the New Testament sense is a grevious sinner, a vile strumpet and whore, and yet Christ himself tells us, *her sins which are many are forgiven her*. Because she loved much, The Lord forgave her.

4. Ye have the instance of Manasseh, which is very suitable to the case of these I am now speaking to.* 2. Chron. xxxiii. 2., where ye find he did evil in the sight of the Lord, like the abominations of the heathen, whom the Lord cast out before the children of Israel. Ye will find he built high places, made groves, and set up altars in the house of the Lord, and caused his children to pass through the fire to Moloch, and used inchantments, and consulted with them that had familiar spirits ; and yet behold an instance of the sovereign grace of God,—that he yet made Israel to sin above the abomination of the heathen, that he greatly humbled himself, and the Lord pardoned him, and was intreated of him. Here is a great instance of the grace of God, which is a great encouragement for all such sinners to close with Christ in order to life everlasting. I might give you more

* It is evident from this, and other places of this Sermon, that the seven persons condemned for witchcraft, were present during Mr. Brown's discourse.

instances,—as the instance of the prodigal, and these, 1 Corinth. vi. 10, where the Apostle, speaking of these that shall not inherit the kingdom of God, Idolators, Fornicators, Adulterers, Drunkards, &c. says he, "and such were some of you, but ye are washed, but ye are sanctified, but ye are justified in the name of the Lord Jesus." One instance more, Acts ii. 36, 37, the Apostle Peter says, *He whom ye crucified is both Lord and Christ;* as if he had said, ye are the folks that have crucified the Son of God, and yet there came a work of grace on their hearts, that made them cry out, *Men and brethren, what shall we do to be saved?* If ever Christ would have stood upon it and not forgiven, it would have been such as were guilty of such an atrocious crime; and yet behold the riches of the grace of God, in that they obtained mercy. Certainly this is a great instance now, I tell you; the Lord hath set up such instances for the encouragement of the worst of sinners to believe on Christ to life everlasting.

In the second place, I come to shew you what way these instances of grace ought to have influence upon great sinners, to encourage them to believe on Christ to life everlasting.

And first, from these instances ye may draw this conclusion, that sure it is not from any inherent worth that God pardons, which may have influence on you to believe. If it had been intrinsic worth, would he ever have forgiven them that crucified him? would he ever have forgiven Paul or Manasseh? What excellency or worth was in them? Should we not therefore reason thus with ourselves, "Thou that forgives, because thou will forgive, wilt thou not have pity upon us?"

Second, ye may from these instances draw this conclusion, that he hath no reason out of himself to forgive, and this is a great foundation to close with Christ; there is no worth in us, therefore all the goodness must be in himself. He hath mercy, because he will have mercy; he sheweth compassion, because he will shew compassion; and if it had not been something in his own bosom, none had ever obtained mercy.

A third conclusion is, that sure there is not ground to think that God cannot find in his heart to forgive. For Christ says, Mat. xii. 31, *All manner of sin and blasphemy shall be forgiven to you.* No sin is unpardonable except the sin against the Holy Ghost. I cannot determine whether any of you be guilty of the sin against the Holy Ghost, but except it be that, all manner of sin may be forgiven, and this may have influence on us to make us haste unto Jesus Christ.

A fourth conclusion is, that the Lord here acts as God,—he acts like himself. When ye read such instances of grace as I have been naming to you, you may draw this conclusion, that he acts like himself. Isaiah xliii. 24.—*Thou hast bought me no sweet cane with money, neither hast thou filled me with the fat of thy sacrifices; but thou hast made me to serve with thy sins, thou hast wearied me with thine iniquities. I, even I, am he that blotteth out thy transgressions for my own sake, and will not remember thy sins.* I am, says he, like myself; I am he, and as he says elsewhere, beside me there is none. So much for the second thing.

In the third place, I shall show you why the Lord is pleased to give such instances of grace for the encouragement of the greatest of sinners to believe in Christ to life everlasting. And the first reason is, because greater sinners have often-times a secret despair, and Satan is ready to suggest that prayers, exhortations, and means are needless, and that now their case is past cure and remedy, and this is ready to occasion either desperation or obduration, that they think God cannot find in his heart to forgive them.

Second, because though there be not a secret despair, yet

at least there is some extraordinary jealousy, and kind of suspicion, and likening God to themselves; thinking they could never forgive others, if others had done to them what they have done to God, and that therefore God will not forgive them. But let such consider, John vi. 37, *He that cometh to me I will in nowise cast out;* and this is very significant with respect to the doubt of poor sinners ; and the doubt lies here, if I would come he would shut the door upon me. No, says he, *him that cometh I will in nowise cast out :* that is, I will receive him, I will open the door and let him in and make him welcome.

Third, the Lord gives such instances of his grace for the encouragement of great sinners to believe on Christ to life everlasting, because that oftentimes when sense of sin and fear of wrath lights upon the conscience, and when there is a sight of the holiness and justice of God, they are extraordinarily damped ; and this doth so seize upon them that it renders them incapable for any duty, and therefore the Lord has set out such instances of his grace : and the Apostle Paul says expressly, God hath set me up as a pattern to them that should hereafter believe on Christ to life everlasting. God hath set me up as a monument of grace, that to whomsoever the sound of this gospel comes, after me never one needs to despair, for God hath shewed mercy to me, and has set me up as a beacon of mercy, that never one needs question God's good will to pardon them after myself.

In the fourth place, I come to shew you what this believing in Christ is, which these instances of grace do encourage great sinners to ; and there are four things in this believing,—1. Knowledge ; 2. Assent to the truth of the gospel ; 3. Consent to take Christ Jesus, and, 4. Recumbency and resting upon him.

1. I say knowledge. And though knowledge be true, yet

it may be without faith; but there can be no faith without knowledge, and sometimes faith is expressed by knowledge. John xvii.—3. *It is life eternal to know thee, the only true God and Jesus Christ whom thou hast sent.* This believing supposes the knowledge of a man's self, the knowledge of his sin, the knowledge of Jesus Christ in his natures and offices. Take heed to this, for I tell you what it supposeth, that ye may not think it the easiest thing in the world to believe. For the Apostle tells us that no less is requisite to it than the mighty power that raised Christ from the dead. The sinner must know the abominableness of his own heart, know his lost state and condition, know how matters stand betwixt God and him, he must know these peculiar evils to which he is subject, he must know Christ Jesus in his fulness—in his willingness to save sinners, he must know him in what he hath done for sinners, he must know him in his excellency, in his answerableness to him, and all the wants he can be trysted with.

2. Again, in this faith there is an assent to the truths of the gospel, and neither is this saving; for there may be an assent where there is not grace. *The Devils,* it is said, *believe and tremble,* and this is a great evidence of many folks' stupidity then, that they have less faith than the devils themselves have; but there must be an assent to the truths of the gospel, because of the authority of God interposed. Thus a man must believe the Bible and the records God hath given of his Son, and that these things that he presses are absolutely necessary in point of obedience.

3. Again, there is a consent, and this is the heart of this faith. A man must be content to take Jesus Christ. Isaiah xliv. 5.—*One shall say, I am the Lord's, and another shall subscribe with his hand to the Lord, and surname himself by the name of Israel.* And in that consent, there is this, to take him for our portion, that we shall not place our happiness in

the world, that Christ shall get our hearts, that we shall take
his law for our rule, and consent to the strictness of holiness,
and that he shall rule our life and conversation. In a word,
to take Christ for all, and to take all for Christ, and to take
him for ever; and to make an everlasting covenant with him
never to be forgotten. This is, indeed, the nature of faith, and
ye that have given your consent to be the Devil's, must be no
more his, but consent to be Christ's.

4. In this believing, there is also a recumbency and resting
upon him. The man, when he hath declared his consent to
take Christ, when he hath considered the offers of the gospel,
he is content with the whole device, and rests there, and there
he casts all his burden; now he answers all his challenges in
Jesus Christ, now he flies from his own righteousness, and
rests in the righteousness of Christ by faith; he renounceth his
own righteousness, and therefore the Psalmist says, *Enter not
into judgment with thy servant, for in thy sight no flesh can be
justified.* Thus, I have told you what this believing takes in,
the consequent of which is life everlasting. I might consider
it as opposed to eternal death, and as it includes the highest
happiness, and the eternity of it. Everlasting life is a freedom
from the wrath to come. Ye will never be able to dwell with
everlasting fire and devouring burnings; and seeing ye may
have Christ and His fulness, will ye, to please the Devil, forego
your inheritance. What will you be able to say, when you
are brought before the tribunal, ere the general judgment
come, if you refuse to take Christ for your pattern, and believe
on him to life everlasting.

But I come to one use of this doctrine. If it be so that the
Lord hath been pleased to give such instances of grace, for the
encouragement of the worst of sinners to close with Christ, in
order to life everlasting, then you may see that instances of
grace are not given you to encourage you in sin; it is that it

z

may be a pattern to them that believe. The reason is not
that ye should continue hard and secure, and delay your
confession, but that you may believe; for I assure you, the
riches of the grace of God has no tendency at all to make folk
secure, if you consider these three things :—1. That it is the
sweetest cord in the world to draw folk from sin. Some have
such undaunted spirits, that nothing but the greatest revelation
of wrath 'can have influence upon them ; but if there be any
true generosity in a soul, there is no greater encouragement to
close with Christ than the riches of His grace and mercy. 2.
If anything be able to break a rocky heart, it is the riches of
His grace ; and when I come to tell you before you go to
eternity, of the riches of His grace, will ye remain so hard that
your hearts cannot be broken so far as to come to Jesus Christ
for life everlasting. 3. If ye consider that we offer Christ and
salvation upon honourable terms. Christ is as a noble prince,
that such as are content to subject tnemselves to Him, He is
willing to save them. The lion of the tribe of Judah is willing
to make peace, but He will make peace upon honourable
terms. You must forsake sin and Satan, and have no corres-
pondence with them, and we can offer you Christ upon no
other terms than these, that you lay down the weapons of rebellion against Jesus Christ indeed.

A second use of this doctrine. Is it so, indeed, that the
Lord hath been pleased to give such instances of His grace for
encouragement of the worst of sinners to believe on Christ to
life everlasting? Then how sad must their case be that cannot be brought to Christ ; and I am come to tell you this day
that the offers of the grace of God will be amongst the
heaviest of their aggravations at that day. I shall first let
you see what great sinners you are, that you may see your
need of closing with Christ to obtain life everlasting ;

2. let you see your dangerous condition if you believe not on
Christ to life everlasting.

And first, to let you see something of the greatness of your
sin. And now consider I am speaking to you that are under
the sentence of death for the sin of Witchcraft, and not in
suspense as if you were not guilty; for since ye are found
guilty by sound evidence, we do not question it to let you
·see then the great evil of Witchcraft, that ye may see the
great need ye have to believe or close with Christ to life
everlasting. 2. It is the highest act of rebellion against the
God of heaven and earth, you have drawn up with God's
greatest enemy, who is the head of the rebellion of the whole
world, and therefore called rebellion. *Rebellion is as the sin
of Witchcraft.* Besides, it is a great apostacy from God. Ye
were given away to God in baptism, and possibly some of
you have given away yourself to Him, and now you declare
you rue it, and all the deed of gift in baptism you declare
you rue it; and, besides, your sin hath in it an eminent
trampling under foot the blood of Christ, *and if he that sinned
under Moses' law died without mercy, of how much sorer punishment must he be worthy that hath trampled under foot the blood
of the covenant.* You have sinned under the gospel many a
day; you have sitten in the house of God and put on a mask
of religion, and have been deep dissemblers with God and
man. And is not this an eminently grevious trampling
under foot the blood of the covenant. Again, in your sin
there is a renouncing of Christ, heaven, and glory. And
you have declared by your practice, and keeping company
with the Devil, and being his servants, that you care not for
Christ, heaven, or glory. There is your sin! and have ye
not need to close with Christ in order to life everlasting.
Again, you have waged war against Christ, against the saints,
and against the world, and stated yourselves enemies to

Christ, heaven and the world ; for where you had access, you
have wrought mischief upon children, ministers, and others,*
so that ye may be looked upon as enemies to the whole creation except the Devil, with whom ye have associated yourselves; and now, by your obstinacy, you declare you are
content to dwell with the Devil and everlasting burnings ;
and since you are in the Devil's service, what can ye expect
but the Devil's reward, as long as your hearts are hardened
from God's fear.

Second, I come to let you see your danger. Will it not be
sad that your heart should be hardened now when ye are
come to your extremity, and when it might be expected that
messengers of grace should be acceptable to you. We are
come to you, when ye are within a few hours of eternity, to
intreat you, before ye perish for ever, to embrace the offers of
Christ. For, first, ye go aback from the remedy if ye close
not with Christ; for though now conscience be secure, yet it
will rise like a roaring lion at the last ; and though ministers
would weep over you, as if we were seeking from you some
great thing for ourselves, yet ye will stand it out. What will
conscience say when the Devil will be at the gallows † foot
ready to harle you down to hell? and no sooner in hell, but
conscience will say, when God sent his ministers to you, ye
believed the Devil and would not yield to Jesus Christ ; and
what will ye say to conscience then ? When conscience will
say, Now, this is your lodging for ever ; now, eternity !
eternity ! what will ye do through eternity ?—ye are laying a
foundation of challenges through eternity. Another thing that
makes your case dangerous, ye declare you will not be in
Christ's reverence for mercy. I will tell how so, if you will be

* *Vide* Narrative, Confessions, &c.
† This shows that the witches were first hanged and then burned.

in His reverence, why will ye not confess your sin, and renounce the deed of gift to the Devil? Ye declared your denial in the face of courts, and frequently since ye have done. O how dreadful will your condition be if you die in such a case!

I come to the third use of this doctrine. If it be so that the Lord is pleased to give such instances of his grace, then the exhortation runs, that ye should come this day and embrace Jesus Christ. As long as ye are impenitent I can but threaten heavy judgments to you, but if you will confess and repent, and come unto Christ, I come to you with the best news ever were heard. The Apostle Paul, 1 Tim. i. 15, was much taken with these news, " *This is a faithful saying, and worthy of all acceptation,*" says he, " *that Jesus Christ came to save sinners.*" This should be the best news to you. The offer of Christ is come to you this day before the execution. And I will tell you two or three things to confirm you that there is mercy for you if ye improve it aright.

First, God hath proclaimed His name to be merciful and gracious, if you will come to Christ, ye will find that He is merciful. Again, Christ was called a friend of publicans and sinners, when He was in the world, because He showed mercy to all, and never put away any that came to Him; and though He be now in heaven, yet He retains His bowels of mercy still. Again, His name is *Saviour*, and He left His Father's glory and came to the world in the likeness of sinful flesh, to save sinners. Sure then, if He had done great things, He will not refuse any thing to those that come to Him. Again, to let you see He is merciful, He commands His disciples to preach remission of sins in His name, beginning at Jerusalem, the very place where He was crucified; and further, the last words He said, are, " He that believeth shall be saved;" so that ye see there is mercy for you, if ye believe to life everlasting.

I would speak to two things here; 1. Offer you some

motives to close with Christ. 2. Give you some directions.
And, I. For the motives to close with Christ. There are two
notions of faith suitable to your case, the first is a flying to the
city of refuge; and there are two things suitable for you. 1.
You are guilty of blood, you have murdered your own souls
and others, therefore run to the city of refuge. 2. You have
little time, your time is nigh a close, your glass is nigh run,
therefore make haste unto Jesus Christ; it is a pity you should
put it off to the last. If ye had confessed in time ye might
have had the prayers of many of the godly. II. Another
notion of faith suitable to you is coming to the market of grace
and buying. "*Ho! every one that thirsteth, come ye to the waters
and buy.*" Now this is suitable to you, for it is said buy without
money, but ye have spent your money for that which is not
bread, Isaiah lv. 2. "*Wherefore do ye spend money for that
which is not bread, and your labour for that which satisfieth not.*"
What fruit have ye now of those things whereof ye may be
ashamed. How aged are some of you, and now what comfort
have ye in the meetings ye had with Satan, or in your corres-
pondings and actings with him. When ye go to eternity you
will say, alas! what satisfaction have I now in Satan's service!
Another part of this notion is coming, and that supposeth a
term from which, and a term to which ye come: Away then
with sin and Satan, and come to Christ and remember Him.

A second thing is, to show ye the necessity ye have of
closing with Christ. It is most necessary for you to embrace
the Son of God, or ye are undone. It is most necessary for
you, for you will never be able to endure the wrath of God.
Who can dwell with devouring fire? O sins! can ye hold out
against the Almighty? Are ye resolved to fight it with the
Lord? Can ye be able to encounter with the wrath of God,
and enter into the sea of wrath? Can ye endure the wrath of
God world without end? O! therefore, come and close with

Christ. Observe the providence of God that has brought to your hand a discovery of your case, and in telling you ye are in the snare of the Devil, and that hath trysted you with a discovery of the remedy, and now ye are inexcusable ; and if ye perish, ye perish justly. I come now to the directions, and intreat you to look upon them as the last directions ye will have in public in this world for anything we know.

What would ye have us to do? I say that ye ought to confess your sin. Acts xix. 18,—Many of them that had used magical art came and confessed their deeds. It is impossible ye can give a convincing evidence of your repentance, if ye do not confess. But say ye, What need we confess our deeds to men, if we repent between God and us? What needs us trouble the world with confession? we will but lose our name and put a stain upon our posterity and friends. But I answer, when folk have stumbled the Church of God, they have confessed their deeds ; even David himself confessed his sins. Again, it is all the folly in the world not to confess your deeds, because they will be brought out before angels and men ; and even in point of policy ye ought to confess your deeds, for ye are captives in Satan's snare, and ye have lost your wills. Ye should confess, therefore, that God's people may pray for you. If ye would be out of the claws of the Devil, it will take all the prayers you can get.

The second direction is,—To be deeply humbled for your sin. Ye remember what is said of Manasseh, 2 Chron. xxxiii. Chap.,—Manasseh humbled himself greatly. And though your heart were like to break, and your sorrow like to bring you to the grave, it were little wonder ; great sin must have great humiliation : and sure if ever God grant you repentance unto life, and show you mercy, there must be deep humiliation with you.

The third direction is,—You must have more than ordinary

prayer, ye must have more frequent and fervent prayer, ye must be more importunate with God; and if ye ask, what should we pray for? I answer, a discovery of the sinfulness of this sin of Witchcraft. For if ye saw it, it would be in hazard to distract you. Pray for brokenness of heart, and that these hard and rocky hearts of yours may be made hearts of flesh. Pray for pardon of sin. *Blessed is the man that hath his iniquities pardoned and his sins forgiven.* Woe to you! if ye get not your sin pardoned. Pray for a sight of your lost estate, that ye may see yourselves under the sentence of the wrath of God, as well as under the sentence of men. Pray for a discovery of Jesus Christ in His fulness, in His suitableness to you, in His offices, and in His glory; that ye may think shame that ever you thought so little of Him. Pray that ye may not go to the grave with a lie in your right hand. Be importunate, then, since your work is so great, the time so short, and eternity so long: be not asleep or unconcerned, for if ye would put off never so confidently, you will have the colour of hell upon you in that day when ye appear before the tribunal of Christ.

The fourth direction is this,—Renounce your deed of gift to the Devil, and if ye should satisfy the people of God, give a declaration that you are grieved for giving yourself to Satan, and give away yourself to the Son of God from head to foot. This is certainly most suitable for you.

But further, another direction is,—That though ye do renounce your deed of gift to the Devil, and give yourself to Christ, yet do not give yourself to Him only in a formal manner, saying,—I give myself to Jesus Christ; but try the sincerity of your hearts in it, and consider ye must have indignation at yourself for your sin as long as ye live. 2 Cor. ii. 11.,—*Lest Satan should get an advantage of us: for we are not ignorant of his devices.* There will be such indignation in your

bosom, if ye be sincere, that ye will be in danger to take
amends of yourselves. Ye will wonder that ye are not sent
down to the pit ere now. There will be an uncouth fight
between hope and fear in your bosoms.

One word further, and that is,—Delay no longer. Ye have
put it off before and since the sentence ; ye have been much
dealt with, and now it comes within a day of your stepping
into eternity, and we are come to you the day before your death
entreating you to put it off no longer. O be serious ! God
hath exercised a great deal of longsuffering towards you, and
ye have hardened your hearts ; and now we are come to you
in your adversity, at last to desire you to take Jesus Christ,
and now we take God to record that we have offered you Jesus
Christ, and if ye will not take him we are free of your blood,
and Jesus Christ is free of your blood ; and if ye should
endure a thousand hells, ye yourselves are only to be blamed
for the slighting the great salvation.

The End of the Sermon.

APPENDIX No. E.

Some passages which fell out before **and** *at the execution of the seven
persons who were condemned and* **burned** *for Witchcraft on the
Gallowgreen of Paisley.*

First printed at **Edinburgh** *in the year 1698.*

There shall be little added anent what passed at the execution of the seven witches (on Thursday, the 10th of June,
1697 *), because there is no subscribed attestation thereanent ; and the design of the publishers has been to advance

* *Vide* Semple's "History of Renfrewshire," and Mr. David Brown's
Sermon, Appendix No. D.

nothing but what stands warranted by testimonies of known credit beyond contradiction. Yet this much is notour, that when they were going to the stake one of the Lindsays was overheard to say to the other, " Now, brother, it is time that we confess since our keeping it up will serve us no purpose," or the like expression ; to which the other answered, "that they should never do that," &c. And Margaret Lang, before and about execution, let drop at minutes of the Devil's inad-vertence—That when the Devil first appeared she knew him not to be such till afterwards ; that he gave her the insensible marks found on her body; she yielded to engage herself in his service by a covenant ; and besides public meetings, she had been about eighty times in private conferences with him. Being enquired by a near relation of her own anent her being in Bargarran's house tormenting Christian Shaw, she answered in these words, " The Devil having an absolute power and dominion over me, carried my shape whither he would ; " and it is known how she confessed unnatural lust and pro-found hypocrisy, &c., though, truly, it did appear from her concurring mien and circumstances that these things fell from her at seasons, when unnatural ingenuity and the vigour of truth got the start of Satan's manacles. So Agnes Nae-smith, &c., frequently told the minister that their heart and tongue were bound up in such a manner that they could not express what they would ; and sometimes it appeared by ocular inspection of their visages that convulsive damps did seize their heads upon getting out the initial words of any such attempt.

There are two remarkable instances in the case of Katherine Campbell, who was chief instrument and author of the girl's trouble, viz., an eminent minister discoursing before famous witnesses to Katharine, and enquiring if she did not distinctly remember the godly counsels and gracious admonitions which

Christian Shaw, while in a fit, mentioned in the Narrative pages 76, 77, 78, gave her a certain time, and instancing some particulars thereof. Her answer was with heavy groans, "Yes, I remember." But being urged wherefore she would not confess the rest as well as that passage, and finding herself to be gravelled, she began to retract and seemed damped, not being able to extricate herself, answered before-mentioned. This occurred while she was in prison before the trial; and after it she, in presence of several witnesses, did get out these words, "That the doom pronounced on her was just, and that she could not free herself of witchcraft." But upon such attempts she fell down dead, strangely distended, and that six or seven times successively, with a suddenness that was both surprising and convincing to the spectators; at which occasion it was observed that immediately before her falling into these fits, and upon her essaying to speak when there were charges laid home on her natural conscience, her mouth seemed to contract, and she uttered heavy moans; whereupon did follow her convulsions, but after rising out of them she turned to be obstinate and inflexible: and whenever there was any appearance of her being more pliant, the foresaid fits did overtake her.

There is one thing further which does abstruct the credibility of what these confessants averred, viz. :—That there are some others, both men and women in the country, who had confessed, and told the same things before some of the best gentry and others, whose case could proceed no further for want of authority, which in due time will, no doubt, not suffer these Witches to live, whom divine and human laws have so justly ordained to be cut off. Wherefore, till the event of a further discovery, there shall only be added some passages which were omitted in the Narrative, though they be attested by some of the same persons that were witnesses to the other matters that were mentioned therein.

Particularly, the girl declares that in one of her conflicts with the Devil, he told her how a certain minister (for whom she had a special respect) did compile his sermons through the week, what books he chiefly made use of, and several other matters anent his method of study in his closet, that no mortal could know by ordinary means ; by which, no doubt, Satan did partly design (though by a very false argument) to raise the esteem of books above sermons collected out of of them ; concealing in the meantime, both the gift of improving helps, and the blessing promised to the hearer of the Word preached. When the Lady Bargarran received the two pieces of red cloth the girl had torn from one of the Witches' sleeves, as is above narrated, she locked up the same and kept the key ; notwithstanding of which caution, some friends having come to visit the girl, and being desirous to see the foresaid pieces of cloth, she being in one of her fits, laughed, and told that her mother needed not to seek for them in the place where they were locked up—the Witches having taken them away, and laid them in a corner of the cellar ; and accordingly being searched for, they were found in the particular place condescended on. There was another like passage which occurred to a friend, who came in with Bargarran, for soliciting a commission from the council : for he having brought alongst with him those pieces of cloth, and buttoned his pocket on them at night, and put it in security as he thought ; behold they are a-missing in the morning ! But after search, are found in a good distance from the pocket, though none visible had been in the room to open it and carry them off. Finally, this girl did, in discourse, discover a great sagacity, yet accompanied with extraordinary modesty ; and among other instances, she did observe the doors and windows open and **shut** again, upon the Witches' entry thereat. There was at no time such a number of them about her as the room might not very well contain, with the visible persons that were present therein. She observed them to shift their place with great agility, when any other came into it, or attacked upon her pointing to them. And she often averred from the instance of the spirit that spoke to her above her head, told their names, and gave her other means of discovering of them, &c. That Satan does often contrive their ruin, by the most undiscernable methods he **can,** because an open deed would scar others to undertake with so faithless a master, &c.

APPENDIX No. F.

Hugo Arnot, Esq., Advocate, author of a Collection and Abridgement of Celebrated Criminal Trials in Scotland, from A.D. 1536 to 1784, calls the title of this trial in 1697, Impostor of Bargarran.* As he takes the opposite side of the subject, I think it fair to give it a place here.

He says, "An impostor appeared in the character of a person tormented by Witches, Christian Shaw, daughter of John Shaw of Bargarran, a gentleman of some note in the county of Renfrew. She is said to have been but eleven years of age: and although it is probable that hysterical affections may in

---

* I think it is proper to apprise the reader from what sources Mr. Arnot got his information concerning Christian Shaw. This I am enabled to do very easy, for Mr. Arnot always gives his authorities in notes at the foot of the page, and the authorities he quotes for the account of this trial are,— "True narrative of the sufferings and relief of a young girl. Edinburgh, printed by James Watson, 1698," and "Records of Privy Council, January 19th, March 9th, and April 5th. 1697."

part have occasioned her rhapsodies to proceed from real illusion, as well as accounted for the contortions which agitated her body, yet she seems to have displayed an artifice above her years, an address superior to her situation, and to have been aided by accomplices, which dulness of apprehension, or violence of prejudice, forbade the bystanders to discover.

"This actress was abundantly pert and lively; and her challenging one of the house-maids for drinking, perhaps for stealing, a little milk, which drew on her an angry retort, was the simple prelude to a complicated and wonderful scene of artifice and delusion,—of fanaticism and barbarity.

"In the month of August, 1696,* within a few days after her quarrel with the house-maid, the girl was seized with hysterical convulsions, which in repeated fits displayed that variety of symptoms which characterise this capricious disease. To these, other appearances were speedily added, which could only be attributed to supernatural influence, or to fraud and imposition. She put out of her mouth quantities of egg-shells, or orange-pill, feathers of wild, and bones of tame fowl, hair of various colours, hot coal cinders, straws, crooked pins, &c.†

"Having by these sensible objects impressed the public with the most complete and fearful conviction of her being grievously vexed with a devil,‡ she found herself capable to command the implicit assent of the spectators in matters that were repugnant to the evidence of their own senses. For this purpose she fell upon the device of seeming to possess the faculties of seeing and hearing, in a manner opposite to that of the rest of mankind. She would address some invisible beings as if actually present; at other times, in her conversation with those invisible beings, she would rail at them for telling her

---

* Page 71.   † Pages 73, 74, &c.   ‡ Mat. xv. 22.

that persons actually present were in the room; protesting that she did not see them, yet at the same time minutely describing their dress. For instance, she spoke as follows to the chief of her alledged tormentors, Katharine Campbell, with whom she had the quarrel, and who, to use the language of those times, was not discernibly present : ' Thou sittest with a stick in thy hand to put into my mouth, but through God's strength thou shalt not get leave. Thou art permitted to torment me, but I trust in God thou shalt never get my life.* I'll let thee see, Katie, there is no repentance in hell. O what ailed thee to be a witch ! Thou sayest it is but three nights since thou wast a witch. O, if thou wouldest repent, it may be God might give thee repentance, if thou wouldest seek it and con- fess : if thou would desire me, I would do what I could, for the Devil is an ill master to serve,' &c., &c.† After that she took up her Bible, read passages and expounded them, and, upon one's offering to take it from her, she shrieked horridly, exclaiming, ' She would keep her Bible in spite of all the devils in hell !'‡ Then she fought, and knocked, and writhed herself, as if struggling with some invisible tormentor. When the sheriff depute of the county, accompanied by a macer of justiciary, came to apprehend some of the persons whom her diabolical malice had accused, and were actually in her presence, she addressed an imaginary and invisible correspon- dent thus : ' Is the sheriff come? Is he near me?' (Then stretching forth her hand, as if to grope, and the sheriff putting his hand into hers, she proceeded) ' I cannot feel the sheriff. How can he be present here? or how can I have him by the hand, as thou sayest, seeing I feel it not? Thou sayest he has brown coloured clothes, and red plush breeches with black

---

stripes, flowered muslin cravat, and an embroidered sword
belt. Thou sayest there is an old grey haired man with him,
having a ring upon his hand; but I can neither see nor feel
any of them. What, are they come to apprehend the gentlewoman? Is this their errand indeed?'*

"These reiterated and awful exercises of the dominion of
Satan (for such they were universally deemed), impressed all
ranks with amazement and terror. The clergy, as was their
duty, were the foremost to embrace the cause of a disciple
that was engaged in more than spiritual warfare with the
grand enemy. Clergymen, by rotation, attended the afflicted
damsel to assist the minister of the parish, the family of
Bargarran, and other pious Christians in the expiatory offices
of fasting and prayer. A public fast was ordained by authority of the presbytery. Three popular clergymen successively harangued the trembling audience; and one of them
chose for his theme this awful text, 'Woe to the inhabitants
of the earth and sea, for the Devil is come down unto you,
having great wrath, because he knoweth that he hath but a
short time. And when the dragon saw that he was cast down
unto the earth, he persecuted the woman.' And the prayers
and exhortations of the Church were speedily seconded with
the weight of the secular arm."

---

* Pages 116 and 117.

APPENDIX No. G.

Written by Dr. Walter Young, *Minister of Erskine,* M.A., F.R.S., *Edinburgh, in* 1792, *extracted from his Statistical Account of the Parish of Erskine.*

"One of the last trials for Witchcraft which happened in Scotland, had its origin in this parish in 1696-7. The person supposed to have been bewitched, or tormented by the agency of evil spirits, or of those who were in compact with them, was Christian Shaw, daughter of John Shaw of Bargarran, then about 11 years of age. A short account of this trial may be seen in Arnot's Collection of Criminal Trials. *

"Three men and four women were condemned to death, as guilty of the crime of Witchcraft, and were executed at Paisley. † A particular account or journal of the extraordinary circumstances of this case was drawn up at the time when it happened; every paragraph of which is affirmed to have been originally subscribed by witnesses, among whom we find the names of almost all the noblemen and gentlemen, and many of the ministers of the neighbourhood. The narrative was afterwards printed ‡ without these subscriptions, along with a very pious and decently written preface, by the publisher. There were subjoined to it the attestations of a physician and surgeon, the judicial confessions of some of the persons accused of Witchcraft, and an abstract of the pleadings of the advocates on the part of the crown, and of their charge

---

* All that Mr. Arnot says about this trial is printed in this volume.

† They were first hanged for a few minutes, and then cut down and put into a fire prepared for them, into which a barrel of tar was put in order to consume them more quickly.

‡ In the year 1698, by James Watson, Edinburgh, and entitled, "True Narrative of the sufferings and relief of a young girl, &c."

to the jury. These last, in their reasonings upon the nature of the evidence, and the credibility of the facts, and in the answers to objections, discover much learning and ability. A few copies of the original publication are still extant, and a new edition of it was, a few years ago, printed in Paisley. * It may furnish ample matter of speculation to those whose object it is to trace the progress and variation of manners and opinions among men. The subsequent history of this lady is, however, more interesting to the political inquirer.

" Having acquired a remarkable dexterity in spinning fine yarn, she conceived the idea of manufacturing it into thread. Her first attempts in this way were necessarily on a small scale. She executed almost every part of the process with her own hands, and bleached her materials on a large slate placed in one of the windows of the house. She succeeded, however, so well in these essays as to have sufficient encouragement to go on, and to take the assistance of her younger sisters and neighbours. The then Lady Blantyre carried a parcel of her thread to Bath, and disposed of it advantageously to some manufacturers of lace ; and this was, probably, the first thread made in Scotland that had crossed the Tweed. About this time, a person who was connected with the family, happening to be in Holland, found means to learn the secrets of the thread manufacture, which was then carried on to great extent in that country, particularly the art of sorting and numbering the threads of different sizes, and packing them up for sale, and the construction and management of the twisting and twining machines. This knowledge he communicated on his return to his friends in Bargarran, and by means of it, they were enabled to conduct their manufacture with more regularity

---

* By Alexander Weir in 1775.

and to a greater extent. The young women in the neighbourhood were taught to spin fine yarn, twining mills were erected,
correspondencies were established, and a profitable business
was carried on. Bargarran thread became extensively known,
and, being ascertained by a stamp, bore a good price. From
the instructions of the family of Bargarran, a few families in
the neighbourhood engaged in the same business, and continued in it for a number of years. It was not to be expected,
however, that a manufacture of that kind could be confined to
so small a district, or would be allowed to remain in so few
hands for a great length of time. The secrets of the business
were gradually divulged by apprentices and assistants. A Mr.
Pollock in Paisley availed himself of these communications,
and laid the foundation of the well established manufacture of
thread, which has ever since been carried on in that town.
From that time the women in this neighbourhood have continued to practise the spinning of fine yarn, which they
disposed of to the Paisley manufacturers."

APPENDIX No. H.

Christian Shaw was married to a Mr. Miller, the parish
minister of Kilmaurs, about the year 1718. The following
quotation from Mr. Alex. Millar's statistical account of the
Parish of Kilmaurs, speaks of Christian Shaw's husband. " A
disposition to secede from the established church hath long
subsisted among the Inhabitants of Kilmaurs : and this
disposition was first excited by the following circumstance.
About the year 1712, Mr. Hugh Thomson, then minister of
this parish, demitted upon the expectation of being called to
Stewarton, but was somehow disappointed ; and either his

pride would not permit him to solicit a re-admission, or a majority of the people, disobliged with his giving them up, refused it. He retired to a small property of his own in the parish, and on Sabbaths preached sometimes at his own fireside, and sometimes from a tent in the fields, to as many of his friends as would hear him. Five or six years elapsed before another minister was elected ; during which time Mr. Thomson had frequent opportunities of reconciling himself to many of his former congregation. After Mr. Miller was chosen and ordained, Mr. Thomson still continued to preach in his own barn, or in the fields, to as many as were willing to hear him. Inconstancy, which always attends the multitude, disposed some to go one way and some another ; directed by humour, local convenience, or the influence of one upon another, they attended sometimes Mr. Miller, at other times Mr. Thomson.

Christian Shaw's husband came to pay his friends a visit at Bargarran, sometime before the year 1725, when he took badly and died there, and was buried in Erskine Church. He was universally lamented by his parishioners, great numbers of whom attended his funeral. After his death Christian Shaw and her family came and resided in Bargarran. Mr. Semple in his History of Renfrew, says,— "About the year 1725, the making of white stitching thread was introduced into the west country by Mrs. Millar of Bargarran, who, very much to her own honour, imported a twist or thread miln, and other necessary utensils from Holland, and carried on a small manufacture in her own family." The Editor saw on the 10th May, 1809, a William Jamieson, an old man, who told him that he had wrought three years and a half on the original thread miln at Bargarran, that he came to Bargarran in the year 1743, and at that time none of the family of Bargarran was alive but Mrs. Shaw, Jean Shaw, (the old sister,) and Mr. Fergusson her husband, who was factor to Lord Blantyre.

APPENDIX No. I.

Mr. Robert Wodrow, Minister at Eastwood, in his History of the Sufferings of the Church of Scotland, from the Restoration to the Revolution, vol. 1, Appendix to Book 2nd No. 11th, in William Sutherland's Declaration and Examination, there is mention made of a person being executed for a Witch about the year 1661. William Sutherland says,—" I being come of poor parents in Strathnaver, (the wildest part of the north Highlands) who were not able to keep me, I was hired with a master who sent me to bring back a horse that Colonel Morgan's party had taken from him ; which party I followed till the enemy fell betwixt me and home, and being afraid to go back, and having a desire to learn the Lowland tongue, I came alongst in a sad condition with the said party, till I came to Spey-side, where I herded cattle for a year in the Parish of Boharm, at a place called the New Kirk ; from thence I came to the Parish of Fyvie in Buchan, where I herded cattle for another year ; from that place I came to the Bridge of Stirling, where I followed the same employment for a third year, which was the year the King came home, (1660) ; and from thence I came to Paisley, where, after herding cattle a fourth year, I fell in extreme want, and that by the reason, the master whom I served being owing to one of the Bailies, called John Weres, the Bailie seized upon my master's goods, so that he ran away, and I lost my fee, and was engaged by the counsel of some honest men, from that scripture,—*Suffer not a Witch to live*, to execute a Witch, and to cleanse chimney-heads, whereby I gained somewhat for livelihood; and having a mind to learn to read, I bought a question book, but finding the people there to fear at my company, so that none would give me a lesson, I came from Paisley to Irvine, about five years since," &c., that is five years before 1666, which makes it to be 1661 the time he was in Paisley.

Mr. Burns, in the Chronological part of his English Dictionary, under the article Paisley, says,—" That five women were burned there for Witchcraft, anno 1667." I suppose this a mistake, as I can find no historical account for this. Hugo Arnot, Esq., says,—" For some time after the Restoration, the records of Privy Council are in a manner engrossed with commissions to take trial of Witches. There is an instance of the Council, at one sederunt, granting fourteen separate commissions to take trial of Witches. Records of Privy Council, November 7, 1661, January 23, 1662." I intend at some future period to notice this of Mr. Burns, and what Mr. Semple says concerning the burning of the Witches on the Gallowgreen of Paisley, in his History of Renfrewshire.

APPENDIX No. K.

*Having shewn how the laws and practice of this country, concern-
ing Witchcraft, stood before A. D. 1736, it is certainly
necessary to let the Public see what the law is at present on
Witchcraft.*

ANNO NONO.

GEORGII II. Regis. 1736.

CAP. V.

An Act to repeal the statute made in the first year of the Reign of King
James the first, intituled, *An Act against Conjuration, Witchcraft,
and dealing with evil and wicked Spirits,* except so much thereof
as repeals an Act of the fifth year of the Reign of Queen Elizabeth,
Against Conjurations, Inchantments, and Witchcrafts, and to
repeal an Act passed in the Parliament of Scotland in the ninth
Parliament of Queen Mary, intituled, *Anentis Witchcrafts,* and for
punishing such persons as pretend to exercise or use any kind of
Witchcraft, Sorcery, Inchantment, or Conjuration.

Be it enacted by the King's most Excellent Majesty, by and
with the advice and consent of the Lords, spiritual and
temporal, and Commons, in this present Parliament assembled,
and by the authority of the same, that the statute made in the
first year of the Reign of King James the first, intituled, *An
Act against Conjuration, Witchcraft, and dealing with evil and
wicked Spirits,* shall, from the twenty-fourth day of June next,
be repealed and utterly void and of none effect (except so
much thereof as repeals the statute made in the fifth year of
the Reign of Queen Elizabeth, intituled, *An Act against Conjurations, Inchantments, and Witchcrafts.)*

II. And be it further enacted by the authority foresaid, that

from and after the said twenty-fourth day of June, the Act
passed in the Parliament of Scotland in the ninth Parliament
of Queen Mary, intituled, *Anentis Witchcrafts*, shall be and is
hereby repealed.

III. And be it further enacted, that from and after the said
twenty-fourth day of June, no Prosecution, Suit, or Proceeding,
shall be commenced or carried on against any person or persons for Witchcraft, Sorcery, Inchantments, or Conjuration, or
for charging another with any such offence, in any Court
whatsoever in *Great Britain*.

IV. And for the more effectual preventing and punishing
any pretences to such arts or powers as are beforementioned,
whereby ignorant persons are frequently deluded and de-
frauded; be it further enacted by the anthority aforesaid, that
if any person shall, from and after the said twenty-fourth day
of June, pretend to exercise or use any kind of Witchcraft,
Sorcery, Inchantment, or Conjuration, or undertake to tell
fortunes, or pretend from his or her skill or knowledge in any
ocult or crafty science to discover where or in what manner
any Goods or Chattels, supposed to have been stolen or lost,
may be found; every person so offending, being thereof
lawfully convicted on indictment or information in that part of
Great Britain called *England*, or on indictment or libel in that
part of *Great Britain* called *Scotland*, shall for every such
offence suffer imprisonment by the space of one whole year
without Bail or Main-prize, and once in every quarter of the
said year, in some market Town of the proper County, upon
the market day, there stand openly on the Pillory for the space
of one hour, and also shall (if the Court by which such judgment shall be given, shall think fit) be obliged to give sureties
for his or her good behaviour, in such sum, and for such time,
as the said Court shall judge proper, according to the circum-

stances of the offence, and in such case shall be further imprisoned until such sureties be given.

APPENDIX No. L.

Hugo Arnot, Esq., in his collection of celebrated Criminal Trials in Scotland, when speaking of the above Act, says,— "Locke had written upon government, Fletcher had been a patriot statesman, Bolingbroke had been a minister in the augustan age of Queen Anne, ere this system of legal murder and torture was abolished. This was an honour which the tardy humanity of their countrymen reserved, almost to the middle of the present century,* for Mr. Conduit, Alderman Heathcote, and Mr. Crosse. These gentlemen brought a bill into the House of Commons, which was passed into a law, repealing the former statutes against witchcraft, Scots as well as English, and discharging prosecutions for that crime, or for accusing others of that offence. On the enactment of this statute vanished all those imaginary powers, so absurdly attributed to women oppressed with age and poverty.

"While we reflect upon the blind and barbarous superstition of our ancestors,—while we bestow the tribute of applause on those humane and liberal senators who introduced this law, we cannot help lamenting that a sect among us looks upon the abolition of the penal statutes against witchcraft not only as an evil, but a sin. The seceders published an act of their associate presbytery at Edinburgh, A.D. 1743. This act† was reprinted at Glasgow so late as the year 1766. In it there

* Eighteenth Century.
† Act for renewing the Covenants, p. 26, 27, 34.

C 2

is contained *the annual confession of sins,* which to this day they
read from the pulpit.‡ Among the sins national and personal
there confessed, are the Act of Queen Anne's Parliament for
tolerating the Episcopal religion in Scotland, the Act for ad-
journing the Court of Session during the Christmas holidays ;
as also the penal statutes against Witches have been repealed
by parliament, contrary to the express law of God.—(Exod.
xxii. 18.) The seceders comprehend a very large body of the
populace in Scotland."

APPENDIX No. M.

*Having got my hands on an old folio volume of acts of the General
Assembly of the Kirk of Scotland, which were passed between
the years 1639, and 1649. The following extracts are curious.*

I see in the year 1640, the General Assembly passed an
Act against Witches and Charmers, as follows : "The Assembly
ordaines all Ministers within the kingdome, carefully to take
notice of Charmers, Witches, and all such abusers of the
people, and to urge the Acts of Parliament to be executed
against them ; and that the Commissioners from the Assembly
to the Parliament, shall recommend to the said supreme
judicatory, the care of the execution of the lawes against such
persons in the most behoovefull way." Also, 5th Aug. 1642,
"The Assembly doe therefore ordain all Presbyteries to give
to the Justice, the names of the Adulterers, incestuous persons,
Witches, and Sorcerers, and others, guilty of such grosse and
fearfull sins within their bounds, that they may be processed
and punished according to the Laws of this kingdome : and

that the Presbyteries and Synods be carefull herein, as they will answer to the General Assemblies," &c. Also Sess. ult. Aug. 19, 1643. I find overtures anent Witchcraft, and Charming, &c., which occupy a page and a half, and beginning with, "the abundance and increase of the sin of Witchcraft, in all the sorts and degrees of it in this time of Reformation, is to be taken to heart by this reverend Assembly, who would to that end consider," &c., and ending with, "The sins aforesaid of Witchcraft, Charming, and consulting with Witches, or Charmers, or such like wickedness, may be tried, restrained, and condignely censured and punished ecclesiastically and civally;" and in the year 1649 there is a "Commission for a conference of Ministers, Lawyers, and Physitians, concerning the tryal and punishment of Witchcraft, Charming, and Consulting," and runs thus :—"The General Assembly taking to their serious consideration the growth of the sins of Witchcraft, Charming, and Consulting, notwithstanding the frequent recommendations for restraining thereof ; and remembering that the General Assembly, 1647, did propose a good way for the tryal and punishment of these sinnes, by appointing conferances with some Ministers, Lawyers, and Physitians, in that matter which hath never yet taken effect ; therefore the Assembly doth appoint Masters Robert Dowglas, Robert Blair, Mungo Law, James Hamilton, John Smith, Robert Traill, George Leslie, John Hamilton, John Duncan, Samuel Rutherfoord, James Wood, John Leviston, James Guthrie, Andro Cant, David Calderwood, John Moncrieff, Frederick Carmichael, James Durhame, Patrick Gillespie, Robert Ker, Ephraim Melville, Ministers ; * to consider seriously of that matter, and to

---

* See the Scots Worthies for an account of these Ministers.

consult and advise therein amongst themselves, as also with
Sir Archibald Johnston of Wariston, Clerk Register; Mr.
Thomas Nicolson, His Majesties Advocate; Mr. Alex.
Peirson, one of the ordinary Lords of Session; Sir Lewes
Stewart, Mr. Alex. Colvill, and Mr. James Robertson,
Justice Deputes; Messrs. Rodger Mowet, John Gilmoir,
and John Nisbet, Lawyers; and with Doctors Sibbald,
Cunninghame, and Purves, Physitians; severally or together
as occasion shall offer, and the Assembly earnestly requests
and confidently expects from these learned and judicious
Lawyers and Physitians before-named, their best endeavours
and concurrence with their brethren of the Ministrie for
advise and counsell herein, and for conference in said
matter; and Ordaine the said brethren to make report of
the result of their consultations and conferences from time
to time as they make any considerable progresse to the
Commission for publick affaires, and the said Commission
shall make report to the next Generall Assembly."

APPENDIX No. N.

*Upon Sunday the 28th of March, 1697, after Sermon, intimation
was made by* Mr. THOMAS BLACKWELL, *the Minister, of a
fast to be kept by the Congregation of Paisley the ensuing
Wednesday, the Causes whereof are below.*

My friends, we have been preaching of Christ to you, we
are now about to speak of the Devil to you,—the greatest
enemy that our Lord and His kingdom hath in the world.
The thing I am about to intimate to you is this,—The
members of the Presbytery having taken to their consideration how much Satan doth rage in these bounds, and which

is indeed very lamentable in our bounds, and in ours only. They have thought fit to appoint a day of fasting and humiliation, that so He who is the lion of the tribe of Judah, may appear with power against him who is the angel of the bottomless pit, and throw him down, who is now come out in great wrath; O! that it may be because his time is short.

As to the causes of the fast, I shall but hint a few things to you, the thing being so well known in the bounds, the Presbytery did not think it needful to be any way large or formal in drawing up of causes; however, I may say in the first place, the causes of our preceding fast * remain yet not sufficiently mourned over, so that though we had no other causes but these, we have ground to observe more fasts than one or two.

But yet a little more close to the purpose. First, Satan is greatly raging in our bounds; he hath in all probability enjoyed a long and old stock of subjects, even among the hearers of the Gospel; it may be, some of them are hearing me just now, conscience being best judge in that matter, and now he hath come that length, no doubt, being permitted of God, that his power is not only to be perceived in keeping many hearts from closing with Christ, but also in tormenting a family extraordinary in our bounds, so that it is known to be the Devil and his instruments, and none else, therefore, Satan who is raging, and who hath gotten many in all probability to devote themselves soul and body to him.

*   *   *   *   *

Again, 2dly, There is the impenitency and obstinacy of

---

* This was at least the second fast kept on Christian Shaw's account.

persons supposed upon many accounts truly to be guilty, their continuing obstinate and impenitent, and refusing to confess guilt in that matter, that God who hath the power of conscience, by the power of His Spirit, in the use of other lawful means for the finding out of the truth, may make these means effectual, and may win in upon their consciences to make them confess guilt.

3dly, The great affliction of that poor child (Christian Shaw,) and that family in whom she is so nearly interested, none of us knows her affliction, and her father's, so as it is in itself. It is easy to look upon one so tormented as she is, be what it would be if we were so tormented ourselves, or yet any one in our family. We would remember them that are in bonds as bound with them, and therefore our petitions have a special respect to them of that family, that is set up as a beacon on the top of a mountain for all to take warning.

Again, in the fourth place, Another reason is, the mysteriousness and difficulty of the process of Witchcraft, so that it is the process of all others, that requires most prudence, solidity, and several other things, to name which, many of you would not understand me; but in a word, it requires much of the presence of the Spirit of God to guide the Judges, and work upon the consciences of the panels, that so the truth may be found out, and judgment accordingly execute; thus we offer several reasons why it is necessary for us to observe a day of fasting and humiliation before God.

And now, my friends, all I add is this;—in the first place, I am sure ministers, and I am sure the godly are called to be very importunate with God in this matter. Would ye know, my friends, why we preach in vain to them that have devoted themselves to the Devil; it is that that makes the Gospel so barren, and who knows but in this congregation there be many who have these many years hence been under vows to Satan, and as for you that are the people of God, ye pray in vain for the success of the Gospel to them, for till once they be brought to see the evil of their sin, and to be convinced of the evil thereof, and to lothe themselves upon account of the same, neither will the Gospel, nor your prayers do them any good; so it is the ministers' and the people of God's duty, and interest, not only to pray that God would find out the guilty among these that are apprehended, but that God would discover all others that are guilty, and who are not apprehended, that the kingdom of Christ may run and be glorified, and the kingdom of Satan destroyed.

FINIS.

APPENDIX.

BY DAVID SEMPLE, F.S.A.

THE names of the persons accused, convicted, and afterwards "worrit" and burnt for the crime of witchcraft on the Gallowgreen of Paisley on 10th June, 1697, are not very distinctly stated. Three men and four women were convicted, and two of these men and the four women were executed, and the other man committed suicide in Renfrew Prison on 21st May previously. The greater number of the names mentioned in the foregoing pages will be found in the Poll Tax Rolls for Renfrewshire for the year 1695,* which corroborate and confirm the authenticity of both records. The names of the seven convicted persons would seem from the foregoing history to have been,—1st, John Lindsay; 2nd, James Lindsay; 3rd, John Reid; 4th, Catherine Campbell; 5th, Margaret Lang; 6th, Margaret Fulton, Dumbarton; and, 7th, Agnes Naismith. From the Poll Tax Rolls it would appear that John Lindsay was a cottar in Barloch of Bargarren; James Lindsay a cottar in Billboe, in Orbistoune's lands of Erskine; Margaret Lang, the wife of William Semple, cottar in Cartympen, also in Orbistoune's lands, all in the parish of Erskine; John Reid was a smith in the Laird of Hapland's lands,

---

* [These Poll Tax Rolls were published in the Glasgow *Herald* on several dates during 1864. They contain the names of all male persons in the county in 1695, with their calling and residence, the maiden names of their wives, children, and servants, &c. These Records, which the compiler sent to several libraries in Scotland, are exceedingly interesting and valuable.—*Ed.*]

in the parish of Inchinnan; Catherine Campbell, Margaret
Fulton, and Agnes Naismith are not to be found in
these Rolls, from the first probably having become a servant
to the Laird of Bargarren at Whitsunday 1696, the second
being resident in Dumbarton, and the third perhaps in
the parish of Kilpatrick, on the opposite side of the River
Clyde from Bargarren. A few excerpts from these authentic
Poll Rolls made up a year before the trial are here given to
show the status of the persons who were brought before the
Commission for a crime that really could not have any existence.

ERSKINE PARISH.

John Shaw and Christian Shaw, page 71 ; *Jean Shaw, page*
209.

Poll Tax Rolls, page 99.

John Shaw, of Barrgarrane, 300lib val., 9lib 6sh ;
Christian M'Gilchrist, spouse, 6sh ; Jo., James,
Christian,* Elez., and Jean, childreine, each 6sh ;
John Bartholemew and Robert Mountgomrie,
servants, each 20lib fie, 10sh ; Ro. Blackwood,
herd, 7lib fie, 3sh 6d ; Elez. Orr, Cat. Dean, and
Agnas M'Cashlane, servants, each 20mks. fie,
6s 8d,   -   -   -   -   -   -   -   -15   1   6

John Lindsay, page 97.

Poll Tax Rolls, page 99.

John Lindsay,† in Barloch, 40mks. val., 5sh 4d ;
Margaret Patiesoune, spouse, 6sh ; Margt. M'Inlay,
servant, 8lib fie, 4sh ; Sara Clerk, in hervest 5lib
fie, 2sh 6d,   :   -   -   -   -   -   - 1   9   10

---

* Christian Shaw. The impostor of Bargarran, who pretended she was bewitched,
and made credulous ministers believe her rhapsodies.

† John Lindsay, a cottar on the lands of Bargarran, who must have been seen every
other day by Christian Shaw.

Pinched **Maggy,** *page* 97 ; *Margaret L———,* *page* 101 : *Margt. Lang, 104 ; Martha Semple, 104.*

Poll Tax Rolls, page 103.

William Semple, in Cartympen, cottar, 6sh ; * Margt. Lang, spouse, 6sh ; Mertha, his daur., 6sh ; Elspe Glasfoord, sert., 8lib fie, 4sh, - - - - 1 8 0

INCHINNAN PARISH.

" *Grandmother's house at Northbar,*" *page* 75 ; *Lady Northbar, page* 104.

Poll Tax Rolls, page 95.

Aikine, Lady Northbarr,† 4lib **6sh as** her pole, **the** third pt. of her husband's **pole, being** 500lib val.

Alexander Anderson, page 78.

Poll Tax Rolls, page 94.

Alexander Andersoune, cotter,‡ - - - - 0 6 0

Margaret Fulton, **page** 100.

Poll Tax Rolls, page 95.

John Gemmell, cordoner, 12sh trade and pole ; Margaret Fulltoune, spouse, 6sh,§ - - - 0 18 0

John Reid, Smith, page 132.

Poll Tax Rolls, page 97.

John Reid,‖ smith, 12sh ; Jennet Hendersoune, spouse, 6sh, - - - - - - - 0 18 0

---

* Margaret Lang was the spouse of a cottar in Cartympen, which was situated a little to the south of the present parochial school of Erskine, and on the north side of the new road leading to Greenock. She was a midwife, an intelligent woman, endowed with abilities at least equal, if not surpassing, those of her superstitious accusers and judges.

† Mrs. M'Gilchrist, maternal grandmother of Christian Shaw.

‡ Residing on the lands of Southbar, in the immediate vicinity of Bargarren.

§ A shoemaker residing on the lands of Northbar, in the neighbourhood of Bargarren.

‖ This unfortunate person committed suicide in Renfrew prison on 21st May, 1697.

4

APPENDIX.

PAISLEY PARISH.

John White, apothecary, page 73.

Poll Tax Rolls, page 59.

John Whyte,* apothecarie, 12lib 6sh Jean Johnstoun,
his spouse, 6sh ; Robert, John, and Agnes Whytes,
his children, each 6sh ; Jean Young, sert., 2lib fee,
1sh, and 6sh general pole, - - - - -13 17 6

Dr. Johnstone, page 73.

Poll Tax Rolls, page 60.

Doctor John Johnstoune,† 12lib 6sh ; Helen Little,
spouse, 6sh ; John, Christian, Helen, and Elizabeth Johnstounes, children, each 6sh ; Elizabeth
McKie and Margaret Johnstoune, servants, each
16lib 6sh 8d fee, 6sh 8d, - : - - -15 1 4

John Campbell, Surgeon.

Poll Tax Rolls, page 61.

John Campbell,‡ appothecarie, 12lib 6sh ; Margaret
Walkinshaw, spouse, 6sh; Mary Houstoune, servt.,
20 merks fie 6sh 8d; Petter Pettersoune and Wm.
Park, prentices, each 9sh ; Jennet Campbell, his
daughter, 6sh, - - - - - - 14 2 8

---

* John Whyte was a near relation of the Shaws, and resided on the west side of
St. Mirin Wynd, Paisley, where the Old Bank of Scotland had since been erected. His
house was burned in 1733 in the great fire of that year. The bank has now been taken
down.

† He resided in Smithhills Street, Paisley, and had a good medical practice.

‡ He resided and carried on business in the house that had been erected by Sir James
Sempill of Belltrees, Sheriff of Renfrewshire, at the north east angle of High Street
and St. Mirin Wynd in which Robert Sempill, born in 1599, author of "Habbie
Simpson," had been brought up. John Campbell was afterwards elected a bailie of
Paisley in 1703 and 1706. A fire occurred in the laboratory in 1733, and burned
both sides of St. Mirin Wynd, and parts of High Street, the Cross, and Causeyside.

Ministers in the County of Renfrew mentioned in the foregoing history.

William Fleming, Innerkip, page 132.

Poll Tax Roll, page 195.

Mr. William Fleming, minister of Innerkippe, his own pole, 3lib 6sh; Agnas Aird, his wife, 6sh; John M'Latchie, servand, 16 merks fie, 11sh 4d; Jennet Miller, 20 mks. fie, 12sh 8d; Anna Tam, 6lib fie, and bounties, 9sh, - - - - - 5 5 0

James Hutchison, Kilalan, page 103.

Poll Tax Rolls, page 114.

Mr. James Hutchesoune, minister, 3lib 6sh; Margt. Gillhugie, spouse, 6sh; Christian, his daur., 6sh; Wm. King, sert., 16lib fie, 8sh; Ann Reid, sert., 12lib fie, 12sh; Jean Hendersoune, sert., 12lib fie, 12sh, - - - - - - - - 5 16 0

James Stirling, Kilbarchan, page 126.

Poll Tax Rolls, page 126.

Mr. James Stirling, minister, 3lib. 6sh; Margt. Dunloap, his spouse, 6sh; Jean and Bessie Stirlings, childreine, each 6sh; James Wayllie, servant, 8lib fie, 4sh; Jennet Murdoch, sert., 14lib fie, 7sh, - - - - - - - - 5 7 0

James Brisbane, Kilmalcolm, page 126.

Poll Tax Rolls, page 155.

Mr. James Birsbane, minr., 3lib. 6sh; Chr. Sheirhun his wife, 6sh; Mar. Chambers and Marion Daviesoune, each 16lib fie, 8sh. each, and 6sh gnall. pole; and   Lang, sert., 10lib fie, 5sh, and gnall. pole 6sh, - - - - - 5 1 0

David Brown, Neilston, page 180.

Poll Tax Rolls, page 35.

Mr. David Broune, minr., 3lib. 6sh, for himself ;
Catharine Blackwall, spouse, 6sh ; Elez., Jennet,
and Catha., childreine, each 6sh ; Will. Sclaitter,
servant, 14lib fie, 7sh; Margt. Gilmour, and
Barbara Airstounes, servants, each 13lib fie per
ann., 7 6sh 6d; and Hugh Fulltoune, schoolmaster,
6sh, - - - - - - - - - 6 4 0

Thomas Blackwell, Paisley, page 136.

Poll Tax Roll, page 60.

Mr. Thomas Blackwall, † minister, 3lib 6sh ; Agnes
Admount, servitrix, 12lib fee, 12sh, - - - 3 18 0

Andrew Turner, Erskine, page 103.

Robert Taylor, Houston, page 126.

Patrick Simpson, Renfrew, page 103.

The Erskine and Houston ministers names are not in
the Poll Rolls; the Roll of the Royal Burgh of Renfrew
was not included in the County Roll, and cannot now be
found.

The foregoing assessments are Scots money.

Scots Money	Sterling Money.
1sh. is	£0 0 1
1 mark, 13/4, is	0 1 1½
1 lib or pound, is	0 1 8

* This is the minister who preached a sermon to the six witches at Paisley on
Wednesday, 9th June, 1697, from 1st Timothy, 1st chap., 16th verse, the day before
before the wretched victims were burnt on the Gallow Green of Paisley. An MS.
volume containing this sermon is in possession of the grandson of Mr. John Millar,
editor of the edition of 1809. Mr. Brown was translated to Glasgow in 1701. Mrs.
Brown was the sister of the minister of Paisley.

† Author of the "Schema Sacra" and "Ratio Sacra," and afterwards Professor of
Divinity in the University of Aberdeen.

www.ingramcontent.com/pod-product-compliance
Lightning Source LLC
Chambersburg PA
CBHW020847270326
41928CB00006B/595